© 2010 Cooperative Cyber Defence Centre of Excellence (CCD COE)

Contact:
Cooperative Cyber Defence Centre of Excellence (CCD COE)
12 Filtri Rd. 10132 Tallinn, Estonia
publications@ccdcoe.org

www.ccdcoe.org

Layout, design and illustrations: Marko Söönurm

ISBN: 978-9949-9040-0-6

# INTERNATIONAL CYBER INCIDENTS:

## LEGAL CONSIDERATIONS

Mike —
enjoy the Pacific!
Eneken

For Mike Loomes
with best regards

Dear Mike,
Enjoy the reading.

Eneken Tikk
Kadri Kaska
Liis Vihul

Best,
Liis

2010

# Contents

# PREFACE

In the twenty-first century, it has become commonly accepted that "cyber security" must be identified as a concern for national and international security. Practical and operational cyber security solutions must be guided by and supported with comprehensive legal and policy analyses. Many countries are still in the process of developing comprehensive understanding of the legal analyses and multi-jurisdictional priorities related to cyber defence. And while there is currently a lack of clarity regarding the international community's role in cyber security, there is a clear recognition that cyber defence must be addressed at an international level. This book directly speaks to these policy needs, and is relevant to individual countries and to international alliances and organisations.

Cyber security and defence are complicated because the cross-jurisdictional authorities, joint public- and private-sector responsibilities, and necessary international collaboration must all be understood, exercised, and legally established as policies for cyber incident management. In the millisecond sectors of communications and information technology, there is often little time to orchestrate response and mitigation efforts. Cyber security, defence, and response options must therefore be predetermined at numerous levels within information and communications technology companies, law enforcement and intelligence offices, military and civilian security departments, foreign affairs agencies, and international alliances and organisations.

However, governments vary widely in their levels of awareness regarding the cyber defence applicability of key concepts such as: the division of roles among the military, law enforcement, emergency response, and information and communications technology (ICT) regulatory/ anti-trust authorities; information sharing and security within government departments and between government and private industry; the different private-sector ICT industry liabilities and regulatory responsibilities; and the ICT industries' contractual obligations and restrictions which support the services and technologies that sustain the existence and resilience of the Internet. If these complexities are not commonly understood by lawmakers and policymakers, any new cyber defence laws and policies may create operational conflicts during a response to a cyber incident, or may have unintended cross-border consequences.

In some countries, new regimes for cyber defence are being considered within governments at the national and sub-national levels. These governments are differently categorising cyber defence, emphasising the role of the military, or law enforcement, or market forces, depending on the governmental definition of "cyber defence" and on the country's regulatory jurisdiction over the various service and asset components required to provide cyber defence. Thus in one country, cyber defence may be primarily a military effort to guard against and respond to cyber attacks; in another country, cyber defence may centre on law enforcement efforts to combat cyber crime; elsewhere, cyber defence may incorporate prevention and response efforts to mitigate cyber damage caused by natural disasters or accidents. A comprehensive cyber defence strategy incorporates the prevention of and response to various types and levels of cyber threats, which may be caused by human error, natural disaster, criminal activity, or politically-motivated attacks.

However, currently there is no common approach for framing the legal authorities and jurisdictions that comprise cyber security. As sovereign nations, most of these countries are properly developing their concepts of cyber defence independently, although they may take advantage of existing bilateral and multilateral agreements for assistance regarding matters of law enforcement, diplomacy, or extradition. Each of these countries' efforts would benefit from a compendium that discusses the various stakeholders, jurisdictions, and policy concerns (which the countries would then weigh appropriately pursuant to their national policies and priorities). Such a framework would provide a comprehensive starting point for countries to develop new cyber defence policies and structures, or to audit their existing cyber security governance frameworks. This series of case studies is our first step toward building that compendium.

Along with new cyber defence policy- and law-making activities within governments, international institutions such as the North Atlantic Treaty Organisation (NATO) and the European Union (EU) have existing or proposed legal authorities that complicate national regulatory activities for cyber defence. As NATO develops its emerging cyber defence policies, and as the EU continues to refine its policies for the information society and for a secure and competitive common market for electronic communications, the different priorities of these two organisations may directly conflict in the area of cyber security. Such conflicts and complexities could cause problems in countries subject to both EU and NATO frameworks, and also to multinational businesses that must operate within the many different and potentially contradictory legal structures for cyber defence. As national, international, and organisational strategies for cyber defence are being developed, it is important to identify early the areas of potential policy conflict and to recommend solutions.

At the same time that governments and international institutions are beginning to consider the frameworks for cyber defence, multinational corporations and other businesses that operate the majority of the international information infrastructure must continue to be able to operate in a reliable manner. These private sector entities have become integral components to both national and international security. However, most legal frameworks of national and international security are still based upon traditional military and intelligence assets, focusing on protecting physical and human resources, and proving a threat via evidence of a pending kinetic attack or similar harm. In the new paradigm that includes cyber defence as a component of national and international security, cyber defence legal frameworks must define the roles and responsibilities of the private sector ICT companies, as well as the values and levels of evidence to show a threat of non-kinetic harm.

In sum, despite their different approaches to cyber defence, governments all have several premises in common: (a) cyber incidents occur swiftly, and most often the origin (whether a politically-motivated attack, criminal hack, accident, etc.) is not immediately known, which means that at the time the incident occurs, a government cannot easily identify a single legal jurisdiction for response, whether military, law enforcement, etc.; (b) global ICT networks are not bounded by the legal jurisdictions of borders and sovereignty, which means that governments must collaborate and coordinate their cyber defence efforts; and (c) national and international security regimes increasingly

rely on interconnected and dependant ICT systems, which means that the legal authorities underpinning these security regimes must be amended to include private-sector ICT systems and assets (human, physical, and informational).

To establish a robust and efficient cyber defence regime, legal and policy frameworks must have a multidisciplinary approach that incorporates legal jurisdictions for prevention and response to all-hazard threats; international collaboration and cooperation; an understanding of private-sector legal rights and responsibilities (under public ordering such as regulations, as well as private ordering such as contracts) for the ICT systems and assets that are the new components of national and international security; and regard for the community of users.

This book presents a series of case studies and legal analyses of four major international cyber incidents, providing a primer of real-world examples of the importance of comprehensive cyber defence efforts. The chapters do not address every legal issue in each case, but rather use the incidents as examples of several areas of concern: (i) the importance of recognising the full spectrum of cyber incidents in national laws, and the need for international cooperation and coordination; (ii) freedom of expression and state responsibility; (iii) the threat of politically-motivated attacks by non-state actors, as well as governmental duties toward the private sector regarding threat warnings; and (iv) the importance of addressing cyber defence in different fields of law (law of armed conflict, criminal law, and legal regulations for the ICT industry).

The Estonian case study provides an example of a country that had extensive laws relevant to cyber incidents, but still lacked legal provision to investigate and prosecute politically-motivated attacks that had no profit motive. This example also illustrates the need for international agreements, or uniform standards of best practice, for response and investigatory authorities and for private industry.

The second case study, involving Radio Free Europe/Radio Liberty (RFE/RL) in Belarus, addresses the right of freedom of expression and government restrictions on citizens' access to information. The RFE/RL Belarus case study elucidates an international standard that includes duties of a state to not unduly restrict information flow; to not allow for information interference by other parties (implying a duty to sanction and to effectively enforce the sanction), and to effectively facilitate the exercise of freedom of speech, both in its active and passive aspects, on the Internet.

The next chapter presents the Lithuania case study, which focuses on defacement attacks, and also provides an example of a government that was prepared for the attacks but who failed to inform the private sector of the threat. This case study also discusses the problem of national laws that require "serious harm" or "great damage" in order to prosecute wrongdoers. The Lithuania chapter shows how political decisions can prompt cyber incidents which have wide-ranging private-sector effects. These effects should be taken into account in both public actions (laws, political speeches, etc.) and in private ordering (e.g., ICT service contracts and contracts to critical infrastructures and vital services).

The final case study, regarding Georgia, covers the confluence of three different fields of law: the law of armed conflict, criminal law, and legal regulations for the ICT industry. These areas of law do not have clear boundaries; in one country they may overlap, and in another they may have gaps. Both the overlap and the gap may create a general murkiness of legal authorities, where a lack of clear policies and procedures can cause problems in cyber security and/or incident response.

In assembling these case studies, the authors' main purpose was to develop a better understanding of current international cyber conflict. It is the authors' hope that this series helps to further national and international understanding of legal issues regarding cyber conflict.

*Maeve Dion*
*Center for Infrastructure Protection*
*George Mason University School of Law*
*Arlington, Virginia, U.S.A.*

# INTRODUCTION TO CASE STUDIES

Conducting legal analyses of current cyber incidents is one dimension of the CCD COE project on legal aspects of cyber defence. The aim of studying real-life cyber incidents is to define the scale and nature of such incidents, identify the actual threats and vulnerabilities, but also to consider the preparedness of the country's legal system to cope with cyber threats and to draw attention to the strengths and challenges in national law that the examples provide. In addition, we hope to provide insights to potential ways ahead in legal thinking.

The first compilation of case studies in this research effort covers some of the cyber incidents that occurred in the world in 2007-2008 and were characterised by a strong political undertone. The cases have been ordered by the timeline of their occurrence. The reports in this series include the case studies and legal lessons identified and learned from the following cyber incidents:

- cyber attacks against Estonia in April-May 2007;

- cyber attacks against Radio Free Europe/ Radio Liberty, in particular its Belarus service in April 2008;

- cyber attacks against Lithuanian websites in June-July 2008;

- cyber attacks against Georgia in August 2008.

The facts about the incidents have been gathered from original observers or incident handlers where possible, including national Computer Emergency Response Teams and/ or IT security analysts. Otherwise, open source reports by international media have been used. The case studies were drafted between April 2008 and August 2009; therefore, later findings and reports are not reflected in this study. Both the technical and legal sections were written by a team of legal professionals; therefore errors may have occurred in terms of technical details of the incidents. We welcome all comments and corrections.

Each chapter is divided into three main subdivisions. The first of these explains the country and political context of the particular incident that directly or indirectly became the trigger of the cyber aftermath, as well as analyses the indicators of national information society – the factor which has a determining role on the effect that the cyber attacks have on each nation and society, but also on the preparedness of the country to effectively conduct mitigation. The second section deals with the incident directly, describing the timeline, methods, targets, and effects of the attacks, as well as the measures that were employed to cope with the attacks. It also discusses the identification of attack origins, based on the evidence that is available through other research efforts we have studied. In the third section, we discuss the legal lessons that these cases draw attention to, and propose some ways forward in the legal thought in this area.

Rather than provide a comprehensive and systematic legal analysis of each incident, complete with the full picture of incident details, the aim and purpose of drafting this book was to identify some of the acute issues for national and international cyber security preparedness, as well as to distinguish the common nominators and emerging trends of legal relevance. If this book triggers ideas for deeper analysis and policy action, it will have served its purpose well.

We are grateful to many people and institutions for their help in the drafting of this book:

- Major Chris Fellows, for asking the right questions, for making us realize that the most important aspects about life are not always strictly legal and for guiding our thinking towards how law, technology and policy interact in on different levels of expertise and decision-making. Chris's questions triggered this series of case studies and his continued support and encouragement to the CCD COE legal team has been invaluable;

- Ms. Kristel Rünnimeri, for her contribution to the Georgian analysis on the applicability of Law of Armed Conflict, and for all her help in compiling the fact material of the incidents;

- Ms. Anna-Maria Talihärm and Ms. Mari Kert, who spent the better part of their internship at CCD COE in August 2008, gathering the scattered pieces of information about events in Georgia and brainstorming over the first version of legal lessons identified from the Georgian cyber attacks, thereby helping to lay the foundation for this series;

- Ms. Maeve Dion, Program Manager at Center for Infrastructure Protection of George Mason

University School of Law (Arlington, Virginia, USA), for providing an added perspective to the book – not only by writing the foreword, but meticulously going through the text and providing her comments, and her help with the grammar revision of the text;

- Mr. Jude Klena, for his comments on the early drafts and impartial recommendations on how to make it a better product;

- Mr. Ulf Häußler, for endless questions that have inspired us in improving our reasoning, correcting the citations and omitting parts of the text we were not really sure about;

- Mr. Rain Ottis from the then CCD COE activation team within the Training and Development Centre for Communications and Information Systems of the Estonian Defence College, for his initiative to document the April-May 2007 events in Estonia and for sharing his observations with us;

- the Lithuanian Communications Regulatory Authority (RRT), the Lithuanian Computer Emergency Response Team, and the Cyber Crime unit of the Lithuanian police who provided valuable remarks to the research team;

- Mr. Tomas Jermalavicius from the International Centre for Defence Studies for his insightful comments and advice on the Lithuanian chapter;

- The readers of our first very raw draft of Georgia analysis of August 2008, who enthusiastically jumped in and shared their suggestions and proposals with us;

- The participants of the CCD COE Cyber Conflict Legal and Policy conference 2009 and all our fellow thinkers, regardless of organisational affiliation, who assured us that time is ripe for a legal discussion on the nature of threats in cyber space and on what can be done to support the functioning of free, modern, and secure information societies.

Finally, we would like to note that the views, opinions, and/or findings and recommendations contained in this analysis are those of the authors and should not be construed as an official position, policy, or decision of NATO or any NATO entity.

# ESTONIA 2007

April-May

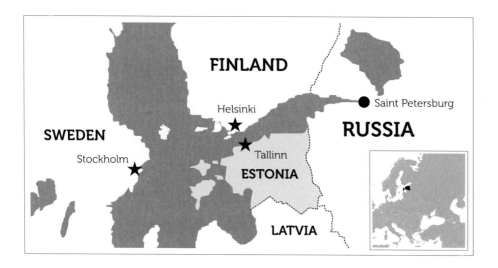

# I Background of the incident

## Political context of the incident

On April 26 and 27 of 2007, Estonia witnessed two nights of unprecedented street riots in the centre of Tallinn, its capital, by youth groups mostly of ethnic Russian origin.[1] The riots had broken out in response to the government decision to remove a Soviet-era Second World War (WWII) memorial, a decision which had been accompanied by intense vocal opposition by the government of Russia[2] and by a series of propagandistic articles in the Russian and international media[3], accusing Estonia of "glorifying Nazism" and "rewriting history".

The memorial in question, the centrepiece of which was a two-metre-high bronze soldier, had been erected in central Tallinn in 1947 as a memorial to the victory of the Soviet Army over Nazi Germany in WWII.[4] While in the early 1990ies many Soviet-symbol statues and memorials throughout Estonia were removed, the Bronze Soldier, as a rather neutral example of the Soviet-era memorials, remained intact, and for years it stood at a small park next to a central intersection without causing concern. On WWII-related holidays formerly celebrated by the Soviet Union, those commemorating their

---

1   Estonia has a sizeable ethnic Russian minority: out of the population of 1,34 million, 344 000 are of ethnic Russian origin. (Statistics Estonia. Statistical Database. Population by Sex, Ethnic Nationality And County, 1 January 2007. pub.stat.ee/px-web.2001/Dialog/statfile1.asp). Within this minority, different groups with various levels of integration into the Estonian society exist. A large percentage holds Estonian citizenship, speak the Estonian language, and consider Estonia as their homeland. Some are citizens of the Russian Federation, of which a number still accept the constitutional order of the Republic of Estonia. Some, however, consider the collapse of the Soviet Union a historical mistake and desire the restoration of Russian dominion over the territory once under Russian control.

2   Among others, the foreign minister of the Russian Federation, Sergey Lavrov, who issued a statement calling the decision „a blasphemy' and threatened 'serious consequences'. See
Socor, Vladimir. 'Moscow stung by Estonian ban on totalitarianism's symbols'. Eurasia Daily Monitor, The Jamestown Foundation, 26 Jan 2007.
Available at http://www.jamestown.org/single/?no_cache=1&tx_ttnews[tt_news]=32427.

3   E.g. Kosachev, Konstantin. 'An insult to our war dead'. The Guardian, 6 Mar 2007. Available at http://www.guardian.co.uk/commentisfree/2007/mar/06/comment.secondworldwar

4   Kaasik, Peeter. 'Common grave for and a memorial to Red Army soldiers on Tõnismägi, Tallinn. Historical statement'. Estonian Foundation for the Investigation of Crimes Against Humanity, 2006. Available at http://www.valitsus.ee/brf/failid/ajalooline_oiend_2006_en.pdf

losses in war laid flowers on the site. However, in recent years, these events increasingly began to turn into more provocative gatherings of groups which were openly hostile towards the Estonian state, and when conflicts arose out of a case where a person carrying an Estonian flag was physically attacked by the gatherers, the area was taken under heightened police supervision.[5] As the site increasingly became a rallying point for national extremists, a public debate arose on the removal of the memorial, along with relocation of the adjoining war graves.

In the early spring of 2007, the government of Estonia announced the start of preparatory works for the excavation of the war graves, re-burial of the bodies to a military cemetery, and relocation of the Bronze Soldier memorial.[6] On April 26, the memorial site was fenced and covered, and preparations for excavations began.

On the evening of April 26, about a thousand people gathered at the memorial site to demonstrate their dissent against the removal of the monument. In later hours, the initially calm protest escalated into violence against the police and later on into street riots with extensive looting and vandalising of buildings and other property in central Tallinn, as well as in the city of Jõhvi north-east of the country. Police arrested 1300 people; about a hundred were injured in the riots, and one person died. The estimated amount of damage directly caused by the street riots was about 70 million kroons (about €4.5 million).[7] The government made a quick decision to move the statue earlier than initially announced, and during the night of April 27, the statue was taken to an unannounced location, and later established at the Tallinn Military Cemetery on April 30.[8]

The decision of relocation set off days of angry protests by Nashi activists in front of the Estonian embassy in Moscow[9] and resulted in physically attacking the Estonian ambassadors at a press conference.[10] Riots in the streets of Tallinn turned into "rioting" in cyberspace when in the late hours of Friday, April 27, web pages of Estonian government institutions and news portals came under a wave of cyber attacks. Attacks against both public and private sector websites lasted, in phases of varying intensity, for more than three weeks; beginning to to subside by May 19 with the overall calming down of political tensions between Estonia and Russia over the Bronze Soldier issue. Some aftermath was still observable at the end of May 2007.[11]

# Estonia as an information Society

To understand the significance that the the spring 2007 cyber attacks had against the Estonian governance and society as a whole, the role of information and communications technology needs a few introductory remarks.[12]

## The evolution of information society services in Estonia

The small size of the population (1.3 million inhabitants), limited resources, and the low population density have challenged Estonia to look for efficient means to provide public services to its residents without requiring excessive resources from the state.

The advance of Estonia as an e-State dates back to the mid-1990s. The first entities to introduce and promote Internet-based service solutions were commercial banks, who were eager to gain market advantage and to reach the

5    'Politsei viis Eesti lipu lehvitaja minema'. Delfi.ee, 9 May 2006 (*In Estonian*). Available at: http://www.delfi.ee/news/paevauudised/eesti/article.php?id=12845410
6    Rand, Erik. 'Ansip: pronkssõdur viiakse Tõnismäelt minema'. Postimees, 29 March 2007 (*In Estonian*). Available at: http://www.epl.ee/artikkel/380087
7    Ojala, Agnes. Pronksiöö hinda mõõdetakse sadades miljonites. Äripäev 10.07.2007. (*in Estonian*)
8    Pronkssõdur avati taas rahvale vaatamiseks. Postimees Online, 30 April 2007. (*in Estonian*) Available at http://www.postimees.ee/300407/esileht/siseuudised/258058.php

9    Arnold, Chloe. 'Russian Group's Claims Reopen Debate On Estonian Cyberattacks.' RFE/RL, 30 March 2009. Available at: http://www.estemb.org/news/aid-2526
10   Myers, Steven Lee. 'Youth Groups Created by Kremlin Serve Putin's Cause'. New York Times, 8 July 2007. Available at: http://www.nytimes.com/2007/07/08/world/europe/08moscow.html?_r=1
11   Landler, Mark; Markoff, John. 'In Estonia, what may be the first war in cyberspace.' International Herald Tribune. 28 May 2007. Available at http://www.iht.com/articles/2007/05/28/business/cyberwar.php
12   Data provided below is as of 2007, to reflect the situation within the timeframe of the cyber attacks. Where available, data references as of end-2008 are given for comparison.

scarcely populated rural areas.[13] High-quality IT solutions in other industries have followed since then. Internet banking has become prevalent (in 2007, 95% of all banking operations were carried out electronically[14]). Mobile solutions such as mobile parking and mobile public transportation tickets have evolved and gained popularity (m-parking constituted more than 50% of the total income gathered from parking fees in major cities in 2005).[15] There are a number of success stories in the Estonian ICT sector, to name Skype, Regio[16] and Mobi Solutions[17] as a few.[18]

For nearly a decade, it has also been an overarching governance policy to use information technology to increase public sector administrative capacity and to ensure an innovative and convenient living environment for the citizens. The legislative ground for the widespread government-to-citizen e-service use was laid by the 2000-2002 administrative law reform, whereby electronic operations were made equal to written operations in administrative procedure.[19] Digital signatures had already been constituted the same legal consequences as a hand-written signatures in 2000.[20]

## Internet access and infrastructure

By 2007, 98% of Estonian territory was covered with Internet access: fixed line, broadband, WiMax, WiFi, and CDMA[21] mobile wireless Internet access solutions.[22] The Internet reaches most of the country's territory, omitting only some small areas because of landscape peculiarities unfavourable for radio transmission. Mobile phone penetration was nearing 100% in 2007[23].

Nearly 50% of the population 16-74 years old was using the Internet in 2007; households having personal computers at home comprised 53% and those having access to the Internet at home, 48%.[24]

## Government e-Services

With the creation and development of the national population registry in 1992 began the era of governmental digital databases and state information systems in Estonia. By 2007, state information systems and databases had been developed into a nationwide state information system with corresponding functional infrastructure that enables service access on the principle of "one stop shopping".[25]

In 2007, the state information administration system consisted of more than 150 public sector information systems, which altogether provided more than 1,000 different electronic services. More than 450 public sector organizations and 30,000 entrepreneurs used the data exchange layer[26] (the "X-road") each day via the State

---

13   Tikk, Eneken; Oorn, Reet. 'Legal and Policy Evaluation: International Coordination of Prosecution and Prevention of Cyber Terrorism.' In 'Responses to Cyber Terrorism'. COE DAT, 2008. Pp. 89-103;

14   In end-2008, there were 1,6 million e-banking clients, and over 98% of transactions concluded online. See 'Pankadel on üle 1,6 miljoni internetipanga kliendi.' Delfi Online, 8 Jan 2009 (in Estonian). Available at http://www.delfi.ee/news/eesti/eesti_uudised/article.php?id=20829300.

15   Arthur D. Little Global M-Payment Update 2005. Available at: http://www.3mfuture.com/articles_epayment/Global_M-Payment-Report_Update_Arthur_D_Little_2005.pdf. P. 17.

16   A provider of various GIS and mobile positioning solutions

17   A developer of different m- applications and m-solutions

18   Talihärm, Anna-Maria. 'Estonia 2007: A Possible Model For Cyberterrorism?' Stockholms Universitet, 2008.

19   Administrative Procedure Act (RT I 2001, 58, 354), passed 6 June 2001, entered into force 1 January 2002. See Art 5 section 6; Art 14, Art 25-27, Art 55. An unofficial English translation is available at http://www.legaltext.ee/et/andmebaas/paraframe.asp?loc=text&lk=et&sk=en&dok=X40071K3.htm&query=haldusmenetluse&tyyp=X&ptyyp=RT&pg=1&fr=no.

20   Digital Signatures Act (RT I 2000, 26, 150), passed 8 March 2000, entered into force 15 December 2000. See Art 3. An unofficial English translation is available at http://www.legaltext.ee/et/andmebaas/paraframe.asp?loc=text&lk=et&sk=en&dok=X30081K5.htm&query=digitaalallkirja&tyyp=X&ptyyp=RT&pg=1&fr=no

21   Code Division Multiple Access (CDMA), a mobile digital radio technology standard.

22   Käo, Merike. 'Cyber Attacks on Estonia: Short Synopsis'. 2007. Available at http://doubleshotsecurity.com/pdf/NANOG-eesti.pdf. P. 4.

23   By end of 2008, this number exceeded 130%. (Data provided by the National Communications Board/Communications Division of the Estonian Competition Authority.) The figure reflects the number of active SIM-cards per population.

24   Implementation Plan 2007-2008 of the Estonian Information Society Strategy. Available at http://www.riso.ee/en/information-policy/policy-document/implementation_plan

25   Tikk, Oorn, supra note 13.

26   The data exchange layer, which constitutes the major part of the X-Road system, integrates the databases through user interfaces to a common network and enables the user, within the limits of his/her authority, to search data from national databases that have joined the system.

Portal *eesti.ee*, and over 500,000 citizens had experienced using public sector e-services via the X-road. The number of individuals having given digital signature had reached 70,000 unique signatories by 2007. [27]

In the year 2008, 80% of natural persons' income declarations were submitted electronically.[28] In local government council elections held in October 2005, Estonia was the first country in the world to use Internet voting.[29] About 90% of the performers of high school state examinations received their exam results via SMS in the 2007 state exams.[30]

Over time, more and more government-to-consumer services have moved online in Estonia, while their on-paper provision has increasingly ceased. Consultation and assistance are provided by the state to people that lack the necessary equipment or skill to use online services.[31]

The high availability of public e-services and wide Internet accessibility that the Estonian population enjoys have, as a negative side effect, also made the country a more attractive target for cyber attacks. The dependency of the population on easily accessible online services has made the society more vulnerable to large-scale disruptions in the availability of Internet access.

# II Facts of the case

## Phases and timeline of the attacks

Cyber attacks started in parallel to rioting on streets in the late hours of Friday, April 27, when web pages of Estonian government institutions and news portals came under a wave of cyber attacks. Estonian e-services and information infrastructure were hit in varying degrees of intensity until the end of May, when the political tensions between Estonia and Russia over the

Bronze Soldier issue finally started to calm down.

The attacks had two distinctly different phases, each consisting of several waves of elevated intensity. The first phase took place from April 27 to 29 and was assessed to have been emotionally motivated, as the attacks were relatively simple and any coordination mainly occurred on an *ad hoc* basis. The first phase was followed by the main, co-ordinated attack phase lasting from April 30 to May 18, which was much more sophisticated, and where the use of large botnets[32] and professional coordination was noticed. Notably, clear correlation was observed between politically significant dates and intensification of attacks.

## Phase I – emotional response (April 27 to 29)

The first attack against government websites was reported to have hit in the late hours of 27 April 2007.[33] Also attacked in the early days were online media outlets carrying news about the street riots and the overall political situation.

Initially, attacks were carried out by relatively simple means, therefore earning the label of "cyber riots"[34]. In various Russian-language Internet forums, calls and instructions were presented to launch *ping* commands (simple commands to check the availability of the targeted computers) with certain parameters on the MS Windows command line.[35] Later on, executable .bat files were made available for users to copy onto their computers and then launch to carry out automated ping requests.[36] This would amount to simple denial of service

---

27    Tikk, Oorn, *supra* note 13.
28    *Id.*
29    EurActiv. 'Estonia first country in the world to introduce internet voting'. 12 October 2005. Available at http://www.euractiv.com/en/egovernment/estonia-country-world-introduce-internet-voting/article-145735
30    Tikk, Oorn, *supra* note 13.
31    *Id.*

32    The nature of a botnet is explained under the section 'Intensity and duration of the attacks' of this paper. For definition, see also the *Abbreviations and Glossary* section.
33    Almann, Lauri. Presentation at the Conference Board of Canada conference 'Cyber Security: Proactive Defence of Critical Systems and Information'. 5 Nov 2008.
34    The title given to the initial phase of the incident by Hillar Aarelaid, head of CERT Estonia. *See* Finn, Peter.' Cyber Assaults on Estonia Typify a New Battle Tactic,' Washington Post, 19 May 2007. Available at http://www.washingtonpost.com/wp-dyn/content/article/2007/05/18/AR2007051802122.html
35    *Id.*
36    Randel, Tarmo. CERT Eesti tegevuse aastakokkuvõte (CERT-EE Annual Report; *in Estonian*). Estonian Informatics Centre, 2007; Evron, Gadi. 'Battling Botnets and Online Mobs. Estonia's Defence Efforts during the Internet War'. *Georgetown Journal of International Affairs*, Winter/Spring 2008, p 121-126.

(DoS)[37] attacks; however, being coordinated, they were effective in disturbing their targets. Attacks were also coordinated via Internet Relay Chat (IRC).[38]

Pinging was soon followed by malformed web queries, which were massively used mainly against the websites of the government and media outlets – this already implied the use of more specific means designed for attack.[39]

As a generalisation, though, the initial attacks on April 27 and 28 were simple, ineptly coordinated and easily mitigated.

## Phase II – Main Attack (April 30 to May 18)

In the second phase, more sophisticated and better-coordinated attacks appeared in four major waves outlined below. Compared to the initial emotional response, phase II was also clearly characterised by use of larger botnets.[40]

In addition to the higher level of sophistication of coordination and attack, the initial model of using Internet forums to distribute instructions and lists of targets to attack was still employed. The instructions were mostly very simple, thus not requiring advanced technical knowledge or skill to follow; a computer with an Internet connection was sufficient to participate. Calls were issued to schedule attacks for specific timings in order to generate greater simultaneous volume of queries for higher effect against targets.[41] Discussions about how to fund the rental of server farms[42] and botnets for distributed denial

of service (DDoS)[43] attack were also present.[44]

The Domain Name Servers (DNS) and routers run by Elion[45] were repeatedly attacked throughout the period between April 30 and May 18, causing temporary service disruptions.[46] Outside the peak days described below, network traffic continued to be above the normal level throughout this period. In the majority, the attacks were manageable, but some sites were affected and remained inaccessible for periods of time.

### First Wave (May 4)

During the night of May 4, DDoS assaults continued against websites and DNSs, while showing remarkable intensification and precision in concentration[47], which indicated the use of botnets. Attackers covered their tracks by various means: by using global botnets, by routing their attacks through proxy servers in other countries (including those in NATO countries) and likely by spoofing their IP addresses[48].[49]

### Second Wave (May 9-11)

Yet another increase in attacks was expected for May 9, 2007. May 9 is the day celebrated annually as Victory Day in Russia, a national holiday which remembers the defeat of Nazi Germany in World War II, and thus of direct relevance to the Bronze Soldier controversy.

As anticipated, the DDoS attacks increased by

---

37  DoS – a Denial of Service attack, where a server is overloaded with irrelevant queries or information packages originating from the same terminal. Technical terms are explained in *Abbreviations and Glossary* of this book.
38  Ottis, Rain. Overview of Events, 30 April 2007. CCD COE Activation Team, TDCCIS.
39  Randel, *supra* note 36.
40  *Id.*
41  Ottis, Rain. Overview of Events, 2 May 2007. CCD COE Activation Team, TDCCIS.
42  A group of networked servers, housed in one location, to streamline internal processes by distributing the workload between the individual components of the farm. For a more detailed explanation, see *Abbreviations and Glossary* of this book.

43  A denial-of-service attack (DoS) occurs when large number of requests are directed to a target URL. The requests occur so quickly that the Web server cannot respond and the site becomes inaccessible. A distributed denial-of-service attack (DDoS) occurs when hundreds or thousands of compromised computers are enlisted. For a more detailed explanation, see *Abbreviations and Glossary*.
44  Ottis, *supra* note 41.
45  Elion Ettevõtted AS is the leading player on fixed electronic communications services markets in Estonia.
46  Cyber attacks against the Republic of Estonia. 10 May 2007. An overview by the Cooperative Cyber Defence Centre of Excellence project team.
47  Overview of Events, 4 May 2007. CCD COE Activation Team, TDCCIS.
48  IP address - the unique 32 bit number assigned to each computer connected to the Internet and used by the TCP/IP protocol to route packets of data to their destinations. For a more detailed explanation, see *Abbreviations and Glossary*.
49  Overview of Events, *supra* note 47.

about 150% at 23:00 EET[50] on May 8 (beginning of May 9 according to Moscow time)[51], and lasted throughout May 9 and 10, then ending abruptly. On May 9, the attacks shut down up to 58 sites at once.[52] This wave of attacks mostly targeted government websites (including official communications channels of the government)[53]; in total intensity however, the attack remained lower than those that had taken place in previous weeks.[54]

The banks experienced more sustained DDoS attacks from May 9 to 11, with the web service of the largest commercial bank of Estonia, Hansapank, being unavailable for customers for ca 1,5 hours on May 9 and for another two hours on May 10.[55]

### Third Wave (May 15)

Strong DDoS attacks (via a large botnet of about 85,000 hijacked computers as reported by the Estonian Computer Emergency Response Team [CERT-EE]) against the websites of government institutions took place from noon until midnight on May 15. Since network capacities had already been increased in response to the earlier attacks, the heightened amount of traffic did not pose significant problems.[56]

The web portal of SEB Eesti Ühispank, the second largest commercial bank, was offline for ca 1.5 hours, and the restoration of service for customers outside of Estonia took longer still. There were lesser incident reports from other banks.[57]

### Fourth Wave (May 18)

Another strong DDoS attack against governmental websites occurred. Banks continued to experience a diminished level of interruptions even after that date.[58]

# Means and types of attacks against Estonia

The means of attack used in the April-May 2007 events included denial of service (DoS) and distributed denial of service (DDoS) attacks, defacement of websites, and large amounts of comment and email spam. Public propaganda, distributed on different Internet forums, and dissemination of attack instructions were employed to encourage, coordinate and aid in carrying out the attacks.

## DoS and DDoS attacks

In the early few days of the Estonian cyber incident, most of the attacks consisted of denial of service (DoS) and distributed denial of service (DDoS) attacks which resulted in the attacked websites becoming inaccessible.

A denial-of-service attack is a concerted malevolent effort to deny access to any electronic device, computer, server, network, or Internet resource by its intended users.[59] This can be accomplished in numerous ways; ping-flooding, UDP flood and malformed queries were mainly used in the case of the Estonian attacks. Malformed GET queries, SYN floods, and the so-called 'ping of death' method were also used.[60]

The effect of the DDoS attacks was more severely noticed by users outside of Estonia, as a large amount of foreign queries were cut off in order to cope with the excessive traffic and to filter out genuine queries.[61]

As the attacks progressed, massive distributed

---

50    Eastern European Time (EET), GMT+2, which, notably, is one hour behind the Russian Standard Time (GMT+3).
51    Ottis, Rain. Overview of Events, 9 May 2007. CCD COE Activation Team, TDCCIS.
52    Nazario, José. 'Estonian DDoS Attacks - A summary to date'. Arbor Networks. May 17th, 2007 Available at asert. arbornetworks.com/2007/05/estonian-ddos-attacks-a-summary-to-date/
53    Randel, *supra* note 36.
54    As demonstrated by data transfer volume graphs recorded by Elion, the major service provider, between 27 April and 11 May.
55    'Hansapanka tabas küberrünne'. Postimees 10 May 2007 (*In Estonian*). Available at http://www.tarbija24. ee/180507/esileht/majandus/259920.php
56    Ottis, Rain. Overview of Events, 15 May 2007. CCD COE Activation Team, TDCCIS.
57    Ottis, Rain. Overview of Events, 16 May 2007. CCD COE Activation Team, TDCCIS.

58    Landler, Markoff, supra note 11.
59    Cyberwarfare: a glossary of useful terms. Stratfor today, 1 March 2008. Available at http://www.stratfor.com/ analysis/cyberwarfare_glossary_useful_terms *See* also *Abbreviations and Glossary*.
60    For explanation on the technical terms, see Abbreviations and Glossary.
61    *See section* 'Measures Taken to Cope with the Attacks' of this paper.

denial of service (DDoS) attacks were targeted against key governmental and private sector web sites, selecting some critical information infrastructure targets (DNS) while using a wide array of offensive techniques. At their peak, the amount of Internet traffic from outside of Estonia, targeting governmental institutions, was nearly 400 times higher than its normal rate. According to Arbor Networks, a global network security solutions R&D corporation that observed the Estonian cyber attacks and provided their observations for part of the attack period, 128 unique DDoS attacks were detected on Estonian websites during that period.[62]

## Defacement of websites

A hacker succeeded at breaking into the Estonian Reform Party website where they placed a forged "official" apology, signed by Estonian Prime Minister Andrus Ansip.

The apology, in contrast with the language of the rest of the website, was offered in Russian. There were also reports of doctoring of a photo of the Prime Minister Ansip to add a Hitler moustache[63].

## Attacking DNS servers

A more dangerous trend was attacking the DNS servers managed by Internet Service Providers. Repeated attacks against DNS and routers run by Elion were observed between April 30 and May 18. Some of the attacks were successful in the short term, temporarily disrupting DNS services in parts of the country.[64]

## Other Types of Attack

Heightened use of mass unsolicited e-mail was observed against government e-mail servers and individual e-mail accounts. Due to public policy applicable since 2001 to publish contact addresses for all public service employees on their entities' websites, these addresses were an easyMass spread of comment spam by robots posting on internet forums and news sites also occurred. These had varying effects, but in gen-

eral, most systems were able to withstand the attacks.[65]

# Attack targets

The prime targets (and also those that experienced major effect) were information distribution channels of both the government and the private sector, and business sector websites, specifically, the banks. The work of vital databases, systems or registers of the public and private sector was not disrupted, but there were attacks directed at the national Internet infrastructure. Also, the common emergency number 112 was targeted so that calls were briefly blocked.[66]

The targets for cyber attack were mainly fourfold (discussed in more detail in following subsections):

- servers of institutions that are responsible for the Estonian Internet infrastructure;

- governmental and political targets;

- services provided by the private sector;

- personal and random targets.

Notably, traditional critical infrastructure objects, such as information systems supporting transportation and energy systems, were not targeted.

## Internet infrastructure providers

CERT-EE reported several occasions of attacks against the Estonian Internet infrastructure and information systems, both governmental and commercial.[67]

Among servers especially pointed out as targets (with instructions given on how to attack) were the national DNS run by the Institute of Chemical Biology and Physics (the institution responsible

---

62   Nazario, supra note 52.
63   Finn, Peter, *supra* note 34.
64   Cyber attacks against the Republic of Estonia, *supra* note 46.

65   *Id.*
66   Estland im Visier: Ist ein Internetangriff der Ernstfall?. Frankfurter Allgemeine Zeitung, 18.06.2007, Nr. 138 / Seite 6. (in German). Available at: http://www.faz.net/s/ RubDDBDABB9457A437BAA85A49C26FB23A0/Doc~E7CC F88CEFB6F467BB8D75A400C07B959~ATpl~Ecommon~S content.html; Ottis, Rain. Overview of Events, 7 May 2007. CCD COE Activation Team, TDCCIS.
67   Tiks, Oliver (ed). 'Küberrünnakuid tõrjuvad sajad spetsialistid' (*In Estonian*). Postimees Online, 2 May 2007. Available at http://www.tarbija24.ee/120507/esileht/ siseuudised/258274.php

for Estonian domain name administration); EENet, which administers the core Internet servers for the Estonian governmental and educational institutions; and also ISP-operated DNSs (a full list of country DNS targets, identified both by their URL and by IP address, was distributed over a Russian-language web forum).[68]

## Governmental and political targets

Among governmental and political websites, those attacked were[69]:

- Estonian constitutional institutions:

  - Government,

  - Prime Minister,

  - President,

  - Riigikogu (the Parliament),

  - State Audit Office.

- Governmental institutions:

  - all ministries (state departments) except for the Estonian Ministry of Culture;

  - state agencies (e.g. the Estonian Police Board);

- Reform Party, the website of the leading coalition party.[70]

CERT-EE confirmed that persistent attacks against the official communications channels of the Estonian government lasted throughout the period between April 27 and May 9.[71]

## Commercial Services

E-banking services of Hansapank and SEB Eesti Ühispank, two of the largest banks that, combined, controlled about 75-80% of the total Estonian banking market, were attacked on various occasions between the period of May 9 to 15.[72] Diminished interruptions continued even after that date. Hansapank's e-banking service had to be shut down from 1,5 to 2 hours on two occasions (May 9 and 10)[73], SEB Eesti Ühispank's online banking service was offline for 1,5 hours on May 15. Both banks reported having to restrict access to customers located abroad in order to cope with the massive amounts of queries originating from outside of Estonia. Considering that the use of e-banking services is almost exclusive in Estonia (in 2007, the share of electronic transactions amounted to about 95-97%), the effect was significant on large parts of the society and economic activities were hindered throughout the entire country. No entities have publicly announced the size of their cyber losses though.[74]

At least three major Internet Service Providers – Elion Ettevõtted, Elisa Andmesideteenused, and Starman – experienced DDoS attacks against their servers.

Three of Estonia's six largest news organisations and news portals (including Postimees.ee, Delfi, EPL Online, Baltic News Service) were also affected. The country's three mobile network operators experienced slight disruptions.[75]

A web hosting service provider (Zone.ee) and a directory service provider (ee.ee) were attacked by DDoS, possibly because these were errone-

---

68    Reference to the original site has been withdrawn from this paper to avoid being a redistribution point. Contact the authors for reference. For an explanation on the abbreviations and terms used, see *Abbreviations and Glossary.*

69    Rantanen, Miska. 'Virtual harassment, but for real.' Helsingin Sanomat International Edition, 6 May 2007. Available at http://www.hs.fi/english/article/Virtual+harassment+but+for+real+/1135227099868; Hyppönen, Mikko. 'Unrest in Estonia'. April 28, 2007. http://www.f-secure.com/weblog/archives/00001181.html; Ottis, *supra* note 66.

70    A 20-*year*-old Tallinn resident Dmitri Galushkevich was convicted for attacking the Reform Party website by DoS attack. (*See* 'Rahutuste ajal Reformierakonna kodulehte rünnanud noormees sai trahvi.' (*In Estonian)* Postimees, 23 Jan 2008. Available at http://www.postimees.ee/250108/esileht/krimi/307821.php.) As of August 2009, this is still the only conviction for any of the cyber attacks under discussion.

71    Randel, *supra* note 36.

72    'Küberründed ei ole vaibunud'. Postimees, 10 May 2007 (*in Estonian*). Available at: http://www.tarbija24.ee/110507/esileht/krimi/259961.php; 'Hansapanka tabas küberrünne'. *supra* note 55.

73    Weiss, Michael. Here Come the Cyber Wars. Are We Ready? Reason.com August 17, 2007. http://www.reason.com/news/show/121896.html

74    In 'Here Come the Cyber Wars. Are We Ready?' Reason.com 17 August 2007. (Available at http://www.reason.com/news/show/121896.html), Michael Weiss reports of the expense of one 1-hour break being at least $1 million. The reliability of this figure is however, not verified; it also only relates to a fraction of the total service disruption.

75    Ottis, *supra* note 66.

ously taken for state information channels.[76]

## Origin of the attacks

According to CERT-EE, the attacks mainly, although not exclusively, originated from sources outside of Estonia.[77] The malicious purpose of the traffic was evident from the commencement of the incident, according to CERT officials – by the nature and setup of the queries, it was apparent that the unusually high traffic flow was not merely caused by a sudden and unexpected increase in foreign interest towards information published on Estonian websites.[78]

Information collated by Arbor Networks showed that attacks were sourced worldwide rather than just from a few locations.[79] According to the State Informatics Centre, there were computers involved from 178 countries[80].

A substantial part of the attackers were crowds affected by nationalistic/political emotions who carried out the attacks according to the instructions provided in Internet forums and websites.[81] As the tension around the Bronze Soldier subsided, this type of protesters quieted down, even though some zealous attackers (such as some activists of the *Nashi* movement) were motivated to carry on longer[82]. The switchover from the simple emotional attacks to botnet use was gradual, not abrupt.

Log analyses affirm that the second phase of the cyber attacks involved coordination and

resources unavailable to *ad hoc* "regular citizen" protest. As was observed, the second phase attacks had the features of central command and control: they were fairly sophisticated, came in (often precisely timed) waves, and required both financial and intellectual resources.[83]

Particularly in the early "emotional" phase, some attackers were identifiable by their IP addresses. A number of those were Russian, including some cases where the IP address involved in the attack belonged to Russian state institutions.[84] However, Russian authorities denied any involvement[85], and cyber security experts also pointed out the possibility of spoofing attacker addresses and pointed out the lack of "evidence of who is behind the attacks supposedly coming from Moscow".[86]

A few self-proclaimed or self-acknowledged attackers were distinguished: one of them was Konstantin Goloskokov (spelled as Goloskov in some sources)[87], a commissar of the pro-Kremlin Russian youth group *Nashi*, another Dmitri Galushkevich, a young IT student from Tallinn who boasted about successfully attacking the Reform Party's website and who was later convicted for this offence.[88] In March 2009, Sergei Markov, a State Duma Deputy from the pro-Kremlin Unified Russia party, stated that the Estonian attacks had been carried out by

---

76   Berendson, Risto. 'Küberrünnakute taga seisavad prof*id.*' (*IN Estonian.*) Postimees, 3 May 2007 Available at http://www.tarbija24.ee/120507/esileht/siseuudised/258409.php

77   Randel, *supra* note 36.

78   Tiks, Oliver (ed.) 'Pahatahtlikud küberründed Eesti vastu tulevad välismaalt'. (*In Estonian.*) Postimees Online, 29 April 2007. Available at http://www.tarbija24.ee/110507/esileht/siseuudised/257862.php

79   'Estonian DDoS - a final analysis'. Heine Online, 31 May 2007. Available at http://www.h-online.com/security/news/item/Estonian-DDoS-a-final-analysis-732971.html

80   Clover, Charles. 'Kremlin-backed group behind Estonia cyber blitz'. Financial Times, 11 March 2009. Available at http://www.ft.com/cms/s/0/57536d5a-0ddc-11de-8ea3-0000779fd2ac.html?nclick_check=1

81   First calls to attack Estonian sites were discovered on 28 April 2007 at Russian hacker sites and internet forums http://2ch.ru and http://forum.xakep.ru, later on also on http://www.web-dozor.ru and others, complete with target lists and instructions.

82   Ottis, Rain. Overview of Events, 3 May 2007. CCD COE Activation Team, TDCCIS.

83   Kash, Wyatt. 'Lauri Almann: Lessons from the cyberattacks on Estonia'. GCN Interview with Lauri Almann, Estonia's permanent undersecretary of Defence. Government Computer News, 13 Jun 2008. Available at: http://gcn.com/Articles/2008/06/13/Lauri-Almann--Lessons-from-the-cyberattacks-on-Estonia.aspx?p=1. Mr. Almann was a member of the Estonian government crisis management committee at the time of the incident. The crisis management committee is responsible for coordination of all crisis-management related government activities.

84   Traynor, Ian. 'Russia accused of unleashing cyberwar to disable Estonia.' The Guardian, 17 May 2007. Available at http://www.guardian.co.uk/world/2007/may/17/topstories3.russia

85   Estonia hit by 'Moscow cyber war'. BBC News, 1 7 May 2007. Available at http://news.bbc.co.uk/2/hi/europe/6665145.stm; 'NATO Sees Recent Cyber Attacks on Estonia as Security Issue'. DW staff / AFP / dpa (nda) 26 May 2007. Available at http://www.dw-world.de/dw/article/0,2144,2558579,00.html

86   Millman, Rene. 'DDoS attacks on Estonia 'not from Kremlin''. ITPro. 1 June 2007. Available at http://www.itpro.co.uk/114570/ddos-attacks-on-estonia-not-from-kremlin

87   Yasmann, Victor. Monument Dispute With Estonia Gets Dirty. Russia Report May 8, 2007. Radio Free Europe/Radio Liberty, 8 May 2007. Available at http://www.rferl.org/content/Article/1347550.html; Clover, *supra* note 80.

88   Postimees, *supra* note 70.

his assistant as part of "a reaction from civil society"[89], which confirms earlier information of *Nashi* activists having been part of the attacks, even though the description of methods that were claimed by Markov and Goloskokov only matches part of the attacks experienced.

# Measures taken to cope with the attacks

## Technical measures

Response to cyber attacks was coordinated by CERT-EE, with the help of system administrators and experts both within and outside of the country. Top Estonian IT specialists from the public and private sectors were engaged on a round-the-clock basis.[90]

The first technical response to the random DoS attacks was to gradually increase the bandwidth of state information system servers (allowing for greater data traffic handling capacity), and to filter out the malicious traffic. By May 9-10, the bandwidth capacity of government networks had been increased to several times above the normal capacity.[91]

Other technical security measures included the application of security patches, firewalling, use of attack detection systems, using multiple servers and/or connections, blocking access, etc. In cooperation with ISPs, the data transmission capacity of incoming connections to Estonia was reduced. This blocked off a part of the attacks, but, as a negative side effect, also part of genuine traffic.[92] As patterns in attacks were distinguished, filtering grew more efficient to block off attacks at the ISP level – both by the Estonian and foreign service providers.[93] Some sites were restored to a "lightweight mode" – e.g. the Police Board that temporarily switched to a simple one-page html-view – to better cope with the amount of incoming queries.[94]

## International cooperation

International support was organised by the Ministry of Defence; EU and NATO nations were informed of the ongoing cyber attacks. In response, international cooperation was offered by several nations to limit the attacks originating or passing their respective jurisdictions.[95]

From May 8 to 10, NATO (NCIRC) and US CERT observers visited Estonia, mainly in order to observe the situation, as well as to provide assistance and advice.[96] United States governmental institutions assisted in locating and shutting down sources of attack.[97] Of foreign partners, CERT Finland was especially helpful in providing contacts and assistance in reaching service providers and computer incident response coordination entities of other countries.[98]

As news was published about Estonia cooperating with foreign authorities to locate the cyber criminals and bring them to justice, the number of spontaneous attackers began to diminish.[99]

# Effects of the attacks

The cyber effects had both a direct economic and a wider societal effect. As many sectors of commerce and industry rely on ICT infrastructure and electronic communication channels in their daily conduct of business, the overload of e-mail servers, network devices and web servers of internet service providers not only affected large entities such as banks, media corporations, and governmental institutions, but also small and medium size enterprises whose daily business activities were seriously impaired.[100] The

89 Behind The Estonia Cyberattacks. Radio Free Europe/Radio Liberty, 6 March 2009. Available at http://www.rferl.org/Content/Behind_The_Estonia_Cyberattacks/1505613.html
90 Tiks, *supra* note 67.
91 Ottis, Rain. Overview of Events, 10 May 2007. CCD COE Activation Team, TDCCIS.
92 Ottis, *supra* note 66.
93 Ottis, Rain. Overview of Events, 14 May 2007. CCD COE Activation Team, TDCCIS.
94 Hyppönen, Mikko. 'Update on the Estonian DDoS attacks.' F-Secure Weblog, 30 April 2007. Available at http://www.f-secure.com/weblog/archives/00001183.html
95 Kash, supra note 83; An Overview of Events, compiled by the CCD COE activation team on 8 May 2007.
96 Ottis, Rain. Overview of Events, 7 May 2007. CCD COE Activation Team, TDCCIS; Ruiz, Maricelle (ed). 1nternet Law - Should We Go To War Over A Massive Cyber-Attack?' Internet Business Law Services, 23 May 2007. Available at http://www.ibls.com/internet_law_news_portal_view.aspx?id=1762&s=latestnews; Finn, supra note 34; Traynor, supra note 85.
97 Ottis, *supra* note 66.
98 Randel, *supra* note 36.
99 Ottis, *supra* note 66.
100 Randel, supra note 36

cyber attacks thus had a perceptible effect to the functioning of domestic economy.[101]

The attacks also had a societal effect. Due to the e-Government reforms of recent years, non-electronic government communication channels and means of dissemination of information have been largely reduced, not to mention the shift in user habits which means that people are unaccustomed to looking for the information elsewhere than online. Because of the unavailability of government websites and the excessive spamming of official e-mail addresses, normal communication with government was impaired for citizens. By law, state authorities are obliged to treat electronically submitted documents or correspondence on equal basis with documents submitted on paper.[102] Ministries and state agencies – being obliged to do so by law[103] – provide detailed information on their services and contacts, as well as information request and application forms on their websites. When the websites closed down and e-mail addresses were flooded with spam, these information and communications channels became inaccessible. Only because the unavailability of government websites was temporary, it can be estimated that cyber attacks on government websites were not critical nor posed significant daily problems for the population in general.

Cyber attacks against online public services provided via the State Portal *eesti.ee* had a discernible effect for certain segments of the population, since these services are widely used for filing tax reports, applying for state benefits and subsidies and for other communication with the government that has a direct practical or monetary significance for the person involved. While the attacks did not cause long-term unavailability of service for users within Estonia, this was the case for those located abroad. It is difficult, if not impossible, to estimate the amount of damages caused to the population; we are only able to offer a conclusion that the unavailability of government websites may have had undesirable effects for parts of the population that went beyond mere inconvenience and also caused material damage or loss.

Last but not least, the attacks also affected the nation's information flow to the outside world.

Large international global/regional media organisations do not have stations or representatives in Estonia. The Estonian government relies on online briefing rooms and online media to distribute information, and these are widely used by the international media. [104] The receipt and dissemination of first-hand information about the Bronze Soldier riots, the siege of the Estonian embassy in Moscow and the cyber attacks was therefore impaired; in fact, local media web outlets and the Estonian government's online briefing room were among the first sites to come under cyber attack.[105] Again, the immediate loss caused by this is difficult to estimate, but the parties involved had to find alternative means of information exchange.

# III Legal considerations

## What response in law?

As the Estonian cyber attacks gained international attention, attempts were quick in trying to label them in terms of existing legal institutions. Parallels to conventional warfare and terrorism were drawn, and while some Estonian politicians initially uttered emotional statements comparing the attacks to conventional military activity, it was clear to the Estonian authorities that the cyber attacks could – and should – be treated as cyber crime under the applicable Penal Code and investigated in accordance with national law and relevant international agreements. The question of invoking article 5 of the Washington

---

101  See the discussion under section "Attack Targets" ("Internet infrastructure providers", "Government and political targets", and "Commercial services").

102  Administrative Procedure Act, § 5 (6). An unofficial English translation of the Act is available at: http://www.legaltext.ee/et/andmebaas/tekst.asp?loc=text&dok=X400 71K3&keel=en&pg=1&ptyyp=RT&tyyp=X&query=haldus menetluse

103  Public Information Act, § 28. Unofficial English translation of the Act is available at: http://www.legaltext.ee/et/andmebaas/tekst.asp?loc=text&dok=X40095K3&keel=en&pg=1&ptyyp=RT&tyyp=X&query=avaliku+teabe

---

104  Almann, *supra* note 33.

105  See *supra* in "Phase I – emotional response (April 27 to 29)".

Treaty was never seriously considered.[106]

## Procedural issues in national law

Identification of the originators of the spring 2007 Estonian cyber attacks was naturally dependent on measures and procedures that were legally permissible. In accordance with the Estonian Surveillance Act, collecting of information concerning data communicated via electronic communications networks – including the fact, duration, manner and form of communication, personal data and location of senders and receivers of such data – is considered a *surveillance activity*, which is strictly available only to surveillance agencies within the limits of their competence and within procedures authorised by law.[107] Unauthorised surveillance, i.e. observation of a person's activities in order to collect information relating to such person, is criminalised and punishable by law.[108] This effectively ruled out the possibility of having the ISPs or CERT monitor and analyse data logs with the objective of identifying particular attackers. Such activities are reserved to law enforcement agencies in investigation proceedings of specific crimes demarcated in the Code of Criminal Procedure ( § § 110–112).

According to the aforementioned provisions of the Code of Criminal Procedure, evidence may be collected by surveillance activities in a criminal proceeding if collection of the evidence by other procedural acts is a) precluded or especially complicated and b) the criminal offence under investigation is, at the minimum, an intentionally committed crime for which the law prescribes a punishment of at least three years' imprisonment. Only in those cases may evidence also be collected by surveillance activities on the basis of an international request for pre-trial investigation assistance.[109]

However, the majority of the criminal acts committed in the Estonian cyber incident failed to meet the 'three years' imprisonment as punishment' criteria. The lawmakers considered computer crimes as crimes directed against the rights and lawful expectations of individual users[110]; such a dimension that the 2007 cyber attacks demonstrated was never foreseen in drafting the Penal Code. The punishment prescribed by law for computer crimes, at the time of the 2007 incidents, was pecuniary punishment or a maximum one year of imprisonment.[111] This put the availability of the one useful surveillance activity – collecting information concerning data communicated via electronic communications networks – out of reach.

For specific computer crimes, procedural law did allow for evidence collecting by a specific type of surveillance activity titled "single inquiry" (defined as "an inquiry for obtaining information specified concerning a *particular* telephone call, a *particular* electronic mail, a *particular* electronic commentary or another communication session related to the forwarding of a single message"[112] [our emphasis]); however, this measure was inefficient to deal with the massive number of DoS and DDoS queries in the 2007 incidents, mainly for the disproportion between the bureaucratic burden contained in procedural requirements and the minuscule potential value derived of this effort. For each single inquiry, all procedural requirements for surveillance activities would have had to be followed – meaning that a reasoned request had to be submitted by the prosecutor to a preliminary investigation judge for the conduct of each surveillance activity, a detailed report had to be drafted on each inquiry, and each such activity was subject to questioning in the later course of proceedings. In other words, single inquiries

---

106   As expressed by Mr. Jaak Aaviksoo, Estonian defence minister, it was clear that 'At present, NATO does not define cyber-attacks as a clear military action. [...] Not a single NATO defence minister would define a cyber-attack as a clear military action at present.' See Traynor, *supra* note 85.

107   These are the Security Police Board, Police and Border Guard Board, the Military Police, the Prisons Department of the Ministry of Justice and prisons, and the Tax and Customs Board. See § 12 (1) section 5, § 6 (1) and (2) of the Estonian Surveillance Act.

108   § 137 of the Estonian Penal Code. Penal Code of Estonia (RT I 2001, 61, 364; 2009, 39, 261). An unofficial English text is available at http://www.legaltext.ee/et/andmebaas/tekst.asp?loc=text&dok=X30068K8&keel=en&pg=1&ptyyp=RT&tyyp=X&query=karistusseadustik

109   § 110, 117 of the Estonian Code of Criminal Procedure

110   Sootak, Jaan; Pikamäe, Priit. Karistusseadustik: kommenteeritud väljaanne. 2nd ed. Juura, 2009 (*The authoritative Commentary of the Estonian Penal Code*). Pp 454-457.

111   Penal Code, § § 206-208. For some cases involving severe damages or a previous offence of the same kind, an elevated term of punishment applied.

112   § 110 (1¹) of the Estonian Code of Criminal Procedure

would in all likeliness have produced "a lot of trees, but no forest".

Combining the complications discussed above with the restriction regarding issuing international requests for assistance (as this measure was not legally permissible in those cases where the "single inquiry" was the only surveillance activity permitted) in a situation where attacks were globally sourced from over a hundred nations, and it becomes apparent that the national legal system was not likely to do too well in identifying the perpetrators.

## International cooperation in criminal matters

According to article 3 of the Agreement on Mutual Legal Assistance between Estonia and Russia[113], signed in 1993, the states render each other legal assistance that includes procedural activities provided by law and conducted by the party who has received the request. Such assistance, according to Article 3, "includes procedural acts foreseen by the law of the receiving party, such as interrogation of parties, accused and accused at trial, witnesses and experts; expert assessments; inspection by court; transfer of physical evidence; initiating prosecution against the person who has committed a criminal offence; and criminal extradition; recognition and execution of court judgments in civil matters; service and transfer of documents; and transfer of data on the punishment of the accused, requested by the other party". As can be derived from the phrasing of the provision (the list of activities is preceded by the phrase "such as"), the list of procedural activities is not exclusive and can include other procedural acts permitted by the law of the receiving country.

Seeking for assistance in criminal investigations to identify persons that participated in the April-May 2007 cyber attacks, and based on the provisions in the Penal Code referring to computer sabotage, damaging a computer network, and the spread of computer viruses, the Estonian Public Prosecutor's Office submitted a letter rogatory to the Russian Federation on 10 May 2007 in accordance with the aforementioned

agreement.[114] The letter rogatory included specific IP addresses and references to web forum users, who were likely located on the Russian territory and whom Russia was asked to assist to identy[115].

In a reply of 28 June 2008, the Russian Federation refused to grant the request, stating that the procedural act requested in the letter rogatory was not foreseen by the mutual legal assistance treaty.[116] According to the reply, the agreement lays down that legal assistance shall be rendered in the framework of procedural actions according to the legal acts of the party who has received the request, but the agreement does not require cooperation in the field of operative surveillance measures (*operativno-rozysknye meroprijatija*) in order to identify a person's location.[117]

Even though the Russian approach to this agreement was formally not ungrounded, refusal was not the inevitable legal solution, considering both earlier cooperation practice with Russia and the practice with other countries with whom identically phrased bilateral agreements apply.[118] According to the prosecutor's office, earlier similarly phrased requests for conducting surveillance activities in criminal proceedings had been met by the Russian Prosecutor's Office, but in the cyber attacks case, the office took a different interpretation to the mutual as-

---

113  Agreement on Legal Assistance and Legal Relations in Civil, Family and Criminal Cases, signed on 26 January 1993. RT II 1993, 16, 27.

114  'Alustati kriminaalasi küberrünnakute uurimiseks.' Press release by the State Prosecutor's Office 2 May 2007. Available at: http://www.prokuratuur.ee/28707

115  'Küberrünnete korraldajaid ähvardab ELi vahistamismäärus.' BNS, 12 March 2009. Available at: http://www.postimees.ee/?id=93564; Pau, Aivar. 'Venemaa keeldus koostööst küberrünnakute uurimisel'. EPLOnline, 6 July 2007. Available at: http://www.epl.ee/artikkel/392271.

116  Pau, *Id.*

117  'Vene saatkond: Eesti ei saatnud korrektset teabenõuet'. Postimees, 10 May 2007 (*In Estonian*). Available at: http://www.euro.postimees.ee/100707/esileht/siseuudised/viimased_sundmused/271542.php

118  Identical phrasing occurs for example in the bilateral treaties for mutual legal assistance with the Ukraine and Poland. See 'Eesti Vabariigi ja Ukraina leping õigusabi ja õigussuhete kohta tsiviil- ning kriminaalasjades'. signed on 15 February 1995, entry into force 07 February 2000 (Published in RT II 1995, 13/14, 63); 'Eesti Vabariigi ja Poola Vabariigi vaheline leping õigusabi osutamise ja õigussuhete kohta tsiviil-, töö- ning kriminaalasjades', signed on 27 November 1998, entry into force 17 May 1996 (Published in RT II 1999, 4, 22).

sistance treaty.[119]

According to Norman Aas, Attorney General of the Estonian Public Prosecutor's Office, criminal cooperation with Russia has been complicated since 2006, when the previous Minister of Justice and Attorney General of the Russian Federation were replaced. Since then, Russia has refused to cooperate in certain aspects stipulated in the mutual assistance treaty, while still granting certain other requests.[120] Specifically, Russia has declared that it will not interrogate a suspect of Russian citizenship nor conduct any other procedural activities directed toward them at the request of another country.[121]

Therefore, in all likeliness, the problematic interpretation of the agreement on mutual legal assistance between Estonia and Russia was not due to a judicial impediment – the ambiguity of the mutual assistance treaty or the letter rogatory being ill-formed – but rather depended on pragmatic will (or lack thereof) to cooperate.

The prosecution of cyber attacks originating from Russia has stood at a standstill since the Russian refusal letter. The Estonian Prosecutor's Office holds that the letter rogatory applies and should be treated in accordance with the applicable agreement between the two countries.[122]

Beside the problematic cooperation with Russia, another specific obstacle that complicated criminal proceedings was the issue that the attackers had purposefully moved botnet C&C servers to less friendly or less advanced jurisdictions[123], thereby avoiding judicial cooperation between nations due to either unwillingness to cooperate on part of the attack source country, or the lack of a legal framework for that purpose. Specifically, unrecognised jurisdictions such as the breakaway Moldovan region of Transdniester were also referred to as having been used as the set-off location for launching attacks.[124]

As of summer 2009, the only person convicted for participation in the cyber attacks is Dmitri Galushkevich, a 19-year-old Estonian citizen of Russian ethnicity and an IT student at Tallinn University of Technology. His role in the incidents was launching ping flood attacks (DoS attacks) against the website of the Estonian Reform Party as an expression of protest against the Government of Estonia. He was prosecuted based on Article 206 (2) of the Estonian Penal Code for illegal blocking of computer data with the purpose of hindering the functioning of the computer system.[125]

Galushkevich admitted to have, upon coordination with other, unidentified persons, used DoS (ping) attacks against the server running the public website as well as the Intranet site of the Reform Party between 25 April to 4 May. By doing this, he caused also other services run on that server to become inaccessible, thereby causing damage to the ISP and the Reform Party in the amount of ca € 2820. Both the ISP and the Reform Party dropped the claim on the condition that Galushkevich agree to a compromise procedure. Galushkevich was fined in the amount of 17 500 kroons (ca € 1120); in addition, he had to pay compensation levies[126] in the amount of 5400 kroons (ca € 345).[127]

## Lessons learned for Estonia: widening the scope of criminal law

Regardless of the cyber attacks being prosecuted as "regular" cyber crime, a perception was there that the Estonian events were something "more" than simply a series of individual cyber crimes. The concertedness, intensity and wide scale, but also the nature of the targets chosen made it clear that the existing cyber crime legal framework with its perception of cyber crime as mainly conducted on the motive of material gain or mere hooliganism was too narrow in fitting these new kind of events.

119 'Riigiprokuratuur: Vene saatkond esitas valeväiteid'. Postimees,
    11 July 2007 (*In Estonian*). Available at: http://www.euro.
    postimees.ee/120707/esileht/siseuudised/271694.php
120 'Venemaa keeldub endiselt koostööst küberrünnakute
    uurimisel'. ERR, 13 Dec 2008. Available at: http://uudised.
    err.ee/index.php?06147571
121 *Id.*
122 *Id.*
123 Kash, *supra* note 83.
124 Yasmann, *supra* note 87.

125 Judgment of Harju County Court of 13 December 2007 in
    criminal matter No 1-07-15185 (Galushkevich)
126 Compensation levies is a payment that the convict is
    obliged to pay upon judgment of conviction. The size of
    the levies is defined based on two criteria: gravity of the
    crime and the applicable minimum salary. The levies is
    collected for state compensation for victims of crime.
127 Judgment of Harju County Court, *supra* note 125.

Due also to the complications that arose in prosecution (that were discussed in more detail above), the Ministry of Justice prepared a comprehensive amendment package to the Penal Code which was presented to the *Riigikogu* (Estonian Parliament) in December 2007 and adopted as law in February 2008.[128]

The amendments itemised in more detail the provisions of the Penal Code relating to attacks against computer systems and data, and updated the extent of some provisions (such as adding the dissemination of spyware and malware) and added a new provision on preparation of cyber crimes. Based on an understanding that the frequency of cyber attacks has been on a steady increase, and that due to the rising availability of Internet and growing use of electronic channels by the population such attacks are becoming increasingly dangerous, the amendments also prescribed higher maximum punishments for such crimes. Moreover, since collecting of evidence is complicated in investigating such crimes, the use of surveillance measures was made more easily available for the police.[129]

The composition of 'terrorist crime' in the Penal Code was amended to include 'interference with computer data or hindrance of operation of computer systems as well as threatening with such acts, if committed with the purpose to force the state or an international organisation to perform an act or omission, or to seriously interfere with or destroy the political, constitutional, economic or social structure of the state, or to seriously interfere with or destroy the operation of an international organisation, or to seriously terrorise the population'.[130] In other words, cyber crimes, if motivated by terrorist aims, are now treated as terrorist crimes by Estonian law.[131]

Similar provisions exist in some other European countries: the French *Code Penal* considers computer crimes committed intentionally with the purpose of seriously disturbing public order by frightening the population (Article 421-1, section 2) to be a terrorist crime; the Austrian *Strafgesetzbuch* considers as terrorist crime "the damaging of computer data if such action causes a threat to life or assets in great extent" (Article 278c section 1 subsection 6); the Luxembourg *Code Penal* in Article 135-1 criminalises any crime that is committed with a terrorist purpose, if at least a three-year imprisonment is foreseen for that crime.[132]

## Lessons learned for Estonia: adopting the Cyber Security Strategy

The attacks accelerated an important undertaking in terms of national security: the drafting and adoption of the Estonian Cyber Security strategy. A Cyber Security Strategy Committee was formed for drafting the strategy for the period of 2008–2013, led by the Ministry of Defence in cooperation with the Ministry of Education and Research, the Ministry of Justice, the Ministry of Economic Affairs and Communications, the Ministry of Internal Affairs and the Ministry of Foreign Affairs.[133] The strategy was submitted to the Government and adopted in May 2008.

While a thorough introduction and analysis of the strategy would be beyond the scope of this paper, we would like to give a short overview of the main concepts the strategy offers, and of the action plan for its implementation.

The strategy points out the importance of understanding that the security risk posed by the asymmetric threat of cyber attacks coupled with the inherent vulnerabilities of cyberspace

---

128   The English translation of the Estonian Penal Code is available at the website of the Estonian Ministry of Justice at: http://www.legaltext.ee/et/andmebaas/tekst.asp?loc=text&dok=X30068K8&keel=en&pg=1&ptyyp=RT&tyyp=X&query=karistusseadustik

129   Explanatory Memorandum to the Draft Act on the Amendment of the Penal Code (116 SE). (*In Estonian.*) December 2007. Available at: http://www.riigikogu.ee/?page=pub_file&op=emsplain&content_type=application/msword&u=20090902161440&file_id=198499&file_name=KarS%20seletuskiri%20(167).doc&file_size=66048&mnsensk=166+SE&etapp=03.12.2007&fd=29.10.2008

130   Estonian Penal Code (RT I 2001, 61, 364; 2009, 39, 261), § 237

131   Explanatory Memorandum to the Draft Act on the Amendment of the Penal Code, supra note 129.

132   As referenced in the Explanatory Memorandum to the Draft Act on the Amendment of the Penal Code, *supra* note 129.

133   'Cyber Security Strategy'. Cyber Security Strategy Committee, Ministry of Defence. Tallinn 2008. The English version of the Estonian Cyber Security Strategy is available at: http://www.mod.gov.ee/static/sisu/files/Estonian_Cyber_Security_Strategy.pdf

is a global one, therefore solvable only by co-ordinated efforts of all nations. It stresses the significance of implementing organisational, technical and regulatory information security measures, but also sets a higher objective of developing a broad and sophisticated cyber security culture. Through these different layers, the Cyber Security Strategy seeks to reduce the inherent vulnerabilities of cyberspace in the nation as a whole.[134]

In order to accomplish these aims, activities are foreseen in five main policy fronts[135]:

- *The development and large-scale implementation of a system of security measures*, where every information system acknowledges the risks related to the disturbance of the service he or she provides, and has up-to-date and economically expedient security measures accessible to them and implemented. Activities are foreseen for increasing the resistance of critical information systems and infrastructure, but also at strengthening the physical and logical infrastructure of the Internet as a core platform for the majority of public services.

- *Increasing expert awareness and competence in cyber security* by developing national expertise in and high awareness of information security to the highest standard of excellence; providing high quality and accessible information security-related training, establishing common requirements for IT staff competence in information security, and by intensifying research and development in cyber security. Also, measures are proposed to ensure readiness in managing cyber security crises in both the public and private sectors.

- *Improvement of the legal framework for supporting cyber security*, including the development of an appropriate regulatory and legal framework to support the secure and seamless operability of information systems, developing legislation on protection of the critical information infrastructure, and participation in international law-making in the field of cyber security.

- *Bolstering international cooperation* by de-veloping cooperative networks in the field of cyber security, and promoting awareness on and adoption of international treaties regulating cyber crime and cyber attacks. Beside the regulatory approach, the activities are directed at achieving a worldwide moral condemnation of cyber attacks, while recognising the need to promote and support human rights and democratic freedoms.

- *Raising public awareness on cyber security* from the grassroots (computer user) level to the widest international field.

The strategy also defines fields of Estonia's critical infrastructure.[136]

According to the strategy, the procurement of national cyber security in Estonia will be pursued by integrating cyber security action plans into the routine processes of national security planning and involving coordinated efforts of all concerned stakeholders, placing the responsibility for awareness and action on every member of the information society: not only the policymakers, law enforcement authorities and service providers, but every information system owner and finally, every computer user. [137]

Despite the high attention to security measures, the strategy stresses that the overall task rests on the need to balance, on the one hand, the risks associated with the use of information systems and, on the other hand, the indispensability of extensive and free use of information technology to the functioning of open and modern societies, wherefore appropriate attention must be paid to the protection of human rights, personal data, and identity.[138]

The practical implementation of the strategy is set out in implementation plans, which focus on the concrete actions and funds needed to achieve the objectives of the Strategy in its various fields of competence. The Implementation Plan covering years 2008–2010, elaborated based on proposals from different state agencies and working groups, was adopted in May

---

134   'Cyber Security Strategy', *supra* note 133. P. 3.
135   *Id.*, pp. 27-34.
136   *Id.*, p. 36.
137   *Id.* pp. 7-8.
138   *Id.* p. 6.

2009.[139] Another one will be developed for years 2011–2013. The implementation and overall efficiency of the Strategy in meeting its stated objectives will be annually assessed and reported by the Cyber Security Council of the Security Committee of the Government of the Republic.

# The emerging trend of "patriot hacking"

The Estonian event was not the first occurrence of the phenomenon of "patriot hacking", but the extent and duration of the attacks to draw renewed attention to the problem. "Patriot hacking" (or "patriotic hacking")[140] is a term that reflects citizen involvement with hacking or cyber attacking the systems of a perceived adversary (e.g. another government or nation).[141]

Patriot hacking is often used as response against a country's political decision that the country where the particular hacker or group of hackers originates from openly or presumably disapproves. As such, patriot hacking is performed by a group of people who take action "pro patria" in cases where they believe that this is the right thing for their government to do or where they perceive the government as unable to do "the right thing". In the Estonian case, such expression took the form of political activists expressing their protest by engaging in coordinated cyber attacks against the online presence and, to a smaller degree, the Internet infrastructure of Estonia.[142]

The definition of "hacking" by itself is motivation-neutral – it does not differentiate whether the aim be material gain, personal revenge, curiosity or a strong political (or other social) opinion. The concept of hacking involves unauthorised access to computer data or network with the purpose of harming the integrity, confidentiality and availability of that data or network.[143]

Most regulation that relates to criminalising hacking is stemming from the understanding of an activity motivated by material gain, as it is there where most harm arises. Likewise, the Council of Europe Convention on Cybercrime[144] also seems to have mainly pecuniary consequences in mind, even though the convention can be applied to tackle hacking in a motivation-neutral way if adequately implemented. Politically motivated attacks seem to have been less in the regulatory focus, probably due to the relatively short history of widespread use of hacking as a political tool. The latter is presumably conditioned by the fact that in contrast to hacking motivated by financial gain, there is little direct reward for "political hacking" – therefore, resources are needed which assumes the involvement of organised activity at some level. Also, the technical base for hacking has in recent years become exponentially more available to regular users, who need not possess advanced technical knowledge or expensive tools to cause significant nuisance.

While patriot hacking may be perceived as more "noble" compared to other types of hacking referenced above in that it is not motivated by financial gain, and has therefore experienced more toleration, it has hazardous effects both toward its target and origin jurisdictions. Patriot hacking is understandably harmful against the target jurisdiction, as it is intended to achieve a political goal by pressuring the authorities or influencing the public. But it also has a hazardous effect towards the jurisdiction of origin in that patriotic hackers assume on their own accord a role on behalf of their governments ("taking the matter in their own hands on behalf of an

---

139  'Valitsus kiitis heaks küberjulgeoleku strateegia rakend-usplaani aastateks 2009–2011'. Postimees, 14 May 2009 *(In Estonian)*. Available at: http://uudisvoog.postimees.ee/?DATE=20090514&ID=204872

140  The actual extent of the activity titled 'hacking' is wider than the common perception of the name indicates, since the same term is also used for actions directed at the availability of computers or computer systems (e.g. committing DoS or DDoS attacks), not only breaching into systems (i.e. the 'confidentiality' and 'integrity' aspect).

141  'An Expert Look at Chinese Information Operations Theory'. IntelliBriefs, 10 November 2008. Available at: http://intellibriefs.blogspot.com/2008/11/expert-look-at-chinese-information.html

142  RFE/RL cites Sergei Markov, a State Duma Deputy from the Unified Russia party, in his comment on the Estonia 2007 cyber attacks: "Turns out it was purely a reaction from civil society […] and, incidentally, such things will happen more and more." *See* Coalson, Robert. 'Behind The Estonia Cyberattacks'. RFE/RL, 6 March 2009. Available at: http://www.rferl.org/Content/Behind_The_Estonia_Cyberattacks/1505613.html

143  *See* Bidgoli, Hossein. 'Handbook of information security', Volume 3. John Wiley and Sons, Inc, 2003. P. 560; Convention on Cybercrime (ETS No. 185), Explanatory Report. Available at: http://conventions.coe.int/Treaty/EN/Reports/Html/185.htm. Section 44.

144  Convention on Cybercrime, Council of Europe (ETS 185). 23.XI.2001. Available at: conventions.coe.int/Treaty/EN/Treaties/Html/185.htm.

incapable state") by going beyond condemning certain activities (which would be a legitimate exercise of freedom of expression) and instead attacking the position of another sovereign, thereby raising the question of state attribution.

The distinction lies in the understanding that a government in a similar political circumstance, if it ordered a cyber attack against another government's information services, would be exposed to state liability, whereas "private hacking initiatives" would be regarded as "ordinary" cyber crime. A convenience for political hackers is that their motivation is covered by the political situation between two governments and therefore will not need to be expressed as part of their identity (which would normally be the case with terrorist groups). This combination leaves patriotic hackers in a gray area of law where their activities may be significantly more disturbing than those of "ordinary hackers", but the legal framework for investigation and prosecution does not recognise any difference.

Regardless of motivation, hacking and cyber attacking cause harm also to communications network infrastructure, including the global Internet infrastructure, in that they overload the normal capacities of networks. Where botnets are used to carry out politically motivated attacks – like the Estonian (and later on also Georgian) examples indicate – the low risk of facing prosecution due to attacks being "only political" feeds the "business incentive" of botnet owners to continue producing and distributing malicious software.

Therefore, there is not much basis for tolerating patriot hacking as "less harmful" or as a semi-legitimate expression of protest. There are legal ways for citizens to express their opinion and attitude without effectively hampering information society in another country. Communications undertakings and infrastructure owners have a legitimate expectation that the state endeavours to provide a secure environment for their business activities. This is also in end user interests, who individually have little chance to defend themselves against the service disruptions caused by cyber attacks. In order to support the functioning and development of information society, the focus of both national and international criminal law needs to widen to take the full spectrum of threat into account. Additionally, widening the scope of national criminal law to include politically motivated cyber attacks in the definition of cyber crime would send a clear message that the government does not condone patriot hacking on its behalf, thereby relieving the risk of government facing international allegations of state involvement in the event that its nationals or residents should engage in such activities.

The Estonian incident offered lessons to be learned for both the target and the originating side; the Georgian incident occurring about a year later demonstrates that lack of a negative reaction from the state encouraged attackers to return to their tools in a more concerted manner when a suitable opportunity arose. To apply the old proverb "Wise men learn from their mistakes, but really wise men learn the mistakes of others": the sooner a general consensus develops regarding the dangerous nature of politically motivated cyber attacks, and the sooner the appropriate legislative steps are taken, the better protected information societies in individual nations, but also information society as a global good will be.

# IV Summary of the Estonian case

## INCIDENT TIME FRAME

*Start*      Friday, 27 April 27 2007

*End*        Friday, 18 May 2007
             (some aftermath until end of May 2007)

*Duration*   3 weeks

## INCIDENT CONTEXT

### Political context and background of incident

- Government decision to relocate a Soviet-era WWII memorial from a central location in the capital city to a military cemetery met by intense opposition from the Russian government and media;

- Protests against the start of removal works break into street riots;

- Siege of the Estonian embassy in Moscow conducted by *Nashi*, a Russian political youth movement. Ambassador physically harassed.

### Information society indicators

- Pioneer since mid-1990ies in state-wide public e-solutions employed by both the private and public sectors (prevalent use of Internet banking; mobile parking and public transportation tickets; online voting in elections since 2005; majority or taxes declared electronically; online State Portal as a one-stop service point for all government e-services)

- Internet access nearly universally available (98% of territory), mobile penetration nearing 100% (in 2007);

- Overarching governance policy, backed by a legal framework, to use information technology to increase public sector administrative capacity and ease citizen-to-government communications. Paperless government since 2001.

## INCIDENT FACTS

### Methods

- DoS and DDoS;
- Website defacement;
- Attacking DNS servers;
- Mass e-mail and comment spam.

### Targets

- Servers of institutions responsible for the Estonian Internet infrastructure;

- Governmental and political targets (parliament, president, ministries, state agencies, political parties);

- Services provided by the private sector (e-banking, news organisations);

- Personal and random targets.

### Origin

- Mainly sourced outside of Estonia, computers involved from 178 countries altogether;

- Early attacks largely carried out by nationalistically/politically motivated individuals and following instructions provided on Russian-language Internet forums and websites;

- The second phase of attacks has features of central command and control;

- A few self-proclaimed or self-acknowledged attackers;

- Russian authorities have denied any involvement.

### Effect

- Perceptible effect to the functioning of domestic economy: affecting sectors of commerce, industry and governance that rely on ICT infrastructure and electronic communications in their daily conduct of business (banks, media corporations, governmental institutions, small and medium size enterprises);

- Societal effect: hindered access to communication with public administration (unavailability of information, means of communication, and access to services);

- Information flow to the outside world impaired;

- Side-effects: attack mitigation means blocked off part of the genuine traffic together with the malicious one.

### Measures taken

- Response coordinated by CERT-EE, with assistance from system administrators and experts both within and outside of the country; IT experts from both public and private sectors engaged round-the-clock;

- Technical measures: increasing bandwidth, using multiple servers and/or connections; firewalling, filtering out malicious traffic; application of security patches; use of attack detection systems, etc. Some sites temporarily switched to "lightweight mode";

- International cooperation, organised by Ministry of Defence: informing partners in EU and NATO; observer and advisory assistance from NATO network incident handling entities; national CERTs (e.g. U.S.A., Germany, Finland) assisted in locating and reporting sources of attack;

- Public awareness: news about Estonia cooperating with foreign authorities to locate cyber criminals and bring them to justice reduced the number of spontaneous attackers.

## LEGAL LESSONS IDENTIFIED AND LEARNED

### Core of the case

- Highlighted the need to raise international awareness about crimes against information society;

- Raised the question of efficiency of mutual criminal assistance treaties in a situation where the receiving party is unwilling to cooperate.

### Summary

- The traditional view of substantive criminal law considers cyber crime foremost as an economically motivated activity, which may not be sufficient to satisfactorily respond to politically motivated cyber attacks where the damaged legal interest is not the integrity, availability, confidentiality or the proper functioning and use of computer data, programs, or networks, but the political, constitutional, economic or social structure of the state;

- There are often differing legal requirements for what is permissible in criminal proceedings in the countries involved; and the attackers may resort their activities to jurisdictions that the attacked country – or the country receiving a request for assistance – does not recognise, which will foreclose the success of criminal proceedings. International law lacks effective enforcement mechanisms to ensure cooperation from the country in which the attacks originate, if the latter in refuses to cooperate. But international cooperation in criminal matters, in its mainly bilateral nature, may be ineffective even if both parties are willing and able to cooperate, as the Internet facilitates easy splitting up of a given illegal act to several small trails that can be left in a number of countries – such as the formation of a botnet to attack servers in a particular country.

### Challenges

- Reorientation from a "whose area of responsibility a particular type of cyber attack might be" to an understanding that a national-scale cyber attack is a problem affecting the society, its security and public order as a whole, and therefore the legal framework needs to specify at what degrees of cyber attacks the different institutions are entitled to and obliged to interfere, and what are the procedural rules and the relevant institutions' terms of reference in case of wide-scale cyber incidents.

- A lack of unison of regulation between countries leads to a fragmented approach toward a phenomenon that knows no borders; a wider platform of multilateral cooperation is therefore needed to handle such threats. Also, the development of international agreements and uniform standards of best practice by the relevant international players would be highly welcome, specifying the organisational framework, terms of reference, and procedural rules applicable in the event of a cyber attack.

# RADIO FREE EUROPE/ RADIO LIBERTY 2008

April

# I Background of the incident

## The political situation in Belarus

Belarus is a former republic of the Union of Soviet Socialist Republics, situated in Eastern Europe. It is a landlocked country bordered by Russia to the north and east, the Ukraine to the south, Latvia to the northwest, Lithuania to the west, and Poland to the southwest.

Belarus gained its independence in 1991 upon the collapse of the Soviet Union. Of all the former Soviet republics, Belarus has retained the closest relations with the Russian Federation.[145]

In July 1994 Alexander Lukashenka was elected President of the Republic of Belarus. By repeatedly extending his opportunities to remain in power via referendums in 1996 and 2004, Lukashenka ensured his re-election to president in 2001 and again in 2006. Both elections have been described as marred by electoral fraud.[146] Since his first election, Lukashenka "has consolidated power steadily in the executive branch through authoritarian means and has dominated all branches of government"[147]. He has earned the criticism of Western governments and human rights campaigners for his authoritarian leadership, and the country is widely referred to as the "last dictatorship of Europe".[148]

The role of political opposition in shaping policies, as well as public support for opposition, are marginal; they also lack available channels to make their position heard.[149]

---

145  Stephens, Hampton. 'Belarusian Cyber Attack'. World Politics Review Blogs, 28 April 2008, available at: http://www.worldpoliticsreview.com/blog/blog.aspx?ID=2012.

146  Belarus. CIA World Factbook, 2009. Available at: https://www.cia.gov/library/publications/the-world-factbook/geos/bo.html; US Department of State – Bureau of European and Eurasian Affairs. Background Notes – Belarus. Available at: http://www.state.gov/r/pa/ei/bgn/5371.htm; Daniszewski, John. 'Election Fraud Belarus'. 11 Sept 2001, Los Angeles Times. http://articles.latimes.com/2001/sep/11/news/mn-44558.

147  US Department of State, Id.

148  'Profile: Alexander Lukashenko'. BBC News, 9 January 2007, available at: http://news.bbc.co.uk/2/hi/europe/3882843.stm; Marson, James. 'Belarus: Can Europe Change Its 'Last Dictatorship'?'. The Time, 25 March 2009. Available at: http://www.time.com/time/world/article/0,8599,1887513,00.html; Jan Maksymiuk 'Belarus: The Slow-Boiling Dictatorship' RFE/RL, 14 June 2005. Available at: http://www.rferl.org/content/article/1059266.html.

149  Meikar, Silver. 'Perestroika imelaps Valgevene' (in Estonian). Diplomaatia, nr 63, November 2008. International Centre for Defence Studies.

## Media freedom in Belarus

Belarus is notorious for having one of the most repressive media environments in the world. Freedom House, a major U.S.-based media rights monitor who conducts annual surveys on freedom of the press, ranked Belarus among the three worst performers (alongside Uzbekistan and Turkmenistan) in the Central and Eastern Europe/Former Soviet Union region and among eight worst performers globally.[150]

According to Freedom House, the state maintains a virtual monopoly on domestic broadcast media and the country's surviving independent media is subjected to constant administrative and economic pressure.[151] Until recently, the Internet was the last channel that went uncontrolled by the state, but the new Statute on Mass Media adopted in the summer of 2008 extended regulation to information published to the World Wide Web.[152]

While about 29% of the Belarus population uses the Internet[153], Internet access is controlled by the state-owned monopoly Beltelekom that, according to Freedom House, "controls all internet access and blocks some critical websites, while the security services reportedly monitor internet communications."[154]

## Radio Free Europe/Radio Liberty

Radio Free Europe/Radio Liberty (RFE/RL) is a private, non-profit corporation funded by the government of the United States through the Broadcasting Board of Governors. It was estab-

lished in 1949 by the National Committee for a Free Europe with the aim to spread pro-Western, uncensored news and to promote democratic values and institutions in countries behind the "Iron Curtain".[155]

Today RFE/RL broadcasts in 28 languages to 20 countries, including Belarus. The organisation is headquartered in Prague, Czech Republic, and has 19 local bureaus in other countries. RFE/RL focuses on providing "news, information, and responsible discussion of domestic and international issues to countries where free and independent media are not permitted, or not yet fully established".[156] The RFE/RL Belarus Service – Radio Svaboda – was established in 1954 and broadcasts daily to the Belarusian audience in the national language; since 1988, they also have an Internet website (www.svaboda.org).[157]

According to Julie Finley, the US Ambassador to the OSCE,[158] "RFE/RL is one of the few sources of outside information about developments in Belarus".[159] It has been suggested that RFE/RL could perhaps be "the most consistent and largest instrument of press freedom in Russia's sphere of influence".[160] During its broadcasting history RFE/RL has experienced a lot of resistance, including regular attempts by the Warsaw pact countries to jam the broadcasting signal of RFE/RL.[161]

150  Freedom of the Press 2009 Table of Global Press Freedom Rankings (pp. 1-5); Freedom of the Press 2009: Press Freedom Rankings by Region: Central And Eastern Europe / Former Soviet Union (p. 10). Available at: http://www.freedomhouse.org/uploads/fop/2009/FreedomofthePress2009_tables.pdf.
151  Freedom Of The Press - Belarus (2008). Freedom House, 2009. Available at: http://www.freedomhouse.org/inc/content/pubs/pfs/inc_country_detail.cfm?country=7351&year=2008&page=16&view=mopf&pf.
152  Meikar, supra note 149.
153  ITU ICT Statistics Database (ICT Eye). Internet indicators: subscribers, users and broadband subscribers: 2008. Available at: http://www.itu.int/ITU-D/icteye/Reporting/ShowReportFrame.aspx?ReportName=/WTI/InformationTechnologyPublic&RP_intYear=2008&RP_intLanguageID=1.
154  Freedom Of The Press, supra note 151..

155  'A Brief History of RFE/RL'. RFE/RL. Available at: http://www.rferl.org/info/history/133.html
156  'RFE/RL In Brief. RFE/RL'. Available at: http://www.rferl.org/info/facts/200.html
157  'RFE/RL's Belarus service'. RFE/RL. Available at: http://www.rferl.org/info/facts/184.html
158  The Organization for Security and Co-operation in Europe. It is the world's largest security-oriented intergovernmental organization. Belarus is a member since 1992.
159  Finley, Julie. 'Statement on Cyber-attacks Against Radio Free Europe in Belarus'. Statement to the OSCE Permanent Council, 8 May 2008, available at: http://www.america.gov/st/texttrans-english/2008/May/20080508115033eaifas0.3709833.html
160  Stephens, supra note 145.
161  'A Brief History of RFE/RL'. Supra note 155.

# II Facts of the Case

## Chronology, targets, methods and origin of cyber attacks

At 8 AM on Saturday, 26 April 2008, the website of Radio Free Europe/Radio Liberty's Belarus service became target of a Distributed Denial of Service (DDoS) attack. The service was inundated with about 50,000 fake pings every second, which the organisation reported as unprecedented in the history of cyber assaults against them. In a few hours after the DDoS attack commenced against the Belarus Service, seven other RFE/RL websites in the Eastern European and Central Asian/Middle East region (Kosovo, Azerbaijan, Tatar-Bashkir [ethnic regions within the Russian Federation], Radio Farda in Iran, South Slavic, and Tajik) were also affected. The attack lasted for two days.[162] By April 28, most of the RFE/RL Internet sites were restored; the primary target, Radio Svaboda, came back online on the evening of April 28.[163]

Political linkage is apparent in the details and timing of the incident. 26 April 2008 was the 22nd anniversary of the Chernobyl nuclear disaster.[164] Over the weekend, thousands of opponents to the Belarusian government held a rally to protest the lack of compensation for the Chernobyl victims and also the government's decision to build a new nuclear power plant.[165] RFE/RL had scheduled a live coverage of the rally and it has been suggested that Belarus' regime may have wanted to limit access to the coverage.[166]

Jeffrey Gedmin, the director of the RFE/RL, believed that the Belarusian government was most likely behind the attacks, describing the cyber attacks as a weapon of dictators who were trying to prevent unfiltered news and information from reaching their people.[167] In an online poll conducted on the Belarus Service's website, 87 percent of respondents blamed the authorities for the attack.[168] Julie Finley stated that "what occurred to RFE was a clear violation of guarantees of media freedom and of freedom of expression that the OSCE as an institution stands for."[169]

According to Alexander Lukashuk, RFE/RL Belarusian Service Director, RFE/RL put questions regarding the cyber attacks to Belarusian officials on several occasions, including at a Belarusian Foreign Ministry press conference, in a phone call to the KGB for comment, and to Internet providers. All denied any involvement in any attacks.[170]

José Nazario of Arbor Networks agreed that the attacks were political in nature, but reported having no evidence that the attacks were carried out by any political agent in general or a government in particular. He also noted the general difficulty of tying this type of attack to specific individuals.[171]

---

162  RFE/RL Belarus Service Director Discusses Cyberattack. RFE/RL 28, April 2008. Available at: http://www.rferl.org/content/article/1109643.html.

163  'RFE/RL Websites Hit By Mass Cyberattack'. Radio Free Europe/Radio Liberty, 28 April 2008, available at: http://www.rferl.org/content/article/1109642.html; Karnej, Ihar; Whitmore, Brian. 'Belarus: RFE/RL Cites Online 'Solidarity' In Face Of Cyberattack' RFE/RL, 29 April 2008. http://www.rferl.org/content/article/1109649.html; 'Global Cyber Attack against Radio Free Europe/Radio Liberty'. Radio Free Europe/Radio Liberty, 28 April 2008, available at: http://www.rferl.org/content/PressRelease/1110126.html.

The last article mentions that a similar attack had been carried out against the same site on the 21st Chernobyl anniversary in 2007, but it lasted only a few hours and did not cause any remarkable damage.

164  The Chernobyl accident was the worst in the history of nuclear power generation. Before the accident a small town of 12,000 people, Chernobyl is located in the northern part of the Ukraine, right on the border of Belarus. When the accident occurred on April 25-26, 1986, not only did it affect the Ukraine, but the wind also spread radioactivity to other countries. About one-fourth of Belarus' territory was affected, causing different environmental and medical problems, among others an increase in cancer deaths and birth defects. *See*, e.g., West, Larry. 'Chernobyl Nuclear Accident'. About.com. Available at: http://environment.about.com/od/chernobyl/p/chernobyl.htm.

165  Goodin, Dan. 'Radio Free Europe hit by DDoS attack'. SecurityFocus, 1 May 2008, available at: http://www.securityfocus.com/news/11515?ref=rss; Mills, Elinor. 'Radio Free Europe DDOS Attack Latest by Hactivists'. CNET News, 1 May 2008, available at: http://news.cnet.com/8301-10784_3-9933746-7.html.

166  'Cyberjamming'. The Wall Street Journal, 29 April 2008, available at: http://online.wsj.com/article/SB120942466671951083.html

167  'Global Cyber Attack Against Radio Free Europe/Radio Liberty'. *supra* note 163.

168  Karnej, Whitmore, *supra* note 163.

169  Finley, *supra* note 159.

170  Heil, Andy, Managing Editor to RFE/RL, in an e-mail to Kadri Kaska/CCD COE on 23 Oct 2009.

171  Nazario, José. 'Radio Free Europe DDoS'. Arbor Networks, 29 April 2008, available at: http://asert.arbornetworks.com/2008/04/radio-free-europe-ddos/.

Nazario points to evidence that "a Russian language DDoS botnet" was partially responsible for the attacks. Other websites were also targeted by the same botnet[172], of which the website of a Belarus-based independent news organisation Charter 97 (www.charter97.org) is visibly linked to the incident in that it carried related content on the political activities in Belarus. Charter 97 has been publishing news from Belarus since 1998[173] and tops the list of Belarusian news websites averaging 20,000 unique queries per day[174] (it is among the ten most popular websites in Belarus[175]). The site has a history of being targeted by frequent cyber attacks deemed to be political in nature.[176] There are also accounts of simultaneous attacks against another news website, "Belorusskii Partizan" (BelPartyzan).[177]

Alexander Lukashuk informed that numerous local websites in Belarus offered their help to carry RFE/RL's news and reports during the April 2008 attacks, until the RFE/RL Belarus website was back to operating.[178]

# III Legal considerations

The RFE/RL case represents an example of the importance of the Internet as a medium for expressing public opinion about the political situation and activities in a country. To a certain extent, also the Estonian, Georgian and Lithuanian cases are about the freedom of expressing one's feelings towards government's activities and decisions. However, the RFE/RL incident is different in that it represents a situation where the possibility of expressing – and accessing

– opinions and views towards authorities has been severely hindered or cut off.

It is for this reason that the RFE/RL case is relevant from the point of view of human rights and fundamental freedoms, most importantly the freedom of expression. As freedom of expression forms the core of the background of the incident, we will take a look at this freedom as guaranteed under international law instruments and the recent developments in Belarus in this field of law. Many conflicts in cyber space touch upon the legal domain of freedom of expression, which is why this aspect needs consideration by nations in forming their nationalcyber security policies and legal framework, as well as consistent attention in the evolution of international law in this field.

## The fundamental freedom of expression

The Universal Declaration on Human Rights (UDHR), adopted by the United Nations General Assembly in 1948, holds freedom of opinion and expression as a fundamental freedom of humanity. Article 19 of the UDHR states:

> "Everyone has the right to freedom of opinion and expression; this right includes freedom to hold opinions without interference and to seek, receive and impart information and ideas through any media and regardless of frontiers."

Moreover, the preamble of the UDHR underlines freedom of speech as a core value of humanity in noting that "the advent of a world in which human beings shall enjoy freedom of speech [...] has been proclaimed as the highest aspiration of the common people".

Likewise, the United Nations International Covenant on Civil and Political Rights (ICCPR), in Article 19 section 2, stipulates the right of everyone to freedom of expression, including the "freedom to seek, receive and impart information and ideas of all kinds, regardless of frontiers, either orally, in writing or in print, in the form of art, or through any other media of his choice."

As defined in both the UDHR and the ICCPR, freedom of expression has an active as well as a passive aspect: active in that it includes the freedom to inform, and passive in including the

---

172  Id.
173  Pauluchenka, Fyodar. 'Internet censorship in Belarus: Politically motivated DDoS-attacks on http://www.charter97.org'. A presentation given at the CCD COE Cyber Warfare Conference on 18 June 2009.
174  Akavita.com: Рейтинг белорусских сайтов. Новости и СМИ. Рейтинг за: среднесуточный. (In Belarus). Available at: http://top.akavita.com/Mass_Media_and_News/daily/visitors/by/ (5.8.2009).
175  According to http://top.akavita.com/ at 5 August 2009, Charter97.org stood on the 7th position in the overall popularity ranking of Belarus websites.
176  Pauluchenka, supra note 173.
177  Id.
178  'Global Cyber Attack Against Radio Free Europe/Radio Liberty', supra note 163.

freedom to receive information.[179]

As a member of United Nations since 1945[180], Belarus recognises the UDHR; it is party to ICCPR since 1973.[181]

Under both of these international treaties, freedom of expression is not an absolute right. Firstly, limitations arise from other fundamental rights and freedoms, such as the right to privacy (Article 12 of UDHR). Secondly, the ICCPR also stipulates that freedom of expression may be subject to certain restrictions due to respect of the rights or reputations of others, and for the protection of national security or of public order, or of public health or morals (Article 19 section 3). Such restrictions may, however, only occur if the following two conditions are met: the restrictions must be provided by law, and they must be necessary to protect the specific personal rights or societal interests referred to above (outlined in section 3 of Article 19).

Freedom of expression is also recognised in European "regional" human rights law, namely, the Council of Europe (CoE) Convention for the Protection of Human Rights and Fundamental Freedoms ("European Convention on Human Rights").[182] While the latter is more detailed than the UDHR and ICCPR definitions, and thus sheds more light on what is considered in Europe as a standard of freedom of expression, especially

on the permissible restrictions[183], Belarus has not joined the CoE[184] (the Convention is open for signature by the member States of the CoE) and thus is formally not bound by the CoE Convention for the Protection of Human Rights and Fundamental Freedoms. This does not, however, undermine the relevance of UDHR and ICCPR for Belarus, and the Convention and the case law of the European Court of Human Rights (ECHR) are helpful in defining the European standard for human rights and fundamental freedoms.

# Freedom of expression and the Internet

The emergence of the Internet has not only brought about a quantitative expansion of opportunities for public expression of opinions, it has also led to a qualitative change by providing (at least potentially) an efficient, quick, and relatively inexpensive means for individuals to publicly express and receive information. As the Internet has become a valued medium in distributing information in and to countries where political speech is suppressed, the question arises: do international law guarantees apply to communication on the Internet, considering that this medium that did not exist when the treaties were drafted?

---

179  See, e.g., Hustad, Richard. 'International Human Rights Law: Substantive Rights'. Lecture 2: Freedom of Expression (HUMR 5120/4120/1120). Norwegian Centre for Human Rights, 2008. P. 8; Dirk Ehlers (Ed.) European fundamental rights and freedoms. De Gryter Recht, 2007. P. 101.

180  Member States of the United Nations. Available at: http://www.un.org/en/members/index.shtml.

181  International Covenant on Civil and Political Rights. New York, 16 December 1966. Available at: http://treaties.un.org/Pages/ViewDetails.aspx?src=TREATY&mtdsg_no=IV-4&chapter=4&lang=en.

182  Convention for the Protection of Human Rights and Fundamental Freedoms as amended by Protocol No. 11. (CETS No.: 005) Rome, 4.XI.1950. Council of Europe. Available at: http://conventions.coe.int/Treaty/en/Treaties/Html/005.htm.

183  Article 10 of the Convention for the Protection of Human Rights and Fundamental Freedoms:
1. Everyone has the right to freedom of expression. This right shall include freedom to hold opinions and to receive and impart information and ideas without interference by public authority and regardless of frontiers. This article shall not prevent States from requiring the licensing of broadcasting, television or cinema enterprises.
2. The exercise of these freedoms, since it carries with it duties and responsibilities, may be subject to such formalities, conditions, restrictions or penalties as are prescribed by law and are necessary in a democratic society, in the interests of national security, territorial integrity or public safety, for the prevention of disorder or crime, for the protection of health or morals, for the protection of the reputation or rights of others, for preventing the disclosure of information received in confidence, or for maintaining the authority and impartiality of the judiciary.

184  It is interesting to note that Belarus is one of three European countries (out of 48) that is not a member of CoE. The other two non-members include the Vatican, and Kazakhstan. See, e.g., http://conventions.coe.int/Treaty/Commun/Cherches ig.asp?NT=005&CM=7&DF=6/25/2009&CL=ENG for the list of CoE member nations. All CoE member nations have ratified and enforced the convention; the newest to enforce the Convention was Montenegro (2006).

It appears to be well established that they do apply. First, the language of the UDHR Article 19 and the ICCPR Article 19.2 is inclusive: "through *any* media"; this consequently includes the Internet.[185] Second, the understanding that the scope of freedom of expression includes information published on the Internet is well established in international legal practice by international organisations (e.g. the UN and the ITU[186]). Therefore, the freedom to both receive and distribute information over the Internet is protected under international human rights law as a fundamental freedom.

Nations and international organisations are increasingly viewing access to the Internet as a specific legal right in democratic (information) societies. The European Parliament has repeatedly adopted resolutions (nonbinding in nature), identifying Internet access a fundamental freedom. The European Parliament, in a 2006 resolution, confirmed the EU's commitment to supporting free expression on the Internet world-wide, describing restrictions on Internet access as incompatible with the right to freedom of expression, and recognising the role of the Internet in strengthening democracy and contributing to a country's economic and social development.[187] In another resolution dating from March 2009, the Parliament further called on the EU Member States to "ensure that freedom of expression is not subject to arbitrary restrictions from the public and/or private sphere and to avoid all legislative or administrative measures that could have a 'chilling effect' on all

aspects of freedom of speech".[188] The same understanding was also reflected in the European Parliament's recent proposals to the EU 2008 telecommunications reform package.[189] In the USA, draft Global Online Freedom Acts were proposed in 2006 and 2007, both of them aiming to promote freedom of expression on the Internet. Neither of the bills became law[190], but the draft acts were reintroduced by Congress in 2009.[191] Section 2 of the bill lays on the United States government a responsibility to "protect freedom of expression on the Internet" as well as to "prevent United States businesses from directly and materially cooperating in human rights abuses perpetrated by repressive foreign governments". The bill contains procedural rules for designation of Internet-restricting countries as well as a system of guarantees regarding data protection related to such countries.

The acceptance of access to Internet as part of fundamental freedoms is settling into case law by national courts as well, with recent examples

---

185  Also in the earlier drafts of the Declaration, the Drafting Committee was consistent in placing no limitations on the means of expression and channels of communication to be protected. Morsink, Johannes. The Universal Declaration of Human Rights. University of Pennsylvania Press, 1999. P. 67.

186  *See* Commission on Human Rights resolution 2000/38, 'The right to freedom of opinion and expression'. The United Nations High Commissioner for Human Rights, 2000. Available at: http://www.unhchr.ch/Huridocda/Huridoca.nsf/0/a10988ef7018d21d802568d4004d04a7?Opendocument; Declaration of Principles by the World Summit on the Information Society, 'Building the Information Society: a global challenge in the new Millennium'. Geneva 2003. Available at: http://www.itu.int/wsis/outcome/booklet/declaration_A.html.

187  *See* European Parliament resolution on freedom of expression on the Internet, P6_TA(2006)0324. Available at: http://www.europarl.europa.eu/sides/getDoc.do?pubRef=-//EP//NONSGML+TA+P6-TA-2006-0324+0+DOC+PDF+V0//EN.

188  European Parliament recommendation of 26 March 2009 to the Council on strengthening security and fundamental freedoms on the Internet (2008/2160(INI)). Available at: http://www.europarl.europa.eu/sides/getDoc.do?type=TA&language=EN&reference=P6-TA-2009-0194.

189  The Parliament proposed the following section to be added in the EU Electronic Communications Framework Directive 2002/21/EC art 8: 'no restriction may be imposed on the fundamental rights and freedoms of end users, without a prior ruling by the judicial authorities [...] save when public security is threatened". The proposal had initially been rejected by the European Council of Ministers, but was reinstated in the Parliament reading by a 407:57 vote. *See* 'No agreement on reform of telecom legislation'. European Parliament press release, 06 May 2009. Available at: http://www.europarl.europa.eu/news/expert/infopress_page/058-55086-124-05-19-909-20090505IPR55085-04-05-2009-2009-true/default_en.htm.

190  Global Online Freedom Act of 2006 (H.R. 4780). 109th Congress, 2005-2006. Available at: http://www.govtrack.us/congress/bill.xpd?bill=h109-4780; Global Online Freedom Act of 2007 (H.R. 275). 110th Congress, 2007-2008. Available at: http://www.govtrack.us/congress/bill.xpd?bill=h110-275.

191  Global Online Freedom Act of 2009 (H.R. 2271). 111th Congress, 2009-2010. Available at: http://www.govtrack.us/congress/bill.xpd?bill=h111-2271.

in France and Estonia, for example.[192]

It should be noted that the concept of freedom of expression is also integrated into the very fundamental principles of Internet governance.[193]

## The extent of government duties in ensuring fundamental freedoms

According to the Preamble of the UDHR, freedom of expression – as all fundamental freedoms – is to be recognised and observable "both among the peoples of Member States themselves and among the peoples of territories under their jurisdiction." As expressed in the Preamble, by adopting the Declaration, all Member States pledge themselves to achieve the observance of human rights and fundamental freedoms.

States have both positive and negative obligations in ensuring fundamental freedoms. As interpreted by the European Court of Human Rights, a positive obligation requires states to undertake specific preventive or protective actions to secure fundamental freedoms, while a negative obligation requires them to refrain from taking certain actions. According to ECHR case law, an example of a *negative obligation* would include not preventing individuals from exercising their rights and freedoms, as well as not placing unnecessary obstacles in the way of

individuals wishing to exercise their rights and freedoms, whether these obstacles be direct or indirect; while a *positive obligation* would include the duty of a state to facilitate and secure the exercise of fundamental freedoms and to protect individuals from obstructive actions of other private parties.[194]

Therefore, genuine and effective freedom of expression cannot be reduced to a mere duty on the part of the state not to interfere; on the other hand, where third parties act in a way that undermines the exercise of freedom, the state may be required to intervene to secure the protection of those rights. [195]

Interpreting these principles in the context of the RFE/RL April 2008 cyber incident, the role and duty of the state would not only be to ensure no government role in the cyber attacks – but to actively *promote respect* for the freedom of expression and *take measures to secure its universal and effective observance.*

As explained previously, freedom of expression on the Internet is imminently a part of the fundamental freedom of expression that UN nations have undertaken an international duty to observe, promote and defend. Based on the negative and positive aspects of a state in promoting and defending freedom of expression, the following three categories can be delineated as regards the obligation of the state to ensure citizen access to information published on the Internet:

- the duty of the state to not unduly restrict information;

- the duty of the state to not allow for third parties to do so – which implies a sanction mechanism in place and an effective enforcement;

- the duty of the state to effectively facilitate the exercise of freedom of speech, both in its active and passive aspect, on the Internet.

Merely remaining on the question of state attribution for cyber attacks is therefore insuf-

---

192  The National Court in Estonia, in a 2007 decision, deemed access to publicly distributable information over the Internet as included in the right to 'freely obtain information disseminated for public use' envisaged by the Constitution of Estonia (art 44.1). *See* Judgment of 31 May 2007 by the Administrative Chamber of the National Court 3-3-1-20-07 (Kalda) (*In Estonian*) RT III 2007, 23, 193. Likewise, the French Constitutional court, in a case concerning cutting off Internet access for persons illegally downloading music files from the Internet, ruled that 'The Internet is a fundamental human right that cannot be taken away by anything other than a court of law, only when guilt has been established there'. *See* 'Internet access a fundamental right, says French court'. Rediff Business, 12 June 2009. Available at: http://business.rediff.com/report/2009/jun/12/net-access-a-fundamental-right-says-french-court.htm.

193  Namely, the principle of *network neutrality*, which integrates both the concept of *universal access to the resources connected to the Internet* and the concept of *freedom of expression*. Mueller, Milton. 'Net Neutrality as Global Principle in Internet Governance'. School of Information Studies, Syracuse University, 2007. Available at: http://www.internetgovernance.org/pdf/NetNeutralityGlobalPrinciple.pdf. Pp. 2-3.

194  'Demonstrating respect for rights? A human rights approach to policing protest.' UK Human Rights Joint Committee Seventh Report, 2009. Sections 15, 17, and 29 Available at: http://www.publications.parliament.uk/pa/jt200809/jtselect/jtrights/47/4705.htm.

195  *Id.*

ficient in analysing whether the state fulfils its international obligations in ensuring freedom of expression. Examining whether a particular government ordered, executed or tolerated cyber attacks against the websites expressing political content is, ultimately, irrelevant. The substantial question is whether the state permits other parties to illegitimately constrain freedom of expression, and whether the state actively pursues the protection of the fundamental freedom of expression by, among other actions, taking measures directed at discouraging other parties from attacking websites carrying political content, thus ensuring unhindered access to legitimately-distributed (within the meaning of international human rights law) information.

In order to effectively promote and support fundamental rights, a legislative response to cyber attacks needs to involve both *substantial* (addressing certain conduct by criminal law) and *procedural* law (giving law enforcement/criminal justice the means to investigate, prosecute and adjudicate cyber crimes).[196] It must also allow for *efficient international cooperation* by harmonising legislation, making provision and establishing institutions for police and judicial cooperation, and concluding or joining international agreements.[197] The Council of Europe Convention on Cybercrime[198], which defines a comprehensive standard for addressing offences against the confidentiality, integrity and availability of computer data and systems, is potentially well equipped to provide a global framework for addressing such cyber offences.[199] As the convention is used as a guideline for legislation around the world[200], its influence reaches well beyond the 46 nations that have so far signed or ratified it.[201] As this standard gains wider international ground, it has a good

prospect for becoming a standard for internat-The applicable law in Belarus and the extent of permissible restrictions in international law

The Belarusian Constitution, adopted on 1 March 1994[202], acknowledges the principles of international human rights law. Articles 8 and 21 of the Constitution state that "[t]he Republic of Belarus shall recognize the supremacy of the universally acknowledged principles of international law and ensure that its laws comply with such principles", and that "[s]afeguarding the rights and liberties of citizens of the Republic of Belarus shall be supreme goal of the State. The State shall guarantee the rights and liberties of the citizens of Belarus that are enshrined in the Constitution and the laws, and specified in the State's international obligations."

Specifically, Articles 33 and 34 of the Belarus Constitution provide as follows:

Article 33 [Expression]

(1) Everyone is guaranteed freedom of thoughts and beliefs and their free expression [Freedom of Expression].

(2) No one shall be forced to express his beliefs or to deny them.

(3) No monopolization of the mass media by the State, public associations or individual citizens and no censorship shall be permitted.

Article 34 [Information]

(1) Citizens of the Republic of Belarus shall be guaranteed the right to receive, store, and disseminate complete, reliable, and timely information on the activities of state bodies and public associations, on political, economic, and international life, and on the state of the environment.

(2) State bodies, public associations, and officials shall afford citizens of the Republic of Belarus an opportunity to familiarize themselves with material that affects their rights and legitimate interests.

On the legislative level, however, severe restrictions apply to freedom of speech and media

---

196  *Id.*
197  *Id.*
198  Convention on Cybercrime, reference in *supra* note 144.
199  Seger, Alexander. 'The Convention on Cybercrime: a Global Framework'. IGF, Geneva, 2009.
200  Including countries in Africa, Asia and Central and South America. In addition to the 46 nations that have signed or ratified the convention, the Council of Europe has established technical cooperation on cyber crime legislation with 52 additional countries, and four countries have been invited to accede to the convention (the convention is open for signature also to non-CoE nations). See Seger, supra note 199.
201  *See* the list of treaty members and signatories at http://conventions.coe.int/Treaty/Commun/ChercheSig.asp?NT=185&CM=1&DF=6/16/2009&CL=ENG.

202  http://www.president.gov.by/en/press19329.html The official Internet Portal of the President of the Republic of Belarus. Constitution of the Republic of Belarus.

freedom[203], rendering the provisions of the Constitution a mere declaration. For example, criminal punishment is envisaged (and reportedly frequently used) for slander and insult of the president and other government entities.[204] Also, Freedom House reports that politicised court rulings and obscure regulations have frequently been used to harass independent media outlets.[205]

Restrictions on online media were cemented by the adoption of the new Statute on Mass Media (О средствах массовой информации), signed into effect by Belarusian President Aleksandr Lukashenka on 4 August 2008, a few months after the cyber attacks against the RFE/RL took place.[206] The statue came into effect six months after publication and replaced the previous Statute on the Press and Other Mass Media. [207] Long prior to its adoption, the draft statute received wide criticism for severe restrictions on freedom of the press due to a sharp cut in journalists' rights foreseen by the earlier law, a non-transparent licensing and journalist accreditation regime, extensive restrictions on funding of public media, and on distribution. This criticism was ignored by the Belarus authorities however.[208]

A wide scope of supplementary regulation to the Statute is left up to the administration to define; further, there is a rather arbitrary procedure for defining information that is not to be released to the public.[209] Liability is envisaged for "disseminating inaccurate information that might cause harm to state and public interests" or for "distribution of information not complying with reality and defaming the honour or business reputation of individuals or the business reputation of legal entities".[210]

A major novelty introduced by the 4 August 2008 statute is the legal treatment of the World Wide Web as a mass media source, which now falls under the same restrictive framework. The publishing of information on the Internet is now not only regulated by law, but the Ministry of Information has been given wide discretionary powers to adopt secondary legislation.[211] The new law allows blocking of all web resources of mass media that are not registered in Belarus and allows prosecution of any Belarusian who presents information to a foreign mass media without accreditation.[212]

As previously discussed, freedom of expression is, under international human rights law, not an unrestricted right and there is a growing trend of content regulation in various countries (China is often referenced as a prime example, but content regulation exists in numerous democratic jurisdictions as well). Deriving from the principles reflected in the UDHR and ICCPR, content regulation is not necessarily incompatible with international human rights law. The Internet need not (and indeed cannot) entirely exist as a legal vacuum. However, any national regulation should be carefully weighed against competing legitimate rights and interests, should conform with international principles of human rights, and limitations should be necessary and proportionate.

Finding the right balance between individual liberties and public interests may be dependent on cultural implications. The international instruments do not provide a list of measures, but a general standard. However, the principles of UDHR and ICCPR are contradicted by restrictions that are disproportionate to the objective of respecting the rights or reputations of other persons or of protection of national security, public order, public health or morals, etc. Delegating the authority to restrict fundamental freedoms to the administration fails to meet the ICCPR requirement that any restrictions of freedom of expression must be provided by law.

---

203 CIA World Factbook, *supra* note 148.
204 'Good Law — Bad Implementation'. Interview with Andrei Richter. Published from 'Media Expert', Russian-Byelorussian quarterly. The Centre for Journalism in Extreme Situations at the Russian Union of Journalists, #4, 2004. Available at: http://www.medialaw.ru/e_pages/publications/goodlaw.htm.
205 Freedom of the Press, *supra* note 151.
206 The text of the Statute (in Belarus) is available at http://pravo.by/webnpa/text.asp?RN=h10800427.
207 Richter, Andrei. 'Belarus: New Media Law Adopted'. IRIS 2008-8:7/9. Media Law and Policy Centre, 2008. Available at: http://merlin.obs.coe.int/iris/2008/8/article9.en.html
208 *Id.*
209 Pastukhou, Mikhail; Taparashau, Yury. 'Authorities to eliminate independent media'. Charter97.org, 13 June 2008. Available at: http://charter97.org/en/news/2008/6/13/7407/; Richter, *supra* note 207.

210 Richter, *Id.*
211 Pastukhou,Taparashau, *supra* note 210; Richter, *supra* note 207.
212 'The most popular websites to be blocked for Belarusians'. Charter97.org, 16 June 2008. Available at: http://charter97.org/en/news/2008/6/16/7428/.

Finally, a balanced criminal law approach in a democratic society would involve not only vigorously defending public interests, but also showing the same kind of vigour in ensuring individual freedoms – both in legislation and in implementation.

# IV Summary of the RFE/RL case

## INCIDENT TIME FRAME

*Start*     Saturday, 26 April 2008, 8 AM

*End*      Monday, 28 April 2008, evening

*Duration*  2,5 days

## INCIDENT CONTEXT

### Political context and background of incident

- Authoritarian leadership: "the last dictatorship of Europe";

- Political opposition protest rally on 26 April in relation to the 22nd anniversary of the Chernobyl nuclear disaster;

- RFE/RL live coverage of the rally scheduled for the day of the anniversary.

### Information society indicators

- Severe restrictions on mass media;

- State control over Internet access;

- Internet communications monitored and regime-critical websites frequently blocked.

## INCIDENT FACTS

### Methods

- Distributed Denial of Service (DDoS).

### Targets

- Website of RFE/RL Belarus service (www. svaboda.org);

- Seven additional RFE/RL websites in the Eastern European and Central Asian/Middle East region;

- Web sites of independent Belarus news organisations (Charter 97; Belorusskiy Partizan).

### Origin

- Undetermined. Technically, this type of attacks is difficult to tie to specific individuals. Political motivation is observable from the pattern of the attacks and from other targets attacked simultaneously;

- The attack victim, RFE/RL, and public opinion align towards believing that the attack was backed by the Belarusian government;

- Objective traffic data provides no evidence that the attacks were carried out by any political agent in general or a government in particular; the Belarus administration has denied any involvement.

### Effect

- The website was inundated with about 50,000 fake pings every second, exceeding the handling capacity of the site.

### Measures taken

- Numerous local websites in Belarus offered help to carry RFE/RL's news and reports until the RFE/RL Belarus website was operational again.

## LEGAL LESSONS IDENTIFIED AND LEARNED

### Core of the case

- Cyber means used to attack fundamental freedom of expression on the Internet;

- The extent of government duty to ensure fundamental freedoms.

### Summary

- There is no dispute that both freedom of expression as well as public order and safety are legitimate values deserving protection. The search for balance between freedom and (inter)national security is still ongoing, and will be as societies change. However, there is also a solid base in international human rights legal theory and practice of defining the standard of proportionality and necessity of restricting the fundamental freedom of expression that is not dependent on the type of media used – whether it is the traditional "physical" media or cyber space.

- Whether states meet the internationally recognised standard in ensuring the observance and protection of freedom of expression on the Internet needs to be assessed from a three-fold prism: whether the state refrains from restricting information in a way that is incompatible with the limits recognised by international instruments; whether the state effectively facilitates the exercise of freedom of speech on the Internet; and finally, whether state-enforced legal mechanisms exist and are employed in protecting the individual rights from suppression by other parties.

**Challenges**

- To secure the Internet as a medium of free speech, international attention needs to focus on how to avoid targeting the global, regional and national communications infrastructure that facilitates information flow. Appropriate organisational, technical and supporting legal means are needed to ensure that public networks (i.e. networks used for the provision of publicly available services) and assets remain accessible for legitimate use by all citizens.

- Setting an international standard by acknowledging the issue of free speech on the Internet in international discussion, developing national laws and procedures to ensure freedom of expression, and supporting similar efforts in young and emerging democratic societies

# LITHUANIA 2008

June-July

# I Background of the incident

## Political context

On June 17, 2008, the Lithuanian Parliament (*Seimas*) adopted an amendment to the Law on Meetings that regulated the implementation of freedom of speech and freedom of assembly.[213]

According to the amendment, public display of Soviet and Nazi German insignia, such as the hammer and sickle, the red star, and the swastika, as well as playing of the Soviet Union and Nazi anthems at public gatherings, were prohibited; violation of the prohibition would constitute a misdemeanour subject to heavy fines and possible cancellation of a political organisation's registration in accordance with the Administrative Law Violations Code.[214]

The passage of the amendment did not cause protests or much outcry from the local ethnic Russian minority, even though it was thought possible that some Lithuanian Russians were upset over it.[215] Russians are the largest minority in Lithuania alongside the Poles, comprising 6.3% (about 220 000 people) of the total population according to the 2001 census.[216]

Following the passage of the amendment, the Russian Federation expressed their discontent with the decision, with both the President and the Parliament issuing condemning statements. On June 22, Russian President Dmitry Medvedev and Belarusian President Alexander Lukashenka jointly denounced the new Lithuanian law as a "politicised approach to history" and condemned what they described as "attempts to

---

213 This legislative measure was initiated by a member of the then opposition right-wing party, Homeland Union-Lithuanian Christian Democrats (the largest party in the governing coalition after the November 2008 elections) and was passed in the midst of the 'war of memories' between the Baltic states and Russia. Since 2000, Russia's official positive re-interpretation of its totalitarian Soviet past, underpinning its ambitions of restoring national self-confidence and returning to the global stage as a great power, has increasingly clashed with the view of the Baltic states that communism was a criminal regime as was Nazism.
The term 'war of memories' is used by some social scientists to describe the clash of divergent historical identities in the public discourse. *See* Pääbo, Heiko 'War of Memories: Explaining 'Memorials War' in Estonia,' Baltic Security & Defence Review, Vol. 10, (2008), 5-28, p.5-8.

214 Roudik, Peter 'Lithuania: 'Constitutional Law - Ban on Nazi and Soviet Symbols,' Law Library of Congress, 2 July 2008. Available at: http://www.loc.gov/lawweb/servlet/lloc_news?disp3_487_text.

215 A comment by Marius Urkis, head of the Academic and Research Network Computer Emergency Response Team of Lithuania (LITNET CERT). Available at: http://www.pcworld.com/article/147960/lithuania_attacks_focused_on_hosting_company.html.

216 Lithuania. CIA World Factbook, November 2008. Available at: https://www.cia.gov/library/publications/the-world-factbook/geos/lh.html.

rewrite wartime history".[217] Also, in a position titled "Regarding actions of the Government of the Republic of Lithuania aimed at undermining relations between Russia and Lithuania", which was approved unanimously by the State *Duma* (the lower house of the Russian Parliament), Lithuania was criticized for the new law which was seen as "insulting the memory of the Soviet soldiers who fought the Nazis in World War II" and an attempt to "rewrite history".[218] Further, a small protest rally was held in front of the Lithuanian Embassy in Moscow by the members of the Communist Party.

In the timeframe coinciding with the adoption of the amendment, on June 28, 2008, a significant number of Lithuanian web sites fell under a defacement attack.[219] About 300 websites were defaced with pro-Soviet and communist symbols as well as profane anti-Lithuanian slogans. Most of the websites were restored by July 2; however, by that time it was unclear whether attacks would subside or continue.[220]

## Lithuania as an information society

The Long-Term Development Strategy of Lithuania, adopted by the *Seimas* in 2002, establishes the 'knowledge society' as the first of three long-term state development priorities for Lithuania (the other two being 'safe society'

and 'competitive economy').[221] Following the conclusions of the Lisbon European Council, which set a strategic goal for the European Union to become the most competitive and dynamic knowledge-based economy in the world capable of sustainable economic growth[222], Lithuania set the creation of a society based on knowledge a goal to be reached by 2015.[223] To achieve this goal, the *Seimas* agreed on four areas to be developed: science and education, competence of the population, state governance and self-government, and culture. The significant role of information society, enhanced ICT use, development of ICT infrastructure, and growth of e-services was recognised in all of those areas.[224]

Lithuania has a 6-year-long Information Society Strategy (adopted in 2005) and a 3-year Information Society Development Program (for the period from 2006 to 2008; adopted in 2005). These initiatives establish, among other aims, Lithuanian key priorities of modernisation of public administration (using information technology) and establishment of the knowledge economy.[225]

In recent years, Lithuania has made considerable progress in the development of its information society and knowledge based economy. A number of legal acts have been passed that support and stimulate the advancement of the information society: Electronic Signatures Act (2002), Act on the Legal Protection of Personal Data (2003), State Registers Act (2004), Electronic Communications Act (2004),

---

217   Dyomkin, Denis. 'Russia condemns rewriting of World War Two history'. Reuters, 23 June 2008. Available at: uk.reuters.com/article/worldNews/idUKL221014120080623?pageNumber=1&virtualBrandChannel=0&sp=true.

218   'Russia Warns Lithuania on US Missile Defense,' The Moscow News, 3 July 2008. Available at: mnweekly.rian.ru/news/20080703/55335914.html. The news cited above did not give a date for the Duma decision, but considering the date of the article, it appears to have been adopted after the cyber attacks had already taken place. While it thus cannot have served as a direct encouragement to attack, it indicates the sentiment prevalent in society rather well.

219   Website defacement involves manipulation of a website that changes the visual appearance of the site.

220   Danchev, Dancho '300 Lithuanian Sites Hacked By Russian Hackers,' Zero Day, 2 July 2008. Available at: blogs.zdnet.com/security/?p=1408.

221   Long-Term Development Strategy of the State. Adopted by resolution No. IX-1187 of the Seimas of the Republic of Lithuania on 12 November 2002. Official translation available at: www3.lrs.lt/pls/inter3/dokpaieska.showdoc_l?p_id=219184.
The Long Term Development Strategy of the State lays down guidelines for the economic, social, environmental protection, and other policies of Lithuania until the year 2015.

222   Presidency Conclusions of European Council, 23 and 24 March 2000, Lisbon. Available at: http://www.europarl.europa.eu/summits/lis1_en.htm.

223   Long-Term Development Strategy of the State, *supra* note 221.

224   *Id.* For more detailed information see section 'Knowledge Society,' Chapter III of the Long-Term Development Strategy of the State.

225   Židonis, Evaldas 'The Development of Information Society in Lithuania – Achievements and Problems,' Information Society Development Committee under Government, 2006. Available at: www3.lrs.lt/home/ivairus/ECPRD_ICT2006/EvaldasZidonis_ICT2006.ppt.

Information Society Services Act (2006) and Management of State Information Resources Act (2007).[226] In addition, an institutional framework was established for the coordination of the Information Society (Electronic Signature Monitoring Authority, Information Society Development Committee).[227] The Lithuanian Computer Emergency Response Team (CERT-LT)[228] was established at the end of 2006 as Lithuanian national CERT, while LITNET CERT[229], which services the clients of the Lithuanian Academic and Research Network (universities, schools, research institutions, and non-profit organisations), is functional already since 1998.[230]

Lithuania's ICT use statistics show steady growth. By the end of 2007, 46% of the Lithuanian households were equipped with a computer, which indicates a 5% increase over 2006.[231] The country's Internet penetration rate (for households) in 2007 was 36%, which was 6% higher than 2006.[232] While broadband use is gaining ground (19% of households by end of 2007, an increase of 2% compared to 2006), Lithuania has a remarkable number of narrowband Internet users (11% of the population, which is slightly above the European Union average).[233] By all these indicators except the last, however, Lithuania remains below the European Union average.

Statistics regarding ICT use by the population show that in 2007, of individuals 16-74 years old, 51.4% used computers, and 48.7% were using the Internet. The most avid internet users were found among the younger generation: out of individuals 16-25 years old, 86% used the Internet daily (61.3%) or at least once a week (25.1%), whereas Internet use among the older popula-

tion (55-74 years) was only 9.4%.[234]

The average score for online availability of public services is 35%, which is below the EU average; that figure has remained constant in the past few years. Significantly, 60% of Lithuanian companies have used eGovernment services (compared to the EU average of 45%).[235]

# II Facts of the case

## Timeline of the attacks

Following the passage of the amendment of the law and its condemnation by the Russian Federation[236], on Saturday, 28 June 2008, cyber attacks against Lithuanian websites started.

The highest amount of simultaneous attacks was registered on Sunday, 29 June 2008, around 17:00 and 18:00 EET (GMT+2). At the peak of the attacks, 300 internet sites were defaced.[237]

In the afternoon of Monday, June 30, Rytis Rainys, the head of the Networks and Information Security Department of the RRT (*Ryšiu reguliavimo tarnyba*), the Lithuanian communications regulatory authority, reported that attacks were still ongoing and that "the network administrators should not relax".[238]

By the afternoon of Tuesday, July 1, most all of the sites had been restored and were back to

226  *Id.*
227  Maskeliūnas, Saulius; Otas, Alfredas. 'Development and Application of Information Society Strategies in Lithuania.' Institute of Mathematics and Informatics, Kaunas University of Technology, 2008. Available at: http://www.scholze-simmel.at/starbus/ws3/lithuania.pdf.
228  Homepage of CERT-LT, available at: http://www.cert.lt/en/
229  LITNET CERT, available at: http://cert.litnet.lt/
230  Inventory of CERT Activities in Europe, ENISA. Available at: www.enisa.europa.eu/cert_inventory/pages/03_li.htm
231  'E-Communications Household Survey,' Special Eurobarometer 293. TNS opinion & social/European Commission, June 2008. P. 50.
232  *Id.*, p. 54.
233  *Id.*, p. 59.

234  DG Information Society and Media. e-Inclusion Policy. Country Profile: Lithuania. European Commission, 2008. Available at: ec.europa.eu/information_society/activities/einclusion/policy/a_documents/lithuania_einclusion.doc.
235  Maskeliūnas, Otas, *supra* note 227.
236  *See* section 'Political context,' Section II.
237  'Cyber Attack Against Lithuania.' Official Statement by Lithuanian Embassy (by e-mail), 1 July 2008.
238  Pavilenene, Danuta 'Cyber attacks against Lithuania do not stop,' The Baltic Course, 30 June 2008. Available at: http://www.baltic-course.com/eng/Technology/?doc=2807.

displaying their normal content.[239]

## Means and types of attacks

### Defacement

The main reported type of the attack was defacement of websites. The original content of nearly 300 websites was replaced with communist images on a red background portraying the flag of the Soviet Union. The pictures included the hammer and sickle motifs as well as slogans and messages containing profanities in the Russian language.[240]

A report released by the Lithuanian Embassy described the attacks having taken place by means of an abrupt break in service, during which website files were modified in three minutes "by using PHP software".[241] According to CERT-LT, after the servers were hacked into and access was gained, automated scripts were launched to modify all index files.[242]

### E-mail spam

According to iDefense[243], attackers also used Internet forums and blasted spam e-mails to spotlight a manifesto called "Hackers United against External Threats to Russia". Their aim was to instigate people to spread the attack to the web sites of the Ukraine, the rest of the Baltic

states, and to "flagrant" Western nations for having supported the expansion of NATO.[244]

## Targets of the attacks

Both private sector and government websites were attacked, the total number of defaced websites exceeding 300.[245] These sites included:

- Chief Institutional Ethics Commission;

- Securities and Exchange Commission;

- Lithuanian Social Democratic Party.

Almost all of 300 defaced web sites were hosted by Hostex, formerly known as MicroLink Lithuania[246], which is a webhosting service provider among the major alternative Lithuanian providers with a market share of around 2,5% (it currently ranks 5th out of 25 providers).[247]

According to the Lithuanian Computer Emergency Response Team (CERT-LT), the majority of the attacked Web sites were hosted on a single Hostex Web server, which had a vulnerability either in the Web server software or the Linux operating system.[248] According to CERT-LT, the hackers launched the attack against all that was accessible in Hostex' servers with no specific regard to particular websites. CERT-LT has estimated that about 95% of the sites that were hit belonged to private sector organisa-

---

239  Krebs, Brian 'Lithuania Weathers Cyber Attack, Braces for Round 2,' 3 July 2008. Available at:  voices.washington-post.com/securityfix/2008/07/lithuania_weathers_cyber_attac_1.html.
    Another cyber incident was reported to have broken out in Lithuania three weeks later. On July 21, the Lithuanian Tax Office reported that its website was hit by a cyber attack over the preceding weekend. The website was swamped with requests, but no damage was sustained. The link between the defacements and the increased traffic on Tax Office's website is unclear. See 'Lithuanian tax office website hit by cyber attack,' Reuters, 21 July 2008. Available at: http://www.reuters.com/article/rbssTechMediaTelecomNews/idUSMAR14153920080721.

240  According to PC Tools, an Irish firm specialising in development of IT security and utility software solutions. Available at: http://www.pctools.com/industry-news/article/cyber_crooks_attack_lithuanian_websites-18663956/; Rhodin, Sara. 'Hackers Tag Lithuanian Web Sites With Soviet Symbols,' The New York Times, 1 July 2008. Available at: http://www.nytimes.com/2008/07/01/world/europe/01baltic.html.

241  Official Statement by Lithuanian Embassy, supra note 237.

242  Rainys, Rytis, RRT. In an e-mail (10 Dec 2008) to the CCD COE Legal Team.

243  A security intelligence firm based in Reston, Virginia, USA.

244  According to an appeal circulated on Russian Internet forums prior to the defacement wave, 'All the hackers of the country have decided to unite, to counter the impudent actions of Western superpowers. We are fed up with NATO's encroachment on our motherland, we have had enough of Ukrainian politicians who have forgotten their nation and only think about their own interests. And we are fed up with Estonian government institutions that blatantly re-write history and support fascism.' Tere, Juhan 'Russian Hackers Plan Cyber Attacks on Baltic Countries and Ukraine,' Baltic Course, 25 June 2008. Available at: http://www.baltic-course.com/eng/baltics_cis/?doc=2699.

245  Danchev, Dancho, supra note 220.

246  Rainys, supra note 242.

247  Most of the Lithuanian web hosting market is divided by two large market players, each with a share of about 30%. The remaining 40% of the market is divided between a number of small players, of which Hostex is one of the largest. See Web Hosting Companies in Lithuania. Webhosting.info. Available at: http://www.webhosting.info/webhosts/tophosts/Country/LT

248  Kirk, Jeremy 'Lithuania: Attacks Focused on Hosting Company'. PC World, 4 July 2008. Available at: http://www.pcworld.com/article/147960/lithuania_attacks_focused_on_hosting_company.html.

tions.[249]

Lithuanian government agencies were warned of an impending Web attack, and therefore mounted appropriate defences and were able to cope with the attacks when they started on June 28.[250] As explained by CERT-LT, after the Estonian TV channel ETV24 and the journal *The Baltic Course* reported the hackers' intention to perform attacks on the cyber space of the Baltic states and the Ukraine, on 26 July 2008 CERT-LT informed government information systems administrators to be ready for possible attacks. The entities informed were those enlisted in the CERT-LT contact list.[251]

Commercial sites were not informed, and over the weekend of June 28 to 29, they took the brunt of the attack.[252]

## Origin of the attacks

As reported by the Lithuanian Embassy in the USA on July 1, the source and origin of the attacks was not clear, as attacks were carried out through intermediary servers, all of them outside Lithuania.[253] Lithuanian official comments from the initial phase of the attack only referred to the attacks having come from outside sources, while not specifying any particular countries. They did suggest that a relation to the Parliament-adopted ban on Soviet symbols was likely[254].

According to comments provided by RRT, the Lithuanian communications regulatory authority, attacks were performed via proxy servers "located in territories east of Lithuania".[255] Also, Rytis Rainys, the RRT expert quoted in international media, found it likely that the attacks were organised in advance, considering the fact that signals, invitations, and agitation were spread on the Internet prior to the attacks.[256] However, the RRT refused to speak of any particular coun-

tries as the initiator of the attacks.[257]

According to Lithuanian researchers, the hackers had used compromised hosts in Western Europe (France and Sweden were named as two specific examples) in order to execute the defacements.[258] As usual, means for cover-up had been used in order not to give away original attack sources[259]; the official statement provided by Lithuanian Embassy reports of a complicated intrusion path (which also supports the idea that the attacks were premeditated and well-planned in advance).[260] The Cyber Police unit of the Lithuanian Police further specified that the attackers used a so-called "onion routing" software ('Tor') for executing the attacks, a system that enables its users to communicate anonymously on the Internet.[261]

iDefense suggests that the cyber attacks could be attributed to nationalistic Russian hacker groups, since a popular Russian hacker web site, hack-wars.ru, was observed to have taken a central role in organizing the attacks.[262] This conclusion is also confirmed by Dancho Danchev[263], who observed a pattern of public justification of the attacks based on nationalism sentiments. For example, discussions across web forums were escalated to the point where conducting cyber attacks against Lithuanian web sites was tied to a demonstration of loyalty to the state ("if you don't take action, you're not loyal to your country").[264] References to various Internet chat

---

249  Rainys, *supra* note 243.
250  Rhodin, *supra* note 240.
251  Rainys, *supra* note 242.
252  Vamosi, Robert 'Hundreds of Lithuanian Websites defaced,' 1 July 2008. Available at: http://news.cnet.com/8301-10789_3-9983940-57.html.
253  Official Statement by Lithuanian Embassy, *supra* note 237
254  Rhodin, reference in supra note 240.
255  Danchev, Dancho, *supra* note 220.
256  *Id.*; Rhodin, cited in *supra* note 240.

257  Pavilenene, *supra* note 238.
258  Danchev, Dancho, *supra* note 220; Kirk, *supra* note 248.
259  Pavilenene, *supra* note 238.
260  Official Statement by Lithuanian Embassy, *supra* note 238.
261  Marcinkevicius, Markas from Lithuanian Cyber Crime Bureau in an e-mail (8 Dec 2008) to the CCD COE Legal Team.
262  Krebs, *supra* note 239.
263  Danchev is an independent security consultant and cyber threat analyst. He runs a blog on information security at http://ddanchev.blogspot.com/ and frequently writes on computer and information security issues on computer news websites such as Zero Day (ZDNet), CircleID, and WindowSecurity.
264  Danchev, Dancho 'Lithuania Attacked by Russian Hacktivists, 300 Sites Defaced,' Circle ID, 8 July 2008. Available at: http://www.circleid.com/posts/87870_lithuania_internet_attack_russian_hacktivists/. Note, however, that prioritising the attack targets, distributing targets list and ensuring coordination in terms of the exact time and data for the attacks to take place is something that didn't happen in the public domain for the mass defacement of Lithuanian sites, the way it happened in the Estonian attack. *See* also Danchev, Dancho, *supra* note 220.

rooms where Russian hackers had been asked "to be unanimous in attacking the websites of Lithuanian, Latvian, Estonian and Ukrainian governmental and administrative institutions" were also shown in the official statement by the Lithuanian Embassy.[265]

## Mitigation and measures taken

Since almost all attacked web sites were hosted by Hostex, the company was advised by the CERT on how to fix the problem.[266]

According to Marius Urkis, head of the Academic and Research Network (LITNET) CERT, the matter was referred to the computer crimes section in the Criminal Police Bureau that handles cybercrime. Since proxy servers were employed to perform the hacking and data anonymising software was used, it was assumed that the investigation would be a complex process, as investigators would have to trace a winding electronic path in an attempt to find the actual perpetrators.[267]

The reaction of the Lithuanian authorities implies that the attack was considered as a cyber crime incident and the responsibility remained primarily with the service provider to regain control of its server.

According to comments provided by Markas Marcinkevicius, Chief of Lithuanian Cybercrime Investigation Board[268], the pre-trial investigation of the June 2008 cyber attacks was still ongoing as of December 2008. A number of mutual legal assistance requests had been sent to different countries, but as no useful leads had yet been collected; therefore, the future of the investigation was uncertain at this phase of the proceedings.

The pre-trial investigations were conducted on grounds of Paragraph 1 of Article 196 and Paragraph 1 of Article 198(1) of the Criminal Code of the Republic of Lithuania, with reference to *illegal damage and change of electronic data*

*and illegal access to the information system by affecting the security measures of information systems.*[269]

Article 196: Illegal Impact on Electronic Data: 'A person who illegally destroys, damages, removes or changes electronic data or restricts the use of such data with the help of hardware, software, or by other means by inflicting great damage shall be punished by community service or a fine, or imprisonment for a term of up to four years. A person who commits the act specified in Paragraph 1 of this Article to the electronic data of information system that has a strategic importance to national security or great significance to public administration, economic or financial system shall be punished by a fine or arrest, or imprisonment for a term of up to six years. A person who commits the act specified in this article by inflicting minor damage, commits a misdemeanor and shall be punished by community service or a fine, or arrest. Any legal entity shall also be held liable for the acts specified in this Article.' Article 198(1): Illegal Access to the Information System: A person who illegally accesses the information system by affecting the information system security means shall be punished by community service or a fine, or arrest, or imprisonment for a term of up to one year. A person who illegally accesses the information system

---

265  Official Statement by Lithuanian Embassy, *supra* note 237.
266  Kirk, *supra* note 248.
267  *Id.*; Marcinkevicius, *supra* note 261.
268  The central unit responsible for investigation of serious and international cybercrime cases in the Lithuanian Criminal Police Bureau.
269  Lithuanian Criminal Code, Article 196: Illegal Impact on Electronic Data:
'A person who illegally destroys, damages, removes or changes electronic data or restricts the use of such data with the help of hardware, software, or by other means by inflicting great damage shall be punished by community service or a fine, or imprisonment for a term of up to four years. A person who commits the act specified in Paragraph 1 of this Article to the electronic data of information system that has a strategic importance to national security or great significance to public administration, economic or financial system shall be punished by a fine or arrest, or imprisonment for a term of up to six years. A person who commits the act specified in this article by inflicting minor damage, commits a misdemeanor and shall be punished by community service or a fine, or arrest. Any legal entity shall also be held liable for the acts specified in this Article.'
Article 198(1): Illegal Access to the Information System: A person who illegally accesses the information system by affecting the information system security means shall be punished by community service or a fine, or arrest, or imprisonment for a term of up to one year. A person who illegally accesses the information system that has a strategic importance to national security or great significance to public administration, economic or financial system shall be punished by a fine or arrest, or imprisonment for a term of up to three years. Any legal entity shall also be held liable for the acts specified in this Article.

that has a strategic importance to national security or great significance to public administration, economic or financial system shall be punished by a fine or arrest, or imprisonment for a term of up to three years. Any legal entity shall also be held liable for the acts specified in this Article.

## Effects of the attacks

According to RRT, state institutions were warned about the possible attacks in advance, and therefore the negative effects were expected to be limited. As reported by the Lithuanian authorities, no real danger to the private sector or strategic State administration was determined, although the cyber attack did disturb the Hostex-operated servers which contained the Internet sites of several hundred companies.[270]

In the official statement circulated by the Lithuanian Embassy, it appears that Lithuania regarded the cyber attacks with much seriousness. "Although more information about these attacks is still needed, there is enough information to assume that preparations to launch the cyber attacks against Lithuanian websites must have been known in advance. [⋯] Taking into account the [⋯] dangers posed by cyber war to the international community of the 21st century and in the spirit of good neighbourly relations we expect that countries concerned put every possible effort to find the perpetrators of these cyber attacks against Lithuania and take appropriate actions to prevent cyber attacks from happening in the future."[271]

# III Legal considerations

One could argue that the incident in Lithuania as an event on "the lower end" of cyber security incidents is of no relevance from an international cyber security perspective and that vulnerabilities in the infrastructure of a single ISP can hardly be something that should raise the question of national security.

Nevertheless, even though the Lithuanian case did not raise issues about "cyber warfare" and "cyber terrorism", it reminds us that the quality of cyber crime regulation will play a role in cyber deterrence. Also, it shows that reactions to politically sensitive decisions and actions of governments may affect random targets and information infrastructure. Further, it may be a "lessons learned" for countries and private businesses about the economic costs of governments not sharing threat information with the private sector (costs not just to the hosting company, but to the business of its clients). Providing for a legal and policy structure for the sharing of such threats, as well as for the businesses to share vulnerability information with the government, may have tangible mitigation effects on future potential attacks.

## The defacement attacks as cyber crime

Depending on the national legislation in the field, the Lithuanian incidents may represent an act provided for in the Council of Europe Convention on Cybercrime[272]. According to Article 4.1 of the convention, each Party shall adopt such legislative and other measures as may be necessary to establish as criminal offences under its domestic law, when committed intentionally, the *damaging, deletion, deterioration, alteration* or *suppression* of computer data without right.

Lithuania ratified the Convention on Cybercrime in March 2004; the convention entered into force in July 2004. Most of the member nations of the Council of Europe have signed the convention (except for Turkey and Russia, and the tiny European nations of Andorra, Monaco, and San Marino), but the total number of signatures not followed by ratification is rather high: 23 countries. Typically (but not extending to all cases), those countries that have ratified the convention and brought it into force are European Union member states. In addition, Canada, Japan, the Republic of South Africa and the United States of America have also signed the convention, but only in the latter has it also been ratified and entered into force.[273]

---

270  Official Statement by Lithuanian Embassy, *supra* note 237.
271  *Id.*

272  Convention on Cybercrime, reference in *supra* note 143.
273  Council of Europe. Available at: http://conventions.coe.int/Treaty/Commun/ChercheSig.asp?NT=185&CM=&DF=&CL=ENG.

As described in the explanatory report of the Convention[274], the legal interest protected by the data interference provision (Article 4.1) is the *integrity* and *proper functioning or use* of stored computer data or computer programs. The terms used in Article 4, '*damaging*' and '*deteriorating*' both refer to acts that constitute a negative alteration of the integrity or of information content of data and programmes. '*Deletion*' of data is to be understood as an action that destroys the data and makes it unrecognisable, while '*suppressing of computer data*' means any action that prevents or terminates the availability of the data to the person who has access to the computer or the data carrier on which it was stored, and the term '*alteration*' means the modification of existing data.[275]

A corresponding clause in the Lithuanian Criminal Code (Article 196) defines these acts as the illegal destruction, damage, removal or change of electronic data, as well as the restriction of the use of such data with the help of hardware, software, or by other means.

From attack descriptions provided by the sources studied in this paper, the Lithuanian defacement attacks appear to correspond to at least some elements of the definition provided in article 4.1 of the Convention on Cybercrime. Due to access restrictions in the criminal proceedings to more specific data, a specific subsumption is not possible nor is it vital in the context of this analysis. It suffices to say that there was enough evidence on the criminal nature of the activities to commence criminal proceedings.

Both by the Convention and the Lithuanian law, the above acts are only punishable if committed "without right" and "intentionally"[276], but neither aspect seems to be problematic here as the lack of authorisation and the presence of some form of intention to commit the defacements are fairly evident in this case.

However, there is a possible restriction to the actual applicability of the national implementation of this article. Paragraph 2 of Article 4 allows the Parties to enter a reservation concerning the offence in that they may require that the

conduct result in serious harm. This is an entitlement that Lithuania used: in accordance with Article 42 and Article 4.2, of the Convention, the Republic of Lithuania declared that *criminal liability occurs if the acts described in Article 4 of the Convention result in serious harm.* [277] Likewise, the Lithuanian Criminal Code Article 196 stipulates that these acts only qualify as crimes if "great damage is inflicted".

By the Convention, what constitutes serious harm is left to domestic legislation to decide.[278] It appears, however, that the Criminal Code of Lithuania does not define the concept of what constitutes "great damage"[279], so it is difficult to determine whether a defacement attack carried out by a particular perpetrator would qualify as cyber crime. (a further complicating fact would be if the damage caused by the particular perpetrator was not properly recorded and aggregated).

Even if the notion of "significant damage" is defined in national law, as it was in the case of Estonia, the complications in identifying the extent, nature and connection of the damages to the particular actor still remain (these are discussed in more detail in the Georgian case study.

An elevated liability is foreseen in the following section (of Article 196 of the Criminal Code of Lithuania) for acts that are potentially or actually more severe: the electronic data of information system that has a strategic importance to national security or of great significance to public administration, economic or financial system, are under particular protection.

As stated in the official report concerning the June 2008 cyber incident, no real danger to the private sector or strategic State administration was determined even if disturbance to a

---

274  Explanatory Report of the Convention on Cybercrime, *supra* note 143.

275  *Id.*

276  Article 4.1 of the Convention on Cybercrime; Article 196 of the Lithuanian Criminal Code.

277  Reservation contained in the instrument of ratification deposited on 18 March 2004 and confirmed by a *Note verbale* from the Ministry of Foreign Affairs of Lithuania, dated 26 April 2004, registered at the Secretariat General on 10 May 2004. *See* List of declarations made with respect to treaty No. 185,' available at: http://conventions.coe.int/Treaty/Commun/ListeDeclarations.asp?NT=185&CV=1&NA=4&PO=999&CN=999&VL=1&CM=9&CL=ENG.

278  Explanatory Report to the Convention on Cybercrime, supra note 143.

279  Special Investigation Service of the Republic of Lithuania. Annual Performance Report 2003, p. 17. Available at: http://http://www.stt.lt/en/files/report_2003.pdf.

private business's server was evident.[280] Thus, the defacement attacks probably would not reach the level of elevated criminal liability where the requirement is that of the harmful act being conducted an information system of "strategic importance to national security" or of "great significance to public administration, economic or financial system". According to the same Article 196, a person that inflicts only minor damage by his/her actions only commits a misdemeanour. Since the European Convention on Mutual Assistance in Criminal Matters[281], to which Lithuania is party, applies only to judicial proceedings as opposed to administrative proceedings[282], Lithuania may not be in position to request international legal assistance even if the perpetrators were identified or at least connected to a particular country so as to identify the relevant nation to consider for cooperation in criminal matters. Efficient international cooperation in criminal matters is often only available between countries that mutually recognise such actions as crimes[283]; Lithuania on its part has reserved the right not to comply with an international request for assistance insofar as it concerns an offence that is not qualified as a "crime" and punishable as a crime under Lit

huanian law.[284]

Therefore, considering the circumstances related to the definition of cyber crimes in national law and limitations to the use and efficiency of international judicial cooperation, in addition to the technical obstacles in locating and identifying the perpetrators in the relative anonymity of cyberspace, the proceedings of the Lithuanian cyber incident are unlikely to meet much success even though Lithuania has a legal framework to investigate such attacks as cyber crimes.

In a wider perspective, this case study reflects the vulnerability of national (including public and private) information infrastructure to this type of attack. It only took a single ISP vulnerability for the hackers to lodge their electronic protests toward the Lithuanian government. As seen in this example, the political protest was communicated via a crime (hacking and defacement), and the results of the protest/crime affected the private sector more than the government, since the government was able to take prevention measures. As we will discuss below, it is thus important for governments to consider third-party effects where political tensions have the potential of resulting in not just legal protest but also those of illegal nature – ones that affect private businesses and information infrastructure.

## Cyber threat risk assessment as due diligence in governmental decision-making

As the facts of the Lithuanian cyber incident illustrate, cyber attacks can become an integral part of political tensions between different countries and ideology-driven groups. It is not known who, if anyone, will be identified as the perpetrator of the defacement of more than 300 websites, but the political context of the attacks is apparent.

While politically motivated attacks mostly protest against government and other public authorities' actions or decisions, they will most

---

280  Official Statement by Lithuanian Embassy, *supra* note 237.
281  European Convention on Mutual Assistance in Criminal Matters. Council of Europe. (ETS 030). 20.IV.1959. Available at: http://conventions.coe.int/Treaty/EN/Treaties/Html/030.htm.
282  *See* Explanatory Report to the European Convention on Mutual Assistance in Criminal Matters, available at: http://conventions.coe.int/Treaty/en/Reports/Html/030.htm.
283  Article 5 of the European Convention on Mutual Assistance in Criminal Matters. A list of declarations and reservations can be viewed at: http://conventions.coe.int/Treaty/Commun/ListeDeclarations.asp?NT=030&CM=1&DF=1/15/2009&CL=ENG&VL=1.
The text of Article 5:
Any Contracting Party may, by a declaration addressed to the Secretary General of the Council of Europe, when signing this Convention or depositing its instrument of ratification or accession, reserve the right to make the execution of letters rogatory for search or seizure of property dependent on one or more of the following conditions:
that the offence motivating the letters rogatory is punishable under both the law of the requesting Party and the law of the requested Party;
that the offence motivating the letters rogatory is an extraditable offence in the requested country;
that execution of the letters rogatory is consistent with the law of the requested Party.
2. Where a Contracting Party makes a declaration in accordance with paragraph 1 of this article, any other Party may apply reciprocity. [Our emphasis]

284  *See* the list of declarations and reservations to the European Convention on Mutual Assistance in Criminal Matters, *id.*

likely be targeted against governmental information systems and specific critical services. As this and other recent cases (including those studied in this book) show, such attacks inevitably result in intrusions against Internet Service Providers and information infrastructure as "random" targets.

The effect of tension caused by political decision-making can therefore also extend to private sector information systems. This may be accidental, as it seems to be in the Lithuanian case (private sector ISPs were affected since the targeted websites were hosted on their servers); but the tension may also trigger attacks that are directly targeted against providers that host services objectionable to the attackers - e.g. online media that publish objectionable information, or, in more severe cases, information systems critical to the society's functioning (e.g. online banking, vital communications, or other services).

Since even a relatively extensive cyber attack does not necessarily require high technical skill or much resource from the perpetrators, the likelihood of a cyber attack against the nation's web presence is high in any evolvement of political tensions. If the cyber incident in Estonia in April-May 2007 and now the Lithuanian event of June 2008 illustrate a pattern – and we believe it does – the targets are not selected among governmental sites only, even if the message of the attackers is to protest against government action. The target appears to be a country's internet presence as a whole, that is to say governmental and commercial. In many cases, a country's public and/or private internet presence may be hosted on, or serviced by 'third parties', i.e. private businesses in other countries.

The fact that the reactions to political and governmental activities may affect the country's private sector and non-affiliated third parties, raises the issue of integrated threat and risk assessment and may, in the light of recent cyber incidents, impose a certain "duty of care" on the government.

"Good governance" principles recognised in the EU require that policy proposals and legislative actions be preceded by an impact assessment, identifying the anticipated or actual impacts of a development intervention on those social, economic and environmental factors which the intervention is designed to affect or may inadvertently affect.[285] A government may thus be required to take the risk of a cyber reaction into account in planning proposals and activities which occur in a highly politicised context.

Prior awareness of a risk of a cyber reaction, and preparedness for one, would help defending entities to withstand a cyber attack. A risk analysis considering the potential political after play of a sensitive decision, and a resulting action plan, could avoid or minimise the harm caused to national information systems and infrastructure. The activities need not be costly or sophisticated, as was well illustrated in the Lithuanian case: the simple fact that governmental agencies were warned to expect cyber attacks gave them an advantage in enduring the attacks and recovering more quickly than the commercial services who had no similar degree of warning (who were not warned as the private sector website owners were not on the CERT's contact list, as CERT-LT later explained[286]).

Risk assessment and notification would not lift the (legal or regulatory) burden of risk assessment from the ISPs, but it would strengthen the overall security level and capacity to withstand attack. Therefore, in situations involving elevated political tension (including cross-border tension) and therefore elevated risk of

---

285    UK Enterprise Development Impact Assessment Information Service. Available at: http://www.enterprise-impact.org.uk/word-files/CoreText-1-WhatisImpactAssessment.doc. *See also* Commission Communication COM(2002)276 of 5 June 2002 on Impact Assessment (available at http://eur-lex.europa.eu/LexUriServ/LexUriServ.do?uri=CELEX:52002DC0276:EN:NOT).

The Göteborg European Council in June 2001 and the Laeken European Council in December 2001 introduced the requirement of impact assessment as an important political consideration.

Impact assessment (IA) is a process aimed at structuring and supporting the development of policies. It identifies and assesses the problem at stake and the objectives pursued. It identifies the main options for achieving the objective and analyses their likely impacts in the economic, environmental and social fields. It outlines advantages and disadvantages of each option and examines possible synergies and trade-offs.

Impact assessment is an aid to *political decision*, not a substitute for it. It informs decision-makers of the likely impacts of proposals, but it leaves it up to them to take the decisions. For more detailed information, see ec.europa.eu/governance/impact/index_en.htm.

286    Rainys, *supra* note 242.

cyber "payback" from outside players or strong internal opinion groups, stakeholders (ISPs and government cyber entities) should be informed of potential risk to systems.

There may be debate over the specifics of the various criteria for determining who should be included on such a contact list, but an early warning measure would support both the providers and the users of electronic communications services and should as such be regarded as part of a country's national cyber security and cyber defence policies and strategies.

## Service Level Agreements

The fact that Lithuanian governmental agencies were informed of the attacks beforehand also raises the issue of the standard of service level agreements (SLAs) for governmental information infrastructure, as well as considerations for the necessity for defining a non-discrimination duty to ensure that both public and private sector ISP-s and web hosts be warned about known threats.

Increasingly, governments make available and the public uses a variety of governmental services online; the Lithuanian eGovernment services with their high record of use of are an excellent example here. All these services are provided under SLAs with mainly private-sector ISPs. Governments in countries with a high degree of cyber threat need to consider additional guarantees for their services and information infrastructure and a way to achieve this would be to apply for a higher level of services in terms of sustainability of electronic services, availability priorities, and reaction time.

The issue of SLAs is, to a great extent, a matter of national legislation or contracts. For Lithuania as well as the other European Union members, the obligations of the service providers in ensuring security of services derives from the ePrivacy Directive 2002/58/EC[287] (which was to be transposed into national law in EU Member States by 31 October 2003 or upon accession for later

entrants, unless the nation negotiated a transition period).The ePrivacy directive foresees a general obligation for the service provider to take appropriate technical and organisational measures to safeguard security of its services. If necessary (and with respect to the security of the network upon which the service provider's services are provided), the service provider must draw upon help from the provider of the public communications network to which it is connected[288].

In accordance with the directive, the technical and organisational measures must correspond to the regular risk level presented to the services and network; however, in case of a particular risk of a breach of the security of the network, the service provider is presented an elevated requirement to inform its subscribers concerning the risk and any possible remedies if the service provider cannot neutralise such risks itself.[289] As part of the warning system, users and subscribers must be informed (free of any extra charge) of measures they can take to protect the security of their communications.[290]

According to this provision, no difference is made between public and private users.

Since the directives do not provide a relevant obligation specifically intended to address wide-scale cyber attacks, any elevated requirements for informing governmental entities, regarding either procedure or content of such information, need therefore either be based on national law or be included in the SLA negotiated between the state and the ISP. For the organisation seeking stronger guarantees to network and service security, the recommendable course of action can be to agree on a notification arrangement with the web host and/or ISP. Even if the relevant obligation does not exist in applicable law, contract parties are free to agree on mutually suitable contract conditions. For state structures, a model contract could be advisable that integrates the best practices from different institutions, takes a requisite level of security into account, and defines the applicable notification regime in case of elevated risk.

---

287 Directive 2002/58/EC of the European Parliament and of the Council of 12 July 2002 concerning the processing of personal data and the protection of privacy in the electronic communications sector (Directive on privacy and electronic communications); OJ L 201, 31/07/2002 pp. 0037 – 0047.

288 Article 4 of the ePrivacy Directive.
289 Preamble section 20 and Article 4 of the ePrivacy Directive.
290 Preamble section 20 of the ePrivacy Directive.

In the Lithuanian case, CERT-LT gave a warning to the governmental agencies that helped these entities to defend their web sites against defacement. Under different circumstances, it may be the case that rather than a national CERT, an ISP or other private sector service provider may know soonest about a potential threat. Some countries may have a law that requires this information to be shared with the government. However, if a country does not legally require a service provider to convey such threat information, the inclusion of early warning guarantees in SLAs with network operators or service providers could help ensure the timely sharing of threat information, thus making the defence of information systems more effective. Likewise, the threat of being exposed to politically motivated cyber attacks raises the issue of service guarantees for critical information infrastructure (CII), where the necessity for similar guarantees needs to be considered.

Considering that the effect of a cyber attack against a website reaches beyond that particular website owner and also affects the webhost, the ISP, and other clients of the ISP, there may be reason to consider national legislation to make it a duty of website owners to provide their contact details to ISPs or CERTs. This could for example be arranged at the point of registering a domain name.

Building a network of cooperation and information between ISPs – possibly connecting them with a central body such as the CERT – can also help to make the networks and services more sustainable. Like we saw in the Lithuanian incident, the fact that the CERT had a contact list for webmasters of public sector websites meant that the public sector site owners were warned in advance, suffered a less severe blow, and were able to resume to their normal business sooner.

Since elevated SLA requirements will result in higher maintenance costs, any business implications of including components of national critical information infrastructure need to be carefully considered in order to avoid disproportional costs to network operators, service providers, and ultimately, users. Also, international obligations that states have taken – e.g. those reflected in NATO Cyber Defence Policy and Concept – may play a role in defining the national CII.

# IV Summary of the Lithuanian case

## INCIDENT TIME FRAME

*Start*     Saturday, 28 June 2008

*End*      Wednesday, 2 July 2008

*Duration* 4 days

## INCIDENT CONTEXT

### Political context and background of incident

- Parliament adopts a law banning Soviet insignia from public use;

- Russian high political level expresses protest against the decision; the local Lithuanian Russian population remains calm;

- Indications received about potential impending cyber attacks.

### Information society indicators

- Information society included under one of the main long-term state priorities; national Information Society Strategy establishes modernisation of public administration by using information technology as a key priority;

- Strong legislative base and institutional framework created to support the functioning of information society;

- ICT use statistics and online availability of public services show steady growth; however, Lithuania has yet to reach the EU average in these areas.

## INCIDENT FACTS

### Methods

- Defacement. Pro-Soviet and communist symbols as well as profane anti-Lithuanian slogans posted on websites.

- Some e-mail spam.

### Targets

- Over 3oo private sector (95%) and governmental (5%) websites;

- The defaced web sites were hosted by one webhosting service provider; the majority of them on a single server with a server software or operating system vulnerability. The attack targeted all that was accessible in that particular provider's server with no specific regard to particular websites.

### Origin

- Undetermined.

### Effect

- Damage largely avoided to the public sector due to timely warning;

- Private sector suffered most.

### Measures taken

- Based on information published in the media about impending cyber attacks, CERT-LT sent a prior warning to their contact list. The latter mainly consisted of Lithuanian government agencies; therefore, commercial sites missed the warning.

## LEGAL LESSONS IDENTIFIED AND LEARNED

### Core of the case

- Reactions to politically sensitive government decisions and actions can affect random targets and information infrastructure. A policy and organisational structure for sharing threat / vulnerability information, both government to private sector and vice versa, may have a tangible mitigating effect on potential attacks;

- Quality of cyber crime regulation will play a role in cyber deterrence.

### Summary

- While politically motivated attacks are most likely targeted against governmental information systems and specific critical services, they will inevitably affect electronic communications network operators and service providers, including ISPs, and could affect non-affiliated third parties. This could impose a certain "duty of care" on the government to take the risk of a cyber reaction into account in planning proposals and activities that occur in a highly politicised context. Such risk analysis with a corresponding action plan could avoid or minimise the harm caused to national information systems and infrastructure.

- The ratification and national implementation of CoE Convention on Cybercrime is important to successful criminal proceedings of politically motivated cyber attacks; however, the fact of ratification and implementation alone will not guarantee success. Circumstances related to the scope of definition of cyber crimes in national law and related limitations to the use and efficiency of international legal cooperation can gravely reduce the likeliness of successful criminal proceedings.

- Activities that are employed for cyber risk management need not be costly or sophisticated: in the case under study, the difference was made by the simple act of informing parties of imminent threats. For stronger guarantees to network and service security, the recommendable course of action could include a notification arrangement between the network and/or service providers and the organisation seeking security guarantees. Even if a relevant obligation does not exist in applicable law, contract parties are free to agree on mutually suitable contract conditions. For state structures, a model contract could be advisable that integrates the best practices from different institutions, takes a requisite level of security into account, defines the applicable notification regime in case of elevated risk.

## Challenges

- Call for a good governance standard, reflected in legal acts, to ensure the dissemination of cyber threat information to both private and public sector; the implementation of such standard by means of legislation, an organsational framework, and service level agreements (SLAs); and finding the balance between a high standard of ICT security and reasonable cost of investment required from network and service operators.

# GEORGIA 2008

June-July

# I Background of the incident

## The political context of the conflict

The cyber conflict under study in this analysis falls within the timeframe and context of a broader armed conflict that broke out in August 2008 between the Russian Federation and Georgia over South Ossetia, an autonomous and *de jure* demilitarized Georgian region on the border of Georgia and Russia.

South Ossetia became *de facto* independent from Georgia during the 1991 Georgian-Ossetian conflict; however, it has remained commonly recognised by the international community as an integral part of Georgia. (The majority of UN nations continue to recognise the territorial integrity of Georgia even after the August 2008 Russo-Georgian conflict.[291])

Despite a declared ceasefire and numerous peace efforts since the 1991 conflict, the tension in the region remained unresolved. To maintain stability in South Ossetia after 1991, a peacekeeping force was formed in 1992 under an OSCE (Organization for Security and Co-operation in Europe) mandate; the force was formed of Russian, Georgian and South Ossetian troops, subjected to the authority of a Russian commander. In practice, these troops failed to cooperate, and tensions kept gradually growing between Georgia on one side and mostly Russian-supported separatists on the other.[292]

Following a period of separatist provocations, on August 7, 2008, Georgian forces launched a surprise attack against the separatist forces.[293] Referring to national obligations to "protect Russian citizens abroad"[294], on August 8, the Russian Federation responded to Georgia's act with military operations into Georgian terri-

291 The Russian Federation recognised South Ossetia's independence on 26th August, 2008; the Russian example was followed by Nicaragua a week later. *See* Statement by President of Russia Dmitry Medvedev on August 26, 2008. Available at: kremlin.ru/eng/speeches/2008/08/26/1543_type82912_205752.shtml; Nicaragua recognizes South Ossetia, Abkhazia. *Reuters.* 3 Sep 2008. Available at: http://www.reuters.com/article/gc07/idUSN0330438620080903.

292 Council of Europe Parliamentary Assembly Resolution 1633 (2008) on 'The consequences of the war between Georgia and the Russian Federation', available at assembly.coe.int/Mainf.asp?link=/Documents/AdoptedText/ta08/ERES1633.htm; Liik, Kadri. 'Tee sõtta'. (In Estonian) International Centre for Defence Studies. 11 Aug 2008. Available at http://www.icds.ee/index.php?id=73&type=98&L=0&tx_ttnews[tt_news]=262&tx_ttnews[backPid]=214&cHash=4de7396400.

293 Liik, *Id.*; Council of Europe Parliamentary Assembly Resolution 1633 (2008), supra note 292, p 4.

294 President Dmitri Medvedev. Statement on the Situation in South Ossetia. 8 August 2008. The Kremlin, Moscow. Available at kremlin.ru/eng/speeches/2008/08/08/1553_type82912type82913_205032.shtml

tory; first into the South Ossetian region, then also beyond the area where the peacekeeping mandate was applicable. Georgian authorities viewed this as Russia's military aggression against Georgia[295]; in response, on August 8, the President of Georgia, Mikheil Saakashvili, informed the international community of having begun mobilisation, and on August 9, Georgia imposed a "state of war".[296] Even though this step foremost served as a national measure in a situation where Georgia perceived a threat to national security and sovereignty, this also set the legal framework within which Georgia dealt with the cyber attacks and as such, is relevant to keep in mind when studying Georgia's response to the cyber attacks.

On August 8, before the Russian invasion into Georgia commenced, cyber attacks were already being launched against a large number of Georgian governmental websites.[297] Whereas military operations were ended by a ceasefire agreement on 12 August 2008[298], cyber attacks continued throughout the rest of the month

of August.[299]

# Georgia as an information society

Statistics about the Georgian ICT sector show that Georgia has 7 Internet users per 100 people (for comparison: Estonia, the country that fell under similar type of attacks in 2007, has 57, and Lithuania who came under coordinated cyber attacks in summer 2008, has 32).[300] The relatively low number of Internet users in Georgia reflects the nation's infrastructural capacity and its lack of overall dependence on IT-based infrastructure. However, the number of Internet users has been steadily growing – the Georgian National Communications Commission (the Georgian regulatory authority in the electronic communications sector) reported an 81% increase in the number of Internet users in Georgia in 2006; much of that growth is based on the growing number of broadband Internet users.[301]

Geographically, Georgia has few options for Internet connectivity via land routes – namely Turkey, Armenia, Azerbaijan, and Russia. Sources vary on Georgia's interconnection dependency on Russia. According to some sources, most of Georgia is, in terms of Internet infrastructure, dependent on Russia: more of Georgia's connections to the Internet pass through Russia than any other country, comprising nearly half of Georgia's thirteen links to the worldwide network.[302] On the other hand, there is indication regarding interconnection with Turkey: according to Renesys[303], most of Georgia's 309 Internet prefixes get routed via Turkish or Azerbaijan service providers; however, the latter is then

295   Information for Press. Georgian Ministry of Foreign Affairs, 8 Aug 2008. Available at: http://www.mfa.gov.ge/index.php?lang_id=ENG&sec_id=461&info_id=7193&date=2008-08-08&new_month=08&new_year=2008.

296   Press release of the President of Georgia. Declaration of Universal Mobilization by Georgian President Mikheil Saakashvili. 8 Aug 2008, available at: http://www.president.gov.ge/?l=E&m=0&sm=1&st=0&id=2689.; [Labott, E., Gotsadze, E.] Russian warplanes target Georgia. CNN, August 9, 2008. Available at: edition.cnn.com/2008/WORLD/europe/08/09/georgia.ossetia/index.html?eref=rss_topstories. According to Georgian officials referenced in the article, the order was not a formal declaration of war and stops short of declaring martial law; it did give the President powers that he would not have had in a peacetime situation, such as issuing curfews, restricting the movement of people or limiting commercial activities.
By a decision of the Georgian Parliament, the state of war was lifted on 3 September 2008.

297   Sources vary on the exact commencement of the attacks, but are united in that the Russian invasion and the commencement of cyber activities against Georgian websites were practically parallel in time. Stratfor dates the commencement of cyber attacks at August 7. See 'Georgia, Russia: The Cyberwarfare Angle'. Stratfor Today, Aug 12, 2008, available at: http://www.stratfor.com/analysis/georgia_russia_cyberwarfare_angle. Note that the situation between Russia and Georgia had been politically very tense for weeks before the actual military intervention.

298   'Russia 'ends Georgia operation''. BBC, 12 Aug 2008. Available at news.bbc.co.uk/go/pr/fr/-/2/hi/europe/7555858.stm.

299   Danchev, Dancho. 'DDoS Attack Graphs from Russia vs Georgia's Cyberattacks'. 15 Oct 2008. Available at: ddanchev.blogspot.com/2008/10/ddos-attack-graphs-from-russia-vs.html.

300   Internet users per 100 population, 2006. Available at: data.un.org/Data.aspx?d=MDG&f=seriesRowID:605.

301   Georgia: Electronic Communications Market Turn Over Exceeds GEL 1 bln. Caucas Euronews, 8 Jun 2007. Available at: http://www.caucaz.com/home_eng/depeches.php?idp=1723&PHPSESSID=d7e84d535388fb8344492715209 9c6967.

302   Stratfor Today, supra note 297.

303   Renesys (founded in 2000, based in New Hampshire, USA, privately held) is a leading provider of intelligence on the state of the Internet worldwide. See http://www.renesys.com/about/.

routed on via Russia.[304] As is apparent, options for dispersing Internet traffic[305] are relatively limited for Georgia, which makes it a good target for coordinated cyber assault and isolation.

Construction of a direct high-capacity link from Georgia to Western Europe was in progress at the time the conflict occurred: a fibre optic cable through the Black Sea (from the coastal city of Poti, Georgia to Varna, Bulgaria) was nearly completely installed by the time the August 2008 Russian-Georgian conflict commenced.[306] This connection is expected to remarkably enhance the country's Internet interconnectivity. It was anticipated that the system would be delivered in the autumn of 2008[307]; and despite a month's delay caused by the conflict[308], the construction project was completed in November 2008. The system passed testing successfully and was, according to Georgian news reports in early 2009, going to be launched for commercial use.[309]

As of 2007, there were five companies operating in the Georgian Internet access and services market; of them, Caucasus Online/ Caucasus Network Tbilisi, the main commercial service provider, held 90% of the market.[310] United Telecom of Georgia (Sakartvelos Elektrokavshiri)[311], the incumbent operator in

the fixed line access market, also provided access to Internet service.[312]

# II Facts of the case

## Timeline of the attacks

A short occasion of turbulence, reflecting the growing tensions in Georgian-Russian relations[313], was visible in the Georgian cyber space on 19 July 2008, weeks before the more coordinated cyber attacks began on August 8. The website of the Georgian President Mikheil Saakashvili (www.president.gov.ge) became unavailable for more than 24 hours because of a DDoS attack. The Shadowserver Foundation[314] observed at least one web-based command and control (C&C) server hitting the website with a variety of simultaneous attacks (TCP, ICMP, and HTTP floods), which took the website offline for more than 24 hours.[315]

However, the main phase of events began

304 The relevant ISPs are TTnet (AS 9121; Turkey), Delta Telecom (AS 29049; Azerbaijan), and TransTelCom (AS 20485; Russia) See Zmijewski, E. 'Georgia Clings to the 'Net', Renesysblog, Aug 11, 2008, available at: http://www.renesys.com/blog/2008/08/georgia_clings_to_the_net.shtml
305 Here in the context of using alternative routes for data transmission in case a certain route becomes unusable.
306 Zmijewski, reference in supra note 304.
307 Tyco to construct undersea fibre-optic system for Caucasus.' Invest In Georgia Investment Agency. Available at: http://www.investingeorgia.org/news/view/274.
308 Georgia's Caucasus Online Invests $40 Mln in Fibre Optic Link to W. Europe via Bulgaria. SeeNews - The Corporate Wire 20 Nov 2008. Available at http://www.seenews.com/news/latestnews/georgiancaucasusonlinelaunchesfibreopticprojectinbulgariaonfriday-153906/.
309 Sarke Infromation Agency. Daily News. November 17, 2008. Available at http://www.sarke.com/cgi/search/issue.asp?Day=17&Month=11&Year=2008&Type=1#5.
310 Georgia Electronic Communications Market Turn Over, supra note 301.
311 Privatised in 2006; a controlling share in United Telecom of Georgia is held by BTA Bank (a Kazakhstan commercial bank). See 'Acquisition of state share of JSC 'United Telecommunications Company of Georgia'. Press release by BTA Bank, 16 May 2006. Available at bta.kz/en/press/news/2006/05/16/1043/; Petriashvili, Diana. 'Georgia Pins Investment Hopes on Kazakhstan.' Eurasianet.org 17 April 2007. Available at http://www.eurasianet.org/departments/insight/articles/eav041707a.shtml

312 Hardabkhadze, V., Kvernadze, L. Georgia. (Part of a report produced for the European Commission on the electronic communications markets in Central and Eastern Europe) Available at: ec.europa.eu/information_society/activities/internationalrel/docs/pi_study_rus_ukr_arm_azerb_bel_geor_kaz_mold/7_georgia.pdf. p. 8.; CERT-EE Report on status in Georgia, 14 August 2008. A public version of the report is available at the website of the Estonian Informatics Centre at http://www.ria.ee/index.php?lang=en.
313 See, e.g, 'Some key events in tense Russia-Georgia relations'. Associated Press, 17 August 2008. Available at: http://www.aol.com.au/news/story/Some-key-events-in-tense-Russia-Georgia-relations/827601/index.html
314 The Shadowserver Foundation (established in 2004) is a volunteer group of computer security professionals from around the world. The mission of the Shadowserver Foundation is to improve the security of the Internet by raising awareness of the presence of compromised servers, malicious attackers, and the spread of malware. The foundation works alongside other security agencies to develop strategies against the threats and to form action plans to help mitigate the threats as they develop. See www.shadowserver.org for more information.
315 Adair, Steven. 'Georgian Attacks: Remember Estonia?' Shadowserver Foundation, Aug 13 2008, available at: www.shadowserver.org/wiki/pmwiki.php?n=Calendar.20080813; Nazario, Jose (Arbor Networks) and DiMino, Andre M. (Shadowserver Foundation). 'An In-Depth Look at the Georgia-Russia Cyber Conflict of 2008'. October 2008. Available at: http://www.shadowserver.org/wiki/uploads/Shadowserver/BTF8_RU_GE_DDOS.pdf

on August 8 [316] when multiple C&C servers hit websites that were either Georgian – such as the website of the Georgian President, the central government site, and the homepages for the Ministry of Foreign Affairs and Ministry of Defence – or sympathetic to the country's cause.[317] Georgian news portals such as Georgia Online (apsny.ge), News.ge, but also non-Georgian, but Georgia-sympathetic news sites and online discussion forums were also attacked.[318]

TBC, the largest commercial bank of Georgia, came under attack on the early morning of August 9.[319]

The Georgian government, reliant on its official websites as information distribution channels, had to look for ways to avoid information blockade. On Saturday, August 9, a Georgian expatriate Nino Doijashvili, chief executive of Atlanta-based hosting company Tulip Systems Inc., offered the Georgian government help and transferred president.gov.ge and rustavi2.com, the Web site of a prominent Georgian TV station, to her company's servers. [320] With Google's permission, the website of the Ministry of Foreign Affairs was transferred to a Blogger account.[321] The Office of the President of the Republic of Poland provided a section on their website for official press releases of the Georgian government, and the Estonian government accommodated the website of the Ministry of Foreign Affairs in a server located in Estonia, as well as sending two CERT-EE information security spe-

cialists to assist in mitigation efforts.[322]

On August 10, Shadowserver reported new attacks against .ge sites: the website of the Georgian Parliament and President were hit with http-flood attacks. In this case, the IP address of the C&C server revealed it was located in Turkey.[323] Again, the attacks were not limited to just government websites. Shadowserver reported at least six different C&C servers attacking various non-governmental websites.

By august 11, the President's website was available again, but the central government site as well as ministries' websites mentioned above still remained down and some commercial websites were also hijacked. [324] A defacement attack against the President's website occurred in this timeframe, where a slideshow was integrated into the page displaying identical images of Saakashvili's and Hitler's public appearances in order to portray Saakashvili as Hitler. As of August 11, the site remained under a sustained DDoS attack. [325]

On August 11, the Georgian Ministry of Foreign Affairs issued a press release, communicating "A cyber warfare campaign by Russia is seriously disrupting many Georgian websites, including that of the Ministry of Foreign Affairs." [326] The statement was released via a replacement website that the ministry had built on Google's blog-hosting service, blogspot.com. The same course of action was also taken by Civil.ge, the largest English-language news site in Georgia, which had come under DDoS attack, and switched to a Blogger account in case the site remained unavailable.[327]

According to Arbor Networks, the attacks were

---

316  The first incidents, as recorded by Shadowserver, occurred on Aug 08 at 2:40 PM. See Nazario, DiMino, Id.; Waterman, Shaun. 'Analysis: Russia-Georgia Cyberwar Doubted,' United Press International, August 18, 2008. Available at: http://www.spacewar.com/reports/Analysis_Russia-Georgia_cyberwar_doubted_999.html

317  Adair, Steven. 'Georgian Websites Under Attack - DDoS and Defacement'. Shadowserver Foundation, Aug 11, 2008, available at: http://www.shadowserver.org/wiki/pmwiki.php/Calendar.20080811; Danchev, Dancho. 'Coordinated Russia vs Georgia cyber attack in progress,' Aug 11, 2008, available at: blogs.zdnet.com/security/?p=1670

318  Adair, supra note 317.

319  CERT-EE Report on status in Georgia, supra note 312.

320  Swartz, Kristie E. 'Tulip Systems Tries to Keep Other Georgia's Web Sites Safe'. The Atlanta Journal-Constitution, 17 August 2008, http://www.ajc.com/business/content/business/stories/2008/08/17/tulip_systems_georgia; Danchev, supra note 317.

321  Shachtman, Noah; 'Estonia, Google Help 'Cyberlocked' Georgia (Updated),' Wired Blog Network/Danger Room, August 11, 2008, http://blog.wired.com/defense/2008/08/civilge-the-geo.html#more

322  CERT-EE Report on status in Georgia, supra note 312; Rand, Erik. 'Gruusia välisministeeriumi kodulehekülg paigutati Eesti serverisse' (in Estonian). EPLOnline. August 12, 2008. Available at: http://www.arileht.ee/artikkel/438306; Kirk, Jeremy. 'Update: Estonia, Poland Help Georgia Fight Cyberattacks,' IDG News Service, August 12, 2008, http://www.computerworld.com/action/article.do?command=viewArticleBasic&articleId=9112399&source=rss_news50; Shachtman, supra note 321.

323  Adair, supra note 315.

324  Danchev, Dancho, supra note 317.

325  Id.

326  'Cyber Attacks Disable Georgian Websites', Georgian Ministry of Foreign Affairs, Aug 11, 2008, available at: georgiamfa.blogspot.com/2008/08/cyber-attacks-disable-georgian-websites.html

327  Danchev, Dancho, supra note 317.

all globally sourced, suggesting one or multiple botnets behind them.[328]

By August 12, most of the observed botnet attacks targeted against .ge sites began to subside and the attack model changed towards using a Microsoft Windows batch file that was designed to attack Georgian websites and was distributed and encouraged to use on Russian forums, blogs, and websites.[329] On August 13, Shadowserver reported large-scale ICMP traffic from numerous Russian computers from several different ISPs throughout the country, covering both dialup and broadband users, and targeting Georgian governmental websites.[330] The effect of it was continuous ICMP traffic via the 'ping' command to several Georgian websites.[331]

The last large cyber attack against Georgian websites was launched on August 27. The main target this time was the Georgian Ministry of Foreign Affairs that together with other sites came under a DDoS attack in the afternoon. The attacks mainly consisted of HTTP queries to the mfa.gov.ge website with the purpose of overloading the web server.[332]

The attacks started to wind down on August 28, due to the reason that most of the attackers were successfully blocked[333]; nevertheless, minor occurrences were detected even after that date that were indistinguishable from regular traffic and could therefore be attributed to regular civilians.

## Means and targets of the attacks

The cyber attacks directed against Georgia primarily involved defacement of public websites and launching Distributed Denial of Service (DDoS) attacks against numerous public and private (financial and media) targets – methods similar to those used in attacks against Estonia in 2007.

Below is a more detailed overview of the main types of attacks used in the Georgian incident.

## Defacement

As reported, defacements were directed at political/governmental and financial sites, including:

www.president.gov.ge

website of Mikheil Saakashvili, the President of the Republic of Georgia

www.nbg.gov.ge

website of the National Bank of the Republic of Georgia

www.mfa.gov.ge

website of the Ministry of Foreign Affairs of the Republic

According to data available, the website of President of Georgia, as well as the Georgian Ministry of Foreign Affairs were defaced and replaced with a collage of photos of Mikheil Saakashvili and Adolf Hitler.[334]

The website of the National Bank of Georgia was reported to have been "defaced and replaced with a gallery of 20th century dictators, President Saakashvili among them".[335] It is not clear from the reporting sources whether all three websites were defaced in the same way or whether two different types of defacements were carried out; the only depiction of defacement that has been presented is a collage of photos of Saakashvili and Hitler.

CERT-EE reported that web sites of several Azerbaijan newspapers and media agencies (www.day.az, www.today.az, www.ans.az) had been defaced in the early days of the incident.[336] The sites were carrying news and analysis on the Georgian events, most of it either neutral or sympathetic to Georgia.

---

328  Nazario, José. 'Georgia DDoS Attacks - A Quick Summary of Observations', Arbor Networks, Aug 12, 2008, available at: http://asert.arbornetworks.com/2008/08/georgia-ddos-attacks-a-quick-summary-of-observations/
329  Nazario, DiMino, *supra* note 315.
330  Adair, *supra* note 315.
331  *Id.*
332  Danchev, *supra* note 299.
333  *Id.*

---

334  *See e.g.* Danchev, Dancho, *supra* note 317; *see also* На сайте МИД Грузии появился коллаж с Гитлером' (in Russian), *Lenta.Ru*, available at: http://www.lenta.ru/news/2008/08/09/defaced/.
335  John Markoff quoting Gadi Evron, a well-known network security expert. *See* Markoff, John. 'Before the gunfire, cyberattacks,' International Herald Tribune, Aug 13, 2008, available at: http://www.iht.com/articles/2008/08/13/technology/13cyber.php.
336  CERT-EE Report on status in Georgia, *supra* note 312.

## DoS and DDoS attacks

According to the information received from CERT-EE and confirmed by the Georgian Embassy in Tallinn, the Georgian websites coming under cyber attack included those in both public and private sectors.[337]

**Government sites:**

www.abkhazia.gov.ge

official website of the government of the Autonomous Republic of Abkhazia

www.mes.gov.ge

Ministry of Education and Science of the Republic of Georgia

www.naec.gov.ge

governmental website providing standardised educational tests for students

www.parliament.ge

the Parliament of the Republic of Georgia

www.president.gov.ge

the President of the Republic of Georgia

**News and media sites:**

www.forum.ge

biggest forum in Georgia

www.civil.ge

largest Georgian news page in English

www.presa.ge

Association Press

www.apsny.ge

Georgia Online, a news portal

www.rustavi2.com

a private television company

www.news.ge

a news portal in English

interpress.ge

a news portal

www.tbilisiweb.info

a news portal

www.os-inform.com

a privately owned Russian-language media site carrying news on Georgia

**Financial institutions:**

www.tbc.ge

Georgia's largest commercial bank

**Other websites:**

www.hacking.ge

Georgian hackers' community website

Attack statistics provided by Arbor Networks show high intensity attacks with data traffic reaching 211.66 Mbps per an average observed attack and 814.33 Mbps at the maximum.[338] Regarding duration, an average attack lasted 2 hours 15 minutes of constant abnormal traffic flow, while the longest one lasted 6 hours.[339]

Analysts point out that, based on observations on Internet traffic patterns, the attacks appeared coordinated from the beginning.[340] In this regard, the cyber events in Georgia differ slightly from the incidents in Estonia, where coordination was recognized only in the second phase of the cyber attacks.[341] The issue of coordination is discussed in more detail under the subsection 'Origins of the attacks' of this case study.

---

337  Steven Adair (Shadowserver) points out that in parallel to the attacks targeted against Georgian websites, certain Russian news portals (http://www.skandaly.ru, http://www.newsgeorgia.ru – the latter a co-project of Russian RIA Novosti and News Georgia) also came under attack – and interestingly, the same groups that were involved with targeting various Russian media outlets were also those that took aim at various Georgian websites. Additionally, the website of Garry Kasparov (http://www.kasparov.ru), a Russian opposition party representative, once again came under attack. See Adair, supra note 317.

338  There are no statistics available to the authors on what was the regular level of Internet traffic per an average site in Georgia in summer 2008. According to José Nazario, 220 Mbps is 'about in the middle of attack sizes', not achievable by a few individual hacktivists. See McMillan, Robert. 'Hackers Hit Scientology With Online Attack'. IDG News Service, 26 Jan 2008 Available at http://www.pcworld.com/article/141839/hackers_hit_scientology_with_online_attack.html.

339  Nazario, *supra* note 328.

340  *See* Danchev, Dancho, *supra* note 318; Stratfor Today, *supra* note 297.

341  In the Estonian case, there was a distinguishable emotional initial phase which was, after some days, followed by clearly more coordinated and professionally conducted waves of attacks.

## Distribution of malicious software and attack instructions

Several Russian blogs, forums, and websites spread a Microsoft Windows batch script that was designed to attack Georgian websites.[342] According to Steven Adair of Shadowserver, this script was posted on several websites and was also hosted on one site as a compressed downloadable file which contained an executable "war .bat" file within it.[343] The same method was used in the emotional phase of cyber attacks against Estonia, where a downloadable script to ping flood Estonian websites (both by Domain Name System (DNS) and Internet Protocol (IP)) was shared on various Russian language message boards.[344]

Instructions on how to ping flood Georgian government web sites were also distributed on Russian language websites and message boards, as well as lists of Georgian sites vulnerable to remote SQL injections[345], facilitating automatic defacement of them.[346] Again, this was similar to the Estonian case, where instructions on carrying out cyber attacks were spread almost exclusively on Russian language sites, regardless of whether those sites were located in Estonia, the Russian Federation, or elsewhere. It is relevant to mention that in both Georgia and Estonia, Russian is a minority language, and in neither of those two is it an official language.[347]

According to the analysis of the Swedish National Defence University[348], and supporting conclusions by Shadowserver, stopgeorgia.ru (also utilizing 'stopgeorgia.info' as a redirect) provided DDoS attack tools for download and indicated a number of.ge[349] web sites as a priority for attack. The findings of an analysis by the Project Grey Goose[350] confirmed evidence of coordinated targeting and attacking of Georgian websites, and pointed out that the same sites (stopgeorgia.ru/stopgeorgia.info) also provided the necessary attack tools for the cyber assault against Georgia for hackers.[351] In summary, 36 major web sites were identified as targets for hackers, among those the Embassies of the US and UK in Tbilisi, the Georgian Parliament, Supreme Court, and Ministry of Foreign Affairs, several news and media resources, and numerous other sites.

## Other types of attacks

The attackers also distributed a list of Georgian politicians's email addresses for spamming and targeted attacks. The list of e-mail addresses had originally been created by a lobbying organisation; during the attacks, it was circulated "in an attempt to convince Russian hackers of the potential for abusing it in spamming attacks and targeted attacks presumably serving malware through live exploit URLs".[352]

Again, the same method was used in the Estonian attacks, where comment and e-mail spam comprised a remarkable load on both

---

342  Adair, *supra* note 315.
343  *Id.* A redacted version of the script can be accessed at http://www.shadowserver.org/wiki/pmwiki. php?n=Calendar.20080813.
344  Note that instructions for cyber attacking Estonian sites continue to be available on the Internet even at the time of this analysis.
345  SQL (Structured Query Language) is a database computer language designed for the retrieval and management of data in relational database management systems (RDBMS), database schema creation and modification, and database object access control management. An SQL injection is a code injection technique that exploits a security vulnerability occurring in the database layer of an application. For a more detailed description, see *Abbreviations and Glossary*.
346  Danchev, Dancho, *supra* note 317.
347  In Georgia, two of the major languages spoken include language Georgian (71%) and Russian (9%); in Estonia, Estonian is the first language for 67.3% and Russian for 29.7% of the population. *See* Georgia. *CIA World Factbook* (Updated as of 6 November 2008). Available at: https://www.cia.gov/library/publications/the-world-factbook/geos/gg.html; Estonia. *CIA World Factbook*, November 2008. Available at: https://www.cia.gov/library/publications/the-world-factbook/geos/en.html

348  Preliminary conclusions on 'Cyberattack against Georgia'. Swedish National Defence University, August 2008. E-mail to CCD COE.
349  ge is the Internet country code for Georgia.
350  Project Grey Goose was a volunteer effort of IT experts, led by Jeff Carr of IntelFusion in cooperation with Palantir Technologies, to understand the nature of recent cyber activities between Russia and Georgia. The Project undertook an in-depth OSINT research into the communications regarding cyber attacks spread over Russian hacker sites in August 2008; a report on the findings is available at http://www.scribd.com/doc/6967393/Project-Grey-Goose-Phase-I-Report. *See also* Krebs, Brian. 'Report: Russian Hacker Forums Fueled Georgia Cyber Attacks' on Computer Security. 17 October 2008. The Washington Post, 16 Oct 2008. Available at voices.washingtonpost.com/securityfix/2008/10/report_russian_hacker_forums_f.html.
351  Project Grey Goose. Phase I Report Russia/Georgia Cyber War – Findings and Analysis. 17 October 2008. Available at: http://www.scribd.com/doc/6967393/Project-Grey-Goose-Phase-I-Report.
352  Danchev, Dancho, *supra* note 317.

private and governmental web and e-mail servers. While Georgia is, as of today, not considered an advanced e-government country[353], the Georgian administration has put effort into being reachable for its citizens via publicly announced e-mail addresses[354], so it is realistic to presume that the spam e-mail interfered with administration to some extent. We have no information on whether e-mail was used for internal government communications during the time of the conflict, but it is reasonable to expect that at least to some degree.

There are references of the attackers redirecting Georgian Internet traffic through servers located in Russia and Turkey, where the traffic was then blocked. Jart Armin, a researcher tracking the activities of the Russian Business Network (RBN)[355], reported that the DDoS-attacked sites had, for a while, been made accessible again for a brief time by re-routing traffic through commercial servers abroad (namely, Deutsche Telekom), but control over the traffic was quickly taken back to servers based in Moscow.[356], Whether this amounts to a "cyber blockade", as one source claimed[357], is uncertain. Still, a similar detail was also reported by Dancho Danchev (ZDNet), who noted that cyber attacks expanded to Turkey and Ukraine, where many of the servers which route traffic to Georgia were commandeered, possibly by the RBN.[358]

Danchev reported another an example of attempts to isolate the Georgian Internet user community and prevent their communication via usual channels: one of Georgia's most popular hacking forums was reported to have come under a permanent DDoS attack for several days on behalf of Russian hackers, an effort which harmed the ability of the Georgian hacker community to exchange information regarding ongoing cyber events, thus potentially delaying mitigation efforts. [359]

## Origin of the attacks

As was the case with Estonia, there is no conclusive proof of who was behind the DDoS or defacement attacks, even though finger pointing at Russia was prevalent in the media.[360] There seems to be a widespread consensus that the attacks appeared coordinated and instructed. [361]

According to Arbor Networks' data traffic analysis, major DDoS attacks were all globally

sourced, suggesting a botnet (or multiple botnets) behind them.[362]

According to the Shadowserver Foundation account from the initial days of the Georgian cyber incident, there were at least six different C&C[363] (Command and Control) servers involved in the attacks; some of the botnets were either "DDoS

353   Department of Economic and Social Affairs of the United Nations Secretariat. 'UN e-Government Survey 2008: From e-Government to Connected Governance.' United Nations, 2008.

354   See, e,g,, the list of national websites at http://www.market.ge/directory/administrative.html for references.

355   Russian Business Network. A cybercrime organisation, specialising in phishing, malicious code, botnet command-and-control (C&C), denial of service (DoS) attacks, and identity theft. Further information is available at: http://www.verisign.com/security-intelligence-service/info-center/webcasts/archived/index.html (last accessed: 27 Aug 2008); Krebs, Brian. 'Shadowy Russian Firm Seen as Conduit for Cybercrime', Washington Post, Oct 13, 2007, available at: http://www.washingtonpost.com/wp-dyn/content/article/2007/10/12/AR2007101202461_pf.html (last accessed: 27 Aug 2008).

356   Markoff, supra note 335.

357   Russian Invasion of Georgia/Russian Cyberwar on Georgia. 9 October, 2008. The report is accessible at http://www.georgiaupdate.gov.ge. It must be noted that the report is anonymous and hosted by Georgia-friendly actors; the conclusions of this report have thus not been relied on in this analysis. It provides a good overview of foreign media review on Georgian cyber events in an annex.

358   Zuckerman, E. 'Cyber Attacks: Misunderstanding Cyberwar in Georgia', Postchronicle, Aug 17, 2008, available at: http://www.postchronicle.com/news/technology/article_212165469.shtml. See also Zuckerman, E. 'Misunderstanding Cyberwar', Aug 18, 2008, available at: http://www.worldchanging.com/archives/008381.html.

359   Danchev, Dancho, supra note 317.

360   'Russian Cyber Attack on Georgia, Government Websites Down or Replaced With Fakes'. Telegraph.co.uk, 11 Aug 2008 ; Hoffman, Stefanie. 'Russian Cyber Attacks Shut Down Georgian Websites', ChannelWeb, 12 Aug 2008. Available at http://www.crn.com/security/210003057 ; 'Expert: Cyber-attacks on Georgia websites tied to mob, Russian government' Los Angeles Times, 13 Aug 2008. Available at latimesblogs.latimes.com/technology/2008/08/experts-debate.html.

361   Danchev, supra note 317; see also, Project Grey Goose Phase I Report. Supra note 351, p 4.

362   According to José Nazario, the DDoS attacks were mostly TCP SYN floods with one TCP RST flood in the mix; no ICMP or UDP floods were detected. See Nazario, supra note 328.

363   Botnet command and control servers, commonly abbreviated by the IT society as C&C.

for hire" or "DDoS for extortion" services which normally employ a regular pattern in attacking sites and rarely go after non-commercial sites. [364] The HTTP-based botnet C&C server was reported to be a MachBot controller, a tool that is frequently used by Russian bot herders[365], and the domain involved with this C&C server had, according to Steven Adair of the Shadowserver Foundation, seemingly fraudulent registration information which tied back to Russia.[366]

There was some indication of the RBN involvement, which was referred to earlier in this paper (see 'Other types of attack' under 'Methods of cyber attack')[367]. The security experts of Shadowserver stated that the involvement of RBN did not amount to more than providing hosting services to the botnet C&Cs, finding that RBN did not commit the DDoS attacks itself.[368]

There is no doubt regarding the involvement of the Russian hacker community in the cyber attacks: the coordination of and support to the attacks took place mainly in the Russian language and was conducted on Russian or Russia-friendly forums. However, there is no evident link to the Russian administration, and the Russian government has denied any involvement in the cyber assaults.[369] The Project Grey Goose team was unable to find, in their research into the Russian hacker sites, any references to state organisations guiding or directing attacks, "be it

because there was none, because the collection efforts were not far-reaching or deep enough to identify these connections, or because involvement by state organisations was conducted in a way to purposefully avoid attribution".[370]

The Project Grey Goose report did provide historical evidence that past and present members of the Russian government have endorsed cyber attacks initiated by their country's hacker population.[371] Jeff Carr, the principal investigator of the Grey Goose project, concluded that the level of advanced preparation and reconnaissance suggests that Russian hackers were primed for the assault by officials within the Russian government and/or military, based also on evidence that the StopGeorgia.ru site was "up and running within hours of the ground assault -- with full target lists already vetted and with a large member population".[372] Don Jackson, the director of threat intelligence at SecureWorks[373], also pointed to the correlation between the types and patterns of activity of DDoS and the suspicious timing of the attacks, claiming it to have been "either one of the most coincidental mass cyber-attacks [he had] ever seen, or [···] some sort of cooperation on some level."[374]

Jackson also reported that incident responders in Georgia had provided logs of network traffic to and from botnet C&C servers, and the latter had IP addresses that were in ranges belonging to Russian state-operated companies. These networks had been launch points for DDoS attacks against Georgian networks. Jackson warned, however, that those addresses could have been 'pwned' (gained unauthorised control over) by hackers.[375]

However, the possible involvement of some officials within the Russian administration is only backed by circumstantial evidence, and does not prove nor amount to official support to the cyber attacks by the Russian government. Many experts remain sceptical that the Russian

---

364  Johnson, M. 'Georgian Websites Under Attack - Don't Believe the Hype', *Shadowserver Foundation*, Aug 12, 2008, available at: http://www.shadowserver.org/wiki/pmwiki.php/Calendar.20080812.
365  Bot herder is a program designed to produce bots anonymously. For a more detailed explanation, see *Abbreviations and Glossary*.
366  Adair, supra note 315; Craciun, G. 'President of Georgia Web Page Down after Hacker Attack - The Russians are believed to be behind it', Security News Editor, available at: http://news.softpedia.com/news/President-of-Georgia-Web-Page-Down-after-Hacker-Attack-90420.shtml.
367  Johnson, *supra* note 364.
368  *Id.*
369  According to Yevgeniy Khorishko, a spokesman at the Russian Embassy in Washington, "Russian officials and the Russian military had nothing to do with the cyberattacks on the Georgian Web sites last year." Gorman, Siobhan. 'Hackers Stole IDs for Attacks'. Wall Street Journal, 24 Aug 2009, available at: http://online.wsj.com/article/SB125046431841935299.html. *See also* Germain, Jack M. 'The Winds of Cyber War'. TechNewsWorld, 16 Sept 2008, available at: http://www.technewsworld.com/rsstory/64494.html?wlc=1263369698; 'Georgia targeted in cyber attack.' AFP, 12 Aug 2008. Available at http://afp.google.com/article/ALeqM5iRuGsssizXAKVgmPqAXOxqB5uHsQ.

370  Project Grey Goose Phase I Report. Supra note 351, p 3.
371  *Id.*, pp. 3, 6-8.
372  Krebs, *supra* note 352.
373  SecureWorks is a leading provider of a wide range of information security services worldwide.
374  Prince, Brian. 'Security Researcher Asserts Russian Role in Georgia Cyber-attacks'. eWeek, 13 Aug 2008. Available at http://www.eweek.com/c/a/Security/Security-Researcher-Asserts-Russian-Role-in-Georgia-Cyber-Attacks/.
375  *Id.*

government had any role in the Georgian cyber attacks and consider them as 'unaffiliated attacks by Russian hackers and/or some rioting by enthusiastic Russian supporters'[376].

Sources indicate a connection between organised crime and the Georgian cyber incidents. According to the above-referred study carried out by the Swedish National Defence University, the organisation provided in the registration details of stopgeorgia.ru was related to different criminal activities, such as forged passports and stolen credit cards – activities that normally should be prosecuted by the authorities. The Russian authorities have remained remarkably passive in prosecuting the organisation in this particular case.[377] The Project Grey Goose report points out that the stopgeorgia.ru site – which provided information and tools for independent hackers to attack Georgian sites – was hosted by SoftLayer Technologies, Inc. (AS36351) of Plano, Texas, USA, the latter being controlled by Atrivo, a host listed as the 4th worldwide among webhosts facilitating the spread of malware, spam, financial scams, and identity theft.[378] Atrivo's connection was cancelled and traffic routing stopped by its service providers in late September 2008 (based mostly on the fraud concerns, not necessarily its participation in the Georgian attack).[379]

Dancho Danchev of ZDNet points out that "an average script kiddie"[380] would not bother with nor understand the psychological effects of coming up with identical gestures of Saakashvili and Hitler and integrating them within the defaced sites.[381] It is obvious from some of the attacks, especially with the amount of photos and the similarities of gestures, that putting this psyops collage together demanded time, commitment and resources.

Based on their data collection and analysis, the Grey Goose Project analysts discerned a pattern in the Georgian attacks, consisting of 5 stages: spreading encouragement to get involved in the cyber war against Georgia; publishing a target list of Georgian government web sites which had been tested for access and/or vulnerabilities; selection of types of malware to use against the target web sites; launching of the attacks; and result evaluation.[382] The conclusions left little doubt that the Georgian cyber attacks were largely coordinated, not simply an *ad hoc* reaction of individual cyber-activists sympathetic to the Russian cause. As stated above, this may constitute a new development compared to the incidents in Estonia, where coordination was recognized only in the second phase of the cyber attacks.

## Mitigation and international assistance

Attack mitigation within Georgia was coordinated by CERT Georgia, who normally provides computer and network security technical support to the Georgian higher education institutions (as a part of the Georgian Research and Educational Networking Association, GRENA)[383] and who assumed the role of national CERT during the cyber attacks.[384]

The immediate response to the attacks had to, naturally, be by the websites under attack. According to Shadowserver, some of the attacked websites remained online and did not really make any changes to defend themselves. A few of the websites temporarily changed their visible IP addresses to loop back to the originating network[385] in an attempt to thwart the at-

376  Evron, Gadi. 'Georgia Cyber Attacks From Russian Government? Not So Fast'. CSO, 13 Aug 2009. Available at http://www.csoonline.com/article/443579/Georgia_Cyber_Attacks_From_Russian_Government_Not_So_Fast.
377  Swedish National Defence University, *supra* note 348.
378  Armin, J. 'Atrivo – Cyber Crime USA: White Paper - Atrivo and their Associates'. Vers: 1.1, September 2008. Available at: hostexploit.com/downloads/Atrivo%20white%20paper%20090308ad.pdf; SoftLayer Technologies - Does the Cyber War '"Buck" Stop There? *Intelfusion*. Available at: http://intelfusion.net/wordpress/?p=452.
379  *See* Krebs, Brian. 'Internet Shuns U.S. Based ISP Amid Fraud, Abuse Allegations' Washington Post, 22 Sept 2008; available at voices.washingtonpost.com/securityfix/2008/09/internet_shuns_us_based_isp_am.html.
380  An intermediate class between everyday computer/Internet users and hackers. For a more detailed description, see *Abbreviations and Glossary*.
381  Danchev, Dancho, *supra* note 317.

382  Project Grey Goose Phase I Report. Supra note 351, p 5.
383  'CERT Georgia'. A description of mission and services is available at: http://www.grena.ge/eng/cert.html.
384  CERT-EE Report on status in Georgia, *supra* note 312.
385  This was done by changing the IP to 127.0.0.1 (*localhost*), which is the standard IP address used for a loopback network connection. The effect of this measure is that upon trying to connect to or target a pingflood attack towards a web server, one is looped back to one's own host. A downside of this measure is that the website becomes inaccessible also for genuine requests.

tacks. A few others also changed hosts.[386]

By order of the Georgian Communication Commission, most Georgian access to Russian websites was blocked at the outset of the conflict with Russia.[387] This was done for information control purposes, but it also freed up some of the existing bandwidth of Georgian servers.

International cooperation was also supplied. The interpress.ge news portal moved to Servage (www.servage.net), a worldwide hosting platform provider. Upon permission from Google, Civil.ge, a Georgian news portal, temporarily switched to publishing their news coverage via an account with Blogger (civilgeorgia.blogspot.com), a tool owned by Google and operated from that company's major resources, thus able to withstand potential DDoS attacks better than the Georgian servers.[388] Georgia's Ministry of Foreign Affairs also opened a Blogger account (georgiamfa.blogspot.com) for distribution of information.

The websites of the Ministry of Defence and the President were relocated to Tulip Systems, Inc., located in Atlanta, in the US state of Georgia[389], and the website of the Ministry of Foreign Affairs was moved to an Estonian server.[390]

The Office of the President of Poland provided a separate section of their website (www.president.pl) for dissemination of information

and helped to get Internet access for Georgia's government after breakdowns of Georgian local servers caused by the cyber attacks.[391]

CERT Poland analyzed IP data and sent out abuse messages, while CERT France helped with collecting log files.[392] From August 12 to 16, two information security specialists from CERT Estonia visited Georgia in order to assist the local CERT by providing their knowhow and experience.[393]

## Effects of the attacks

CERT-EE provided information on the effects of the cyber attacks on two main players on the Georgian Internet access and services market: United Telecom and Caucasus Network. United Telecom of Georgia router (Cisco 7206 series) was unavailable and incapable of providing service for several days.[394] Caucasus Network Tbilisi was flooded with excessive queries; according to data provided to the Estonian CERT by Caucasus Network, rerouting of traffic to help Caucasus Network Tbilisi may have adversely affected smaller Internet providers.[395] The problems were exacerbated by the fact that the Caucasus Network infrastructure runs through the war activity zone, which also caused physical disconnections.[396]

The DoS and DDoS attacks severed communication from crucial Georgian government websites in the early days of the Georgian-Russian conflict – a period that was doubtless the most critical in the events and where the Georgian government had a vital interest in keeping the

---

386  Adair, *supra* note 342.
387  Mchedlishvili, Niko. 'Georgia cuts access to Russian websites, TV news'. Reuters, 19 Aug 2008. Available at http://www.reuters.com/article/internetNews/idUSLJ36223120080819?sp=true. Here, it is appropriate to recall that the Georgian 'state of war' was still applicable.
388  Shachtman, *supra* note 321.
389  The Ministry of Defence website was reported to have been made unavailable for an extended period as a result of an attack, but the source reporting it does not cite verifiable sources nor have we been able to specify the means of attack or verify the report. (Coordinated Cyber Attacks Hit Websites Due To Russian-Georgian Conflict. Cyberinsecure, 12 Aug 2008. Available at cyberinsecure.com/coordinated-cyber-attacks-hit-websites-due-to-russian-georgian-conflict/.) Thus, the only reliable information we have is about the MOD website having been moved.
390  CERT-EE Report on status in Georgia, supra note 312; Rand, supra note 322. According to information exchanged in a meeting at the Estonian Ministry of Foreign Affairs in September 2008, the initiative of the Estonian Ministry of Foreign Affairs to host the Georgian Ministry of Foreign Affairs website could not have happened, and certainly not in such a short timeframe (the site was reportedly moved within 24 hours), without Estonia learning lessons from 2007.

---

391  'Cenne polskie wsparcie dla Gruzji' (in Polish), *RMF FM*, 9 Aug, 2008, available at: http://www.rmf.fm/fakty/?id=141305. *See* also: 'Information about the latest developments in Georgia', *President of the Republic of Poland*, available at: http://www.president.pl/x.node?id=479.
392  *Id.*
393  Eesti aitab Gruusiat küberrünnete tõrjumisel' (*in Estonian*), Estonian Informatics Centre, Aug 12, 2008, available at: http://www.ria.ee/index.php.
394  According to CERT-EE, CPU utilization at UTG was 100%, which made it almost impossible to get console access. The cause seemed to be some sort of BGP upload activity. L3 switches on the way to the router were unaffected. See CERT-EE Report on status in Georgia, supra note 312.
395  The Caucasus has a 1G backbone and an uplink (probably 3 x STM1) via Turkey and Azerbaijan. Caucasus was reported to have been flooded with 150Mbit/s traffic, TCP SYN flood towards interpress.ge port 80. *Id.*
396  Danchev, Dancho, *supra* note 315.

information flowing to both the international public and to its own residents. The unavailability of core state institutions' websites can additionally be seen as serving a discouraging effect on Georgian morale and public confidence.

Given the different context of the Georgian cyber event compared to the Estonian cyber attacks in spring 2007, the damage was manifested in different categories as well. Whereas in Estonia, the core of the damage consisted of obstructed access to socially vital electronic services provided by both the public and private sector (such as e-government and e-banking services), in Georgia the main damage was in limiting the nation's possibilities to distribute information about the ongoing military conflict– in "making its voice heard" to the world and in communicating with the Georgian pThe cyber incidents also affected the provision of public services. As a consequence of the attacks, on August 9, the National Bank of Georgia ordered all banks to stop offering electronic services. These electronic banking services were out of function for ten days[397]; on Monday, August 18, the National Bank reported that all commercial banks in Georgia were back to operating business as usual.[398]

As the scale of ICT dependence is rather different in Georgia compared to Estonia, the significance of service disruption was also different. As dependence on ICT for everyday services and communication correlates with the level of harm that could be caused by the attacks, generally, countries with a higher degree of ICT development are more exposed to cyber attacks and face greater damage, and the same is true in reverse. Regarding the Georgian case, Josè Nazario (Arbor Networks) was quoted in media as not observing devastating effects.[399]

However, even though the relatively low ICT dependence of Georgia limited the damages caused by the cyber attacks on the service providers, Georgia also illustrates another trend in the effect of cyber attacks: namely, countries whose ICT availability is low, may still suffer in terms of efficiency of information flow.

The difference between the short-term and long-term effects of cyber attacks must also be kept in mind. While the attacks did not have a permanent or even a long-run devastating effect on the Georgian Internet infrastructure, the damage caused by the attacks was most acutely experienced at the time when Georgia was the most dependent on the availability of information channels. This brings up another characteristic of cyber attacks: unlike the effect of kinetic force, cyber attack can be designed in a way to cause only temporary harm in a particular timeframe.

As is the case with Estonia, the amount of damage caused by the Georgian cyber attacks is difficult to estimate monetarily[400] – even more so in the case of Georgia since the timing of the cyber incidents coincided with physical damages caused by the ongoing armed conflict. A conclusive estimation of damages would require a systematic and inclusive effort from all parties involved – government, private sector as well as the users. In many cases, reluctance of the private sector to provide exact data on the kind and size of the damages occurred may be predicted, as there are reasonable and genuine concerns as to the negative effect of revealing such data both in terms of business interest and security considerations; such data may also fall under the protection of business confidentiality, which means that there is no legal obligation to the private sector enterprises to provide data. Further, the lack of information flow may have affected Georgian government decision-making during wartime; in such a situation, it is hard to distinguish a separate cost of the cyber attacks.

In summary, this means that while it is possible to describe the kinds of damages that extensive cyber attacks may produce, just like in the case of Estonia it is unlikely that exact figures on the

---

397   Compared to Estonia, where online banking services were out of function for two hours, this is a lengthy period. However, given the hight dependence on Estonians on e-banking (over 90% of all banking transactions are conducted via electronic means), even this relatively short timeframe was already considered critical. This illustrates well that the facts of a particular cyber incident must be studied against the specific national situation.

398   'All commercial banks in Georgia are operating business as usual', *National Bank of Georgia*, Aug 18, 2008, available at: http://www.nbg.gov.ge/index.php?m=340&newsid=832.

399   Arnoldy, B. Cyberspace: New Frontier in Conflicts. ABC News, 17 Aug 2008. Available at: http:// abcnews.go.com/Technology/AheadoftheCurve/ Story?id=5590834&page=2.

400   Linnamäe, L. 'Küberrünnakute kahjusid hakatakse arvutama hiljem' (*in Estonian*). *Postimees*, 5 May 2007. Available at: suusk24.postimees.ee/110507/esileht/ majandus/259796.php.

size of damages will be available.

However, a discussion of the effects of cyber attacks would not be complete without also taking note of the benefits that resulted from the Georgian cyber incidents, foremost to Georgia, but also to the international community. In this context, international media attention to Georgia, the international cooperation and mitigation assistance offered, and international awareness these events have raised, has certainly been beneficial to both Georgia and the international community.

# III Legal considerations

Due to the simultaneous occurrence of the cyber attacks to the South-Ossetian war, the Georgian cyber attacks raised with a previously unparalleled acuteness the question of the nature of cyber attacks. Was this the much-spoken "cyber war"? What legal regime was applicable to the cyber incident and what could Georgia do? And equally, what could the nations and international organisations Georgia called for help from, do?

A cyber incident may fall within categories ranging from a simple deviation of internal regulations (corporate or agency/department rules or best practices) to cyber terrorist acts and cyber warfare. Therefore, response to the incidents may be governed by different fields of law (such as IT regulatory framework, criminal law, law of armed conflict) and thus fall under different legal provisions under national and international law. The law determines the authorities' capability to act, the nature and extent of their involvement, the legal remedies available and a number of practicalities related to cyber incident management. Legal categorisation of the incident is therefore the starting point for identifying which existing rules are applicable for a particular cyber incident, but also for identifying any gaps in the legal framework.

# Applicability of the law of armed conflict

## Rationale of questioning the applicability of law of armed conflict

International media was quick to title the cyber attacks against Georgia a "cyber war"[401] and security experts pointed out similarities of the Georgian incidents to the cyber events in Estonia in April 2007, a conflict that has frequently been referred to as "Cyber War I"[402]. These allegations raised the issue of the nature of the incident in legal terms, and, deriving from there, the binding set of rules for the parties involved.

The discussion on the applicability of the law of armed conflict to cyber attacks is not recent in itself: substantial works on the topic already date from the late 1990s.[403] There are several reasons for considering the applicability of the respective legal provisions to the Georgian cyber incident: the nation was in a situation where it perceived a threat to its territorial integrity and political independence (thus the prerequisite to the use of force was there); some of the targets attacked by cyber means were military in nature (e.g. the Georgian Ministry of Defence website); the simultaneous timing between the cyber attacks and Russian military operations into Georgian territory caused, at least initially, allegations by some of a state-on-state "cyber attack". Another issue was the question of the standard of government action in suppressing non-state-affiliated cyber attackers within the nation's territory and while the government was waging war with the country to which these attackers were sympathetic.

---

401   E.g. Markoff, supra note 335; Swaine, Jon. 'Georgia: Russia 'conducting cyber war". Telegraph, 11 Aug 2008. Available at: http://www.telegraph.co.uk/news/worldnews/europe/georgia/2539157/Georgia-Russia-conducting-cyber-war.html.

402   Landler, Markoff, supra note 11.

403   Such as Schmitt, Michael N. 'Computer Network Attack and the Use of Force in International Law: Thoughts on a Normative Framework.' Research Publications 1, Information Series (1999).; Sharp, Walter Gary, 'Cyberspace and the Use of Force'. Falls Church, Va.: Aegis Research Corp., (1999).

## General prerequisites for the applicability of LOAC

The law of armed conflict (LOAC) is a term comprising two major sets of rules: *jus ad bellum* that focuses on the criteria for going to war in the first place (covering issues such as right purpose, duly constituted authority, last resort, etc.) and *jus in bello* that creates the concept of just war-fighting (covering the concepts of lawful targets, proportionality, civilian-military discrimination, etc.). Due to the level of abstraction of this analysis, the term LOAC is used without specifically referring to *jus ad bellum* or *jus in bello*. Where only certain aspects of LOAC are referred to, they are identified.

First, it needs to be noted that in order for LOAC to apply to a particular armed conflict, neither a formal declaration of war, nor recognition of a state of war is required. Instead, the requirements of LOAC become applicable "as from the actual opening of hostilities"[404] *(ex nunc)*. An international armed conflict is perceived as "[a]ny difference arising *between two States*[405] and leading to the *intervention of armed forces···* even if one of the Parties denies the existence of a state of war"[406] [emphasis added]. Since the situation between Georgia and Russia in August 2008 involved armed forces in a cross-border conflict, the applicability of LOAC to the Russian-Georgian conflict raises little doubt[407] regardless of the fact that the Georgian declaration of a "state of war"[408] was a domestic measure rather than one rooted in international law, and regardless of the claims of the Russian Federation that it only entered the territory of Georgia in order to "defend the lives and dignity of its citizens" in South Ossetia and Georgia, describing its intervention as a peacekeeping operation (even though Russian forces went beyond the area where the peacekeeping mandate was applicable).[409]

This does not, however, automatically mean that LOAC would also be applicable to the cyber attacks that took place in conjunction with the ongoing kinetic armed conflict.

In order to make a legal assessment of the situation, both the notions of "cyber war" and "cyber attacks" must be defined in legal terms, and for doing that, it must be examined whether the cyber incidents in Georgia satisfy the criteria of an "armed attack" that triggers the applicability of *jus in bello*.

As stated above, the involvement of armed forces in the conflict is an important prerequisite for the applicability of LOAC. As regards assessing a cyber incident, most countries do not have a specialised "cyber force" within their military

---

404   The authoritative Commentary of the International Committee of the Red Cross on the 1949 Geneva Conventions states that '[t]here is no longer any need for a formal declaration or war, or for recognition of the state of war, as preliminaries to the application of the Convention. The Convention becomes applicable as from the actual opening of hostilities.' *See* Pictet, J. (ed.). Commentary on the Geneva Convention for the Amelioration of the Condition of the Wounded and Sick in Armed Forces in the Field. *ICRC*, Geneva, 1952, p. 32.

405   Nevertheless, after the terrorist attacks of 11 September 2001 in the United States, the international community has acknowledged the changes regarding parties in armed conflict. The terrorist attacks against the United States were conducted by the terrorist network al-Qaeda led by Osama bin Laden and were considered armed attacks both by the UN and NATO. In addition, US president George W. Bush also held the Taliban regime of Afghanistan responsible for the attacks because it allowed al-Qaeda to operate on Afghanistan territory. After the attacks on the World Trade Center and the Pentagon, the US President started his War on Terror, which was first demonstrated by the invasion into Afghanistan by the troops of the USA and several of its allies. Hence, the attacks of 11 September 2001 expanded the traditional definition of armed conflict, e.g. armed conflict does not necessarily have to arise between two States but instead one of the parties can be, for example, a private group supported by a state. In this case, the question of state attribution and state responsibility arises.

406   Pictet, *supra* note 404, p. 32.

407   This position is shared by e.g. Human Rights Watch ('Q & A: Violence in South Ossetia'. Human Rights Watch, 15 Aug 2008. Available at: http://www.hrw.org/en/news/2008/08/15/q-violence-south-ossetia; Council of Europe Parliamentary Assembly Resolution 1633 (2008), reference in supra note 292.

408   *See* above under subsection 'Political context of the conflict'.

409   Statement of the President of Russia on August 8, 2008. Medvedev, D. 'Statement on the Situation in South Ossetia', August 8, 2008 available at: http://www.kremlin.ru/eng/speeches/2008/08/08/1553_type82912type82913_205032.shtml In his statement, the President relied on the Constitution of the Russian Federation to justify the interference in Georgia, as Article 80 (2) of the Constitution stipulates 'The President of the Russian Federation shall be guarantor of the Constitution of the Russian Federation, of the rights and freedoms of man and citizen. According to the rules fixed by the Constitution of the Russian Federation, he shall adopt measures to protect the sovereignty of the Russian Federation, its independence and state integrity, ensure coordinated functioning and interaction of all the bodies of state power.', *See* The Constitution of The Russian Federation, available at: http://www.constitution.ru/en/10003000-01.htm.

command structure, a fact that makes drawing a direct connection practically impossible. In the case of the Georgian incident, the Russian Federation denied any state involvement in the cyber attacks, and data traffic analyses conducted by independent parties failed to draw a direct connection between the cyber attacks and Russian authorities. Also, as Prof. Michael Scmitt, the leading scholar to address the issue of applicability of LOAC to computer network operations, explicitly reasons, the engagement of armed forces (or lack thereof), even if established, is not the sole decisive criterion.[410]

According to Prof. Schmitt, the decisive criteria in qualifying certain activities as "armed attacks" are the nature and, more importantly, the effect of the conduct under question.[411] Based on the reasoning established for defining traditional armed conflicts, Schmitt suggests that an action could be defined as an "armed attack", thus triggering the applicability of LOAC, if that action "is either intended to cause injury, death, damage or destruction, or such consequences are foreseeable".[412]

To make use of this argument, it is necessary to examine whether the incidents in Georgia meet the criteria listed above. Economic harm and loss of tangible property can be considered as damage and destruction, while significant human physical and mental suffering is logically included in the concept of injury, being, however, dependent on the level of human suffering involved – mere inconvenience, harassment or diminishment in the quality of life do not reach the level of injury.[413] Therefore, when evaluating the consequences of cyber attacks, both the physical and mental sides must be taken into account.

As demonstrated previously[414], the direct effect of the Georgian cyber attacks is difficult to estimate. Whereas negative implications on access to information and information society services are evident, the extent of monetary loss and human suffering is difficult to calculate due to a lack of a proper methodology, and because the damage caused by the armed conflict was far more severe, and the collection of evidence on losses was objectively hindered due to more acute concerns. It can be assumed, given the low overall dependence of the Georgian population on online services and the nature of the websites attacked (online distribution of information to the public, which is normally not a life-sustaining service nor necessary to economic stability) that the effect of cyber attacks was not serious enough to amount to severe economic damage or significant human suffering. All the more, it is hard to distinguish the damage and suffering caused by cyber attacks from the overall damage and suffering caused by the "traditional" armed conflict.

And even if the effects were easily measurable and could be deemed as sufficiently severe, the role of the state on behalf of the attacking party would still need to be established, which brings us back to the question of state involvement and responsibility.

## General principles of state responsibility

In order to hold a state responsible for cyber attacks under international law, it must be established, in addition to the "effect test" discussed above, that the cyber attacks can be directly connected with that particular state (e.g. due to state attribution or sponsorship).

The governing principle of state responsibility under international law has traditionally been that the conduct of private actors – both entities and individuals – is not attributable to the state, unless the state has directly and explicitly delegated a part of its tasks and functions to a

---

410  Schmitt, Michael N. Wired Warfare: Computer Network Attack and *jus in bello*, IRRC June 2002, Vol. 84, No. 846, page 372ff.
411  Schmitt explains the seeming widening of the definition of armed conflict by reasoning that at the time when the LOAC instruments were drafted, national armed forces were the only entities that were capable of conducting armed attacks.
412  See, e.g. Schmitt, supra note 410, page 372ff.
413  *Id.*
414  *See* subsection 'Effects of the attacks' of the Georgia case study.

private entity.[415] A shift in this rigid paradigm can be observed in the developments of recent years: e.g. by the International Criminal Tribunal for the former Yugoslavia in the *Tadic* case[416] and further by the international community in relation to the U.S. Operation Enduring Freedom in 2001.[417] However, the current view for attribution still requires some form of overall control by the state over the private actor.

The law on state responsibility is based on the concept of agency.[418] Hence, in determining whether responsibility can be attributed to a state, the key questions are (a) whether a person has acted as an *agent* of a particular state and (b) whether his actions qualify as *actions* of that state.[419] While state responsibility is apparent when a state commits certain acts as a direct result of exercising its public functions, *indirect* responsibility is also possible if the state tolerates the private action in question or is incapable of preventing it. Here, the wrongdoing of the state lies in its inadequate efforts to prevent the private action.[420]

The rules governing state responsibity were codified in 2001 into Draft Articles on Responsibility of States for Internationally Wrongful Acts[421], which can be considered as a reflection of *customary international law* – the latter being binding upon all states.[422] According to article 12 of the Draft Articles, a breach (that entails liability under international law) occurs when an act of a state does not conform to what is required of that state by the particular obligation under international law, regardless of the origin or character of that act. What is considered an internationally wrongful act is determined by international law.[423]

Still, the right of the injured state to use force as a response against another state depends on the level of involvement of the source state. While state *direction* and/or *support* of attacks can be seen as active involvement and therefore justify a stronger reaction, mere *toleration* (making no effort to suppress or stop those committing the attacks) or *inaction* (being unable to effectively deal with the perpetrators) on behalf of the source state as passive forms of involvement do not make the source state a target of lawful military operations.[424] Also, the remedy has to

---

415  In the *Nicaragua* case, the International Court of Justice (ICJ) noted that the state may be held responsible for the conduct of private actors only *if it executed effective control over such actors.* Hence, the ICJ could not hold the United States responsible for the conduct of the *contra* rebels, because the United States did not exercise effective control over the contras. The Court also noted that, in order for the conduct of private actors to give rise to legal responsibility of the state, it would have to be proved that the state indeed had effective control over the conduct of private actors. *See Military and Paramilitary Activities in and against Nicaragua* – ICJ Reports, 1986; Jinks, Derek. 'State Responsibility for the Acts of Private Armed Groups', *Chicago Journal of International Law,* 4 (2003), 83-95, p. 88.

416  In comparison with the Nicaragua case and the ICJ rule, the ICTY in the Tadic case lowered the threshold for imputing private acts to states and concluded that states only need to exercise overall control over private actors in order to attribute to the state any unlawful acts of the actors. The ICTY in its reasoning held that the 'effective control' criterion of the ICJ was contrary to the very logic of state responsibility and that it was inconsistent with state and judicial practice. See Prosecutor v. Tadic - ICTY Case No. IT-94-1, 1999.; Jinks, reference in supra note 415, p. 88-89.

417  Compared to the Tadic case, the U.S. Operation Enduring Freedom in turn lowered the threshold for attribution because the U.S. sought to impute al Qaeda's conduct to Afghanistan simply because its official regime Taliban had harboured and supported the terrorist group (irrespective of whether Afghanistan exercised effective or overall control). The international community along with several important international organisations endorsed the U.S approach and determined that under international instruments the attacks of September 11 constituted armed attacks which triggered the U.S inherent right of self-defence. The U.N, NATO and the OAS also attributed the terrorist attacks of al Qaeda to the Taliban regime. See Jinks, supra note 415, pp. 85-87.

418  Värk, René, 'State Responsibility for Private Armed Groups in the Context of Terrorism', XI *Juridica International*, 2006, 184-193, p. 185.

419  Under international law, the conduct of formal state organs and their officials is usually attributable to the state (as they have been authorised by the state to exercise public functions) and therefore it is considered that the state itself has committed that act, whereas the conduct of private actors, both entities and persons, is attributable to the state when it is sufficiently connected with the exercise of public functions. *Id.*

420  This is the case in state-on-state situations; the private actors are still responsible before the state for breaching their obligations arising from national legislation.

421  Draft Articles on the Responsibility of States for Internationally Wrongful Acts, text as it appears in the annex to General Assembly resolution 56/83 of 12 December 2001.

422  Värk, supra note 418, p. 185.

423  Id.

424  Id., p. 187.

be proportionate to the threat[425] – therefore, the less apparent the linkage of cyber attacks to a source state *and,* at the same time, the smaller the overall harm arising from the attacks, the less there is reason to speak of holding the state responsible for cyber attacks.

Considering this threshold, it is highly problematic to apply Law of Armed Conflict to the Georgian cyber attacks – the objective evidence of the case is too vague to meet the necessary criteria of both state involvement and gravity of effect. Therefore, the potential remedies arising from the law of armed conflict and international humanitarian law, as well as their usefulness, remain beyond the scope of this analysis.

## Technical assistance and the principle of neutrality

A separate concern that arose in the course of providing international assistance to Georgia to tackle the cyber attacks was whether countries such as Poland and Estonia, by agreeing to host on their websites or servers the content of Georgian websites targeted by cyber attacks, violated neutrality in international law and therefore made themselves parties in the Russo-Georgian conflict. Considering that some of the websites were also relocated to U.S. servers, albeit privately owned, the same question from a different angle arises in the case of the United States as well.

The principle of neutrality, set out in the Hague Conventions, provides for the rights and duties of belligerents and neutral states to maintain their neutrality during armed conflict. The Conventions stipulate the inviolability of the territory of a neutral state: belligerents may not move troops, weapons, or other materials of war across the territory of a neutral state.[426] Specific provisions are directed at the use of military

aircraft and marine vessels in the jurisdiction of a neutral state[427], but also the use of telecommunications assets.[428] According to Article 8 of the 1907 Hague Convention V, "[a] neutral Power is not called upon to forbid or restrict the use on behalf of the belligerents of telegraph or telephone cables or of wireless telegraphy apparatus belonging to it or to companies or private individuals." This rule is tied to the requirement of impartial treatment of all parties of the conflict, i.e. the neutral state must impartially permit the use of those structures for both belligerents.[429]

So even if the applicability of law of armed conflict to the Georgian cyber incident was an issue, interpreting the above clause in the context of modern technology, the fact that a neutral state permits use of its telecommunications infrastructure and equipment does not automatically entail breach of neutrality for that state. Of course, the level of state activism in permitting the use of telecommunications may range, from simply accepting data flow through private infrastructure to lending server space as was the case with Poland and Estonia, to actively supporting the functioning of telecommunications. Not all activities on this scale need necessarily be interpreted in a similar measure in the light of Article 8 of the Hague Convention cited above, but the smaller the degree of state activism, the less there is reason to speak of the state violating neutrality.

Due also to the fact that the Russian Federation clearly and sharply distanced itself from the cyber attacks[430] and that there is no evidence of state involvement in the attacks, the Georgian cyber attacks cannot be regarded as a military action. Therefore, it is safe to assume that helping Georgia to deal with the cyber attacks did not counter any Russian military efforts. Neutrality is only an issue during armed conflicts. According to information available to the authors, including the information provided by CERT-EE ob-

---

425  The co-called "Webster formula", defined in 1841, describes the "necessity of self-defence, instant, overwhelming, leaving no choice of means, and no moment for deliberation", and requires the party exercising self-defence to 'avoid doing anything unreasonable or excessive; since the act justified by the necessity of self-defence must be limited by that necessity, and kept clearly within it'. *See* Brownlie, Ian. 'The rule of law in international affairs: international law at the Fiftieth Anniversary of the United Nations'. The Hague Academy of International Law, 1998. Pp. 202-203.
426  Rights and Duties of Neutral Powers and Persons in Case of War on Land (Hague V); October 18, 1907. Art. 1 and 2.

427  Rights and Duties of Neutral Powers in Naval War (Hague XIII); October 18, 1907, Art. I and II.
428  *Id.*; Hague V, supra note 426, Art. 8.
429  *Id.*, Art. 9.; Kelsey, Jeffrey T. G. 'Hacking into International Humanitarian Law: The Principles of Distinction and Neutrality in the Age of Cyber Warfare'. 106 Michigan Law Review, 1427-1452 (2008). P. 1442-1443.
430  See the statement of the  spokesman at the Russian Embassy in Washington, Yevgeniy Khorishko, supra note 369.

servers on location, neither did Georgia officially react to the attacks by "cyber retaliation" by the military but instead treated the cyber incident as a computer security issue. So in conclusion, not only was this *not* an armed conflict, but neither Poland nor Estonia nor the United States interfered into the military purposes of either party, and thus did not violate the rules of the Hague Conventions on neutral conduct.

This two-fold test of level of state activism in permitting (in a non-discriminating manner) the use of its telecommunications infrastructure and equipment on the one hand, and the abstention from interfering into the military purposes or activities of either party on the other hand, could be used for giving countries assurance of the preservation of their neutral status when they assist a country (that is simultaneously a conflict party) to tackle cyber attacks of non-military nature in the midst of an armed conflict. What makes the distinction simpler in the Georgian case was the clear stances that both parties took regarding state roles in cyber attacks. Also, the institutions that came under attack provided communications channels and were not military in nature (the Ministry of Foreign Affairs in the case of Estonia, and the President of Georgia in the case of Poland). Neither is there evidence of impartial treatment since Russia never requested similar help. Therefore, it can be concluded that international assistance provided to Georgia to handle the cyber attacks cannot be interpreted as a position of the assisting countries to become parties to armed confApplicability of criminal law

## The rationale of questioning the applicability of criminal law

As we concluded above, it is problematic to apply the law of armed conflict to the Georgian cyber attacks due both to the lack of provable state involvement in the attacks and the small degree of damage directly caused by the attacks. The question remains: if the Georgian events were not cyber war, what were they? And more importantly, in the absence of law of armed conflict as a useful tool for countering cyber attacks, what tools does law offer to manage a phenomenon such as the Georgian cyber incident?

As information technology has evolved, many countries have included provisions of computer crimes in their criminal law to fight the hostile trends of intrusion into networks and data, computer fraud, and spread of malicious code. The rationale behind this is to avoid activities that have the potential of causing extensive societal and financial damage, and to counter the evolution of hostile trends.

In 2001, the Council of Europe adopted the first international agreement in the field – the Convention on Cybercrime[431] that contains both substantive and procedural aspects of investigating cyber crimes. While a valuable instrument for the purposes of shaping national criminal law and for planning and conducting collaboration between law enforcement agencies, the Convention on Cybercrime has, especially in implementation on the national level, been targeted mainly against the economic harm of cyber incidents. There have been few possibilities to test the usefulness of the Convention for the purposes of investigating and prosecuting politically motivated cyber attacks – the Estonian April 2007 cyber incident was perhaps the most wide-scale with more than a hundred countries involved – and the results, while too few to draw comprehensive conclusions, give little reason for complacency. An important deficiency of the Convention is the fact that it has only been ratified by 26 countries so far (the number is showing a small but steady growth though).[432]

## Georgian criminal law in the field

Georgia signed the Council of Europe Convention on Cybercrime in April 2008 but had, as of August 2008, not yet ratified the convention. The investigation of the incidents

---

431  Convention on Cybercrime, supra note 144.
432  Most of the member nations of the Council of Europe have signed the convention (except for Turkey and Russia, and the tiny European nations of Andorra, Monaco, and San Marino), but the total number of signatures not followed by ratification is rather high: 23 countries. Typically (but not extending to all cases), those countries that have ratified the convention and brought it into force are European Union member states. In addition, Canada, Japan, the Republic of South Africa and the United States of America have also signed the convention, but only in the latter has it also been ratified and entered into force. *See* Council of Europe. Convention on Cybercrime: Status as of 25 Aug 2009. Available at: conventions.coe.int/Treaty/Commun/ChercheSig. asp?NT=185&CM=&DF=&CL=ENG.

therefore can only be based on what then existed in Georgia's national substantive and procedural law. The following analysis is not intended to cover all aspects of Georgian national criminal law and only highlights the key elements worthy of consideration in deciding on further action.

Chapter 47 of Georgian Criminal Code[433] criminalises the following activities as computer crimes: "unlawful infiltration into computer information" (Art. 303), "creating, applying and disseminating a program damaging computers" (Art. 304), and "infringement of the rules for exploiting computers, computer systems or their networks" (Art. 305).[434] Specifically, "unlawful infiltration into the computer information, or the information reflected in the computer network system, if this action [···] disrupted the work of computers, computer systems or networks", are prohibited and punishable (Art 303 (1)), as are "creating a program damaging computers or making changes in existing programs that intentionally cause unsanctioned [···] disruption of the work of computers, computer systems or network" (Art 304). Thus, the Georgian authorities had a basis in law to instigate criminal proceedings to investigate the cyber attacks that took place in August 2008.

Taking the assumption that the same deeds are punishable also in (at least some of) the countries that the attacks originated from – which is generally the prerequisite for international criminal cooperation with those countries – Georgia may lean on the provisions of mutual legal assistance treaties of the Council of Europe. Nearly all of the 47 Council of Europe member countries, including Georgia and Russia, have acceded and ratified the European Convention on Mutual Assistance in Criminal Matters and Additional Protocol to the European Convention on Mutual Assistance in Criminal Matters.[435]

According to Article 1 of the Mutual Assistance Convention, the contracting parties undertake to afford each other "the widest measure of mutual assistance in proceedings in respect of offences the punishment of which, at the time of the request for assistance, falls within the jurisdiction of the judicial authorities of the requesting Party". According to Article 3.1, "the requested Party shall execute in the manner provided for by its law any letters relating to a criminal matter and addressed to it by the judicial authorities of the requesting Party for the purpose of procuring evidence or transmitting articles to be produced in evidence, records or documents". Assistance may be refused, under Article 2, only if the request concerns an offence which the requested Party considers a political or fiscal offence or an offence connected with a political offence (as for Russia, it has made a declaration to the convention defining the characteristics of crimes it may consider as such), or if the requested Party considers that execution of the request is likely to prejudice the sovereignty, security, public order or other essential interests of the country. Any refusal for mutual assistance must be reasoned. In accordance with Article 26, the Convention supersedes the provisions of any treaties, conventions or bilateral agreements governing mutual assistance in criminal matters between any two Contracting Parties.

However, as has also been demonstrated by earlier cases, the efficiency of international treaties that provide a framework for international cooperation is very much tied to the nations' willingness to cooperate in a particular case

---

433  The CCD COE Legal Task Team received the text of Georgian Criminal Code from Academy of the Ministry of Internal Affairs of Georgia via the OSCE Mission in Georgia; the authors of this paper cannot ensure that the provisions of the Georgian Criminal Code cited in this paper are up-to-date.

434  According to the Georgian Criminal Code: Unlawful infiltration into the computer information, or the information reflected in the computer network system, if this action destroyed, blocked, modified or copied the information, or disrupted the work of computers, computer systems or networks, are punishable by a penalty to from 70 to 360 times the daily salary or correctional work for a period of up to two years, or deprivation of liberty for the same period. According to Art 303 (2), the same action committed by a group by a prior agreement, are punishable by a penalty equal to 240 to 360 times the daily salary or correctional work for a period of up to five years, or imprisonment for a period of up to four months, or deprivation of liberty for a period of up to five years. Under Article 304, creating a program damaging computers or making changes in existing programs that intentionally cause unsanctioned destruction, blockage, modification or copying of information, disruption of the work of computers, computer systems or network, are punishable by a penalty equal to from 100 to 360 times the daily salary or correctional work for a period of up to three years or deprivation of liberty for the same period.

435  European Convention on Mutual Assistance in Criminal Matters, supra note 281; Additional Protocol to the European Convention on Mutual Assistance in Criminal Matters. CETS No.: 099. Strasbourg, 17.III.1978. Available at: http://conventions.coe.int/Treaty/EN/Treaties/Html/099.htm.

and, as is the case with public international law in general, no effective mechanism for sanctions exists should a nation refuse to comply with an international obligation. Russia, which is one of the nations of most interest to Georgia in the investigation of the August 2008 cyber incidents, has not acceded to the Cybercrime Convention and has announced its intent not to ratify the convention.[436] Therefore, even existing treaties on legal cooperation may be insufficient for carrying out effective investigation. Still, the ratification of the Council of Europe Convention on Cybercrime would be an advisable step for Georgia, as it would at least ensure basic international cooperation in the field of cybercrime with nations that do not avoid cooperation, thereby strengthening the capacity to handle any similar future events and make the nation a less attractive target.

## Applicability of ICT legal framework

### The rationale for choosing a model ICT legislation

As information societies have developed hand in hand with the technologies supporting them, law has entered into new domains such as personal data protection, access to information, electronic commerce, and also the general requirements for the setup of information infrastructure and provision of information services. For nations and organisations pursuing ambitious information society agendas, such regulations are inevitable to maintain trust among different stakeholders of the information communities.

Even though there is a certain degree of uniqueness to any country and its legal system, certain regional and universal standards of IT legal regulation have evolved which, when adapted for the particular country, are capable of providing sound legal support to the functioning and stability of a nation's information society. This was a particular legal lesson learned from the 2007 Estonian cyber attacks – the systematic and well-developed ICT legal framework that set

national standards for IT security proved to be a strength in coping with and recovering from the attacks.

Georgia has, in recent years, put much effort into modernising the country's ICT regulation and policy. For example, the nation has developed an electronic communications legal framework and draft legislation in the field of data protection, based on the key elements provided for in the relevant principles of European Union (EU) law.[437]

Even though Georgia is neither an EU member state nor a candidate country, the nation has expressed aspiration toward integration to the European Union and sees membership as a long-term goal.[438] Furthermore, the EU and Georgia have had a bilateral Partnership and Cooperation Agreement (PCA) since 1999, and Georgia is part of the European Neighbourhood Policy (ENP) program, which sets ambitious objectives for partnership with neighbouring countries based on commitments to shared values, key foreign policy objectives and political, economic and institutional reforms, including reforms in the information society. The ENP Action Plan of 2006 involves a significant degree of economic integration and political cooperation. Georgia has expressed its interest in aligning its legislation with EU law, and the field of information society and electronic communications law is highly relevant for Georgia.[439]

### EU legal framework in the field of ICT

Since mid-1980s, the EU has gradually developed what is now a wide-ranging legal framework to support information society – covering aspects of competitive common market for electronic communication and content services, a comprehensive set of user rights and interests' guarantees, and network and data security regimes.[440] This framework is today implemented

---

436   Putin defies Convention on Cybercrime. *Computer Crime Research Center*, March 28, 2008. http://www.crime-research.org/news/28.03.2008/3277/.

437   Hardabkhadze, Kvernadze, *supra* note 312.
438   European Union External Relations: Georgia. *European Commission.* Available at: ec.europa.eu/external_relations/georgia/index_en.htm.
439   Hardabkhadze, Kvernadze, *supra* note 312.
440   For an extensive overview on the European Union information society policy and regulation, *see* the webpage of the European Commission Information Society and Media Directorate-General http://ec.europa.eu/dgs/information_society/index_en.htm.

in the 27 EU nations[441] and four European Free Trade Area (EFTA)[442] countries. Three candidate countries[443] are at various stages of aligning their legal norms with EU information society and common market requirements.

There are several legal mechanisms in EU law that oblige both the state and private actors to maintain a sufficient level of network and information security and that could be an efficient example for countries like Georgia in further developing their IT legislation. The directives of the electronic communications regulatory framework[444] serve as cornerstones for ICT regulation in the EU. While the framework is not entirely aimed at ensuring network security, it does provide for a sustainable and balanced ICT infrastructure and facilitate stable provision of electronic communications services in the market. Of the electronic communications regulatory framework directives, the ePrivacy directive 2002/58/EC[445], in particular articles 4 ('Security') and 5 ('Confidentiality of the communications') also address the network security issue by providing an outline of technical and organisational measures to safeguard security of services. Essential technical requirements for radio and telecommunications terminal equipment, together with a safeguards mechanism to

ensure their observance, are set out in the Radio & Telecommunications Terminal Equipment (R&TTE) directive 1999/5/EC[446] to ensure no harmful interference to the networks and their functioning, to prevent misuse of network resources, to ensure the protection of personal data and user privacy, and to avoid fraud. User rights to privacy are protected under the "legal security standard" set forth in the Personal Data Protection Directive 95/46/EC.[447] This Directive provides for terms of exchange of personal data between public and private authorities, potential rights and claims of data subjects, as well as the security measures to be taken by data controllers. Proper implementation of these rules will create a clear understanding of the rules for using data about cyber incidents for purposes of investigation and future prevention. Directive 2000/31/EC on E-Commerce sets the standards for information society services and ISP liability as well as the legal framework of spam.

And finally, the Data Retention directive 2006/24/EC[448] sets out a framework that includes preservation of log files of online activities, thus facilitating investigation efforts against cyber crime.

Implementing these measures nationally would support the development of a more resilient infrastructure and service capacity, and would also provide a legal basis to collect the data necessary for investigation of any future cyber attacks.

It is important to note that the "everyday" network security legislation usually determines the model of cyber incident management for a given jurisdiction. While EU countries tend to impose rather high standards on information security assets for different types of information systems, there are countries who have only little

441  Austria, Belgium, Bulgaria, Cyprus, the Czech Republic, Denmark, Estonia, Finland, France, Germany, Greece, Hungary, Ireland, Italy, Latvia, Lithuania, Luxembourg, Malta, the Netherlands, Poland, Portugal, Romania, Slovakia, Slovenia, Spain, Sweden, and the United Kingdom.
442  Iceland (applied for full EU membership in July 2009), Liechtenstein, Norway, Switzerland.
443  Turkey, Croatia, and FYR Macedonia.
444  Directive 2002/21/EC of the European Parliament and of the Council of 7 March 2002 on a common regulatory framework for electronic communications networks and services (Framework Directive), OJ L 108, 24/04/2002 pp. 0033-0050; and four specific Directives: Directive 2002/20/EC of the European Parliament and of the Council of 7 March 2002 on the authorisation of electronic communications networks and services (Authorisation Directive), Directive 2002/19/EC of the European Parliament and of the Council of 7 March 2002 on access to, and interconnection of, electronic communications networks and associated facilities (Access Directive), Directive 2002/22/EC of the European Parliament and of the Council of 7 March 2002 on universal service and users' rights relating to electronic communications networks and services (Universal Service Directive), Directive 97/66/EC of the European Parliament and of the Council of 15 December 1997 concerning the processing of personal data and the protection of privacy in the telecommunications sector).
445  Directive 2002/58/EC of the European Parliament and of the Council (Directive on privacy and electronic communications), supra note 287.

446  Directive 1999/5/EC of the European Parliament and of the Council of 9 March 1999 on radio equipment and telecommunications terminal equipment and the mutual recognition of their conformity; OJ L 91, 7.4.1999, pp. 0010–0028.
447  OJ L 281, 23 Nov 95, pp. 31-39.
448  Directive 2006/24/EC of the European Parliament and of the Council of 15 March 2006 on the retention of data generated or processed in connection with the provision of publicly available electronic communications services or of public communications networks and amending Directive 2002/58/EC. OJ L 105 , 13/04/2006 pp. 0054 – 0063, available at: eur-lex.europa.eu/LexUriServ/LexUriServ.do?uri=OJ:L:2006:105:0054:0063:EN:PDF.

legislation in the field. It is difficult to engage these types of nations in proactive cyber security initiatives until proper national legislation is in place.

# IV Summary of the Georgian case

## INCIDENT TIME FRAME

*Start* Friday, 8 August 2008

*End* Thursday, 28 August 2008

*Duration* 3 weeks

## INCIDENT CONTEXT

### Political context and background of incident
- Armed conflict between the Russian Federation and Georgia over South Ossetia.

### Information society indicators
- Low Internet penetration (7% of population in 2008), but percentage rapidly growing;
- Low overall dependence on IT-infrastructure;
- Limited options for Internet connectivity via land routes, strong interconnection dependency on Russia.

## INCIDENT FACTS

### Methods
- DoS and DDoS attacks;
- Distribution of malicious software (MS batch script) together with attack instructions; exploiting SQL vulnerability;
- Defacement;
- Using e-mail addresses for spamming and targeted attacks.

### Targets
- Government sites (President, Parliament, ministries; local government of Abkhazia);
- News and media sites, online discussion forums;
- Financial institutions.

### Origin
- Organised Russian hacker groups most likely behind the exploit attacks;

- No evident link to the Russian administration or state organisations guiding or directing attacks; the Russian government has denied any involvement in the cyber assaults;
- No conclusive proof of who was behind the DDoS or defacement attacks.

### Effect
- Limiting Georgia's options to distribute information regarding the ongoing Georgian-Russian military conflict to the outside world and the Georgian public, especially during the critical early days of the conflict;
- Main communications network operators affected; problems exacerbated by physical disconnections in the communications network infrastructure caused by war activities;
- Side-effects: smaller ISP-s adversely affected by countermeasures applied.

### Measures taken
- Attack mitigation coordinated by Georgian academic sector CERT who assumed the role of national CERT during the cyber attacks;
- A state-mandated block on access to Russian websites for the dual purpose of information control and freeing up bandwidth;
- Relocating services to servers or hosts located abroad;
- Assistance from national CERTs of other countries.

## LEGAL LESSONS IDENTIFIED AND LEARNED

### Core of the case
- Applicability of Law of Armed Conflicts to cyber attacks occurring during conventional armed conflict;
- Measures available in national law to deal with wide-scale cyber attacks.

### Summary
- The right of the injured state to use force as a response against another state depends on the level of involvement of the source state. While state *direction* and/or *support* of attacks can be seen as active involvement

and therefore justify a stronger reaction, mere *toleration* (making no effort to suppress or stop the perpetrators) or *inaction* (being unable to effectively deal with the perpetrators) on behalf of the source state as passive forms of involvement do not make the source state a target of lawful military operations. Also, the remedy has to be proportionate to the threat – the smaller the overall harm arising from the attacks, the less there is reason to speak of holding the state responsible for cyber attacks. While the direct effect of the Georgian cyber attacks is difficult to estimate, the low overall dependence of the Georgian population on online services indicates that the effect of cyber attacks was not serious enough to amount to severe economic damage or significant human suffering. Considering this threshold, it is highly problematic to apply Law of Armed Conflict to the Georgian cyber attacks – the objective evidence of the case is too vague to meet the necessary criteria of both state involvement and gravity of effect.

- Effective response to cyber attacks of scale and type like the Georgia incident are quite limited under law. In the long-term perspective, most value is to be derived from developing a legal and organisational structure that supports the development of a resilient infrastructure and service capacity, and provides a lawful basis to collect the data necessary for investigation of any future cyber attacks. Also important is the promotion of effective international cooperation, as there is no way for a country to coordinate defences against attacks originating from other jurisdictions.

### Challenges
- New approaches needed to traditional LOAC principles to provide effective legal remedies under this area of law;
- Continued development of national ICT legal frameworks.

# CONCLUSIONS. General Observations from Cyber Conflicts 2007-2008

# I Introductory remarks

The conclusions drawn from the four case studies indicate that after years of debate on how to improve cyber deterrence, and despite a number of international instruments introduced, a coherent approach to cyber security is still wishful thinking.

There seems to be a rather wide understanding on the threat environment: increased dependence on sophisticated information systems and related vulnerabilities, the limited relevance of territorial defence principles to cyber space, as well as rapid development of technology which has become accessible to virtually everyone at low cost and entry barriers. Our conclusions in this regard support many earlier observations.

On the other hand, the cases studied show a trend that seems not to have been addressed by the many attempts to tackle cyber security from the perspective of international peace and the use of force, simply because this legal area presumes a significant element of state involvement to be present in any case of relevance. In all these cases we see that state attribution is not only nearly impossible, but that the habitual pattern of seeking state attribution often leads to misinterpretation and an incorrect assessment of the situation, and causes confusion in terms of response and defences.

The cases analysed indicate that real-life cyber incidents differ slightly from the threat characteristics that the nations have been preparing for – in practice, obvious state involvement in a cyber incident is unlikely (in many cases, it lacks completely, and in any case, it rarely reaches the necessary threshold even if it can be detected), the application of LOAC will rarely come into question. At the same time, the cases in question do not fit into what is usually perceived to be the effective response under cyber crime regulation, simply because they fail to meet the traditional purpose of this field of law, which has been developed mainly for defending against personally motivated activities and localised impact of damages. Moreover, as these cases repeatedly demonstrate, enforcement of criminal law is often impaired due to complexities of international cooperation in matters of criminal justice.

Deriving from these two categories of conclusions, we therefore first suggest a slightly shifted legal approach to (inter)national cyber security building – combining the old with the new, i.e. further implementation of current instruments in international law (specifically, the Council of Europe Convention on Cybercrime) with a review of national criminal policy to critically implement the legal lessons learned from cyber victimised nations.

Secondly, and more precisely, we have identified a number of legal concepts that suggest additional conceptual thinking in the fields of LOAC and criminal law, and may need reconsideration in the light of our findings. Those are related mainly to the borderline between, or overlap of, these two legal areas and are meant to bridge two areas of law thereby decreasing the gray area currently facilitating and shielding highly disturbing cyber activities.

Ten years have passed since Phillip A. Johnson outlined the characteristics of cyber network attacks (CNA) that distinguish it from other elements of warfare.[449] Analysis of the major cyber incidents of 2007-2008 confirms that Johnson's observations are still valid, although improvements have been made on international level to counter cybercrime and cyber terrorism.[450] Effective responses to cyber attacks of scale and type like the Georgian and Estonian incidents are still quite limited under law. Most importantly, they include the promotion of effective international awareness and cooperation, as there is no way for a country to coordinate defences against attacks originating from other jurisdictions. Since no national or international entity has universal authority to legislate in the field, national efforts will have to work together with international instruments in different fields, some of which may have different motivations or original objectives (such as market efficiency or privacy protections.

---

449   Johnson, Phillip A. "Is It Time for a Treaty on Information Warfare?" In International Law Studies, Vol. 76, edited by Michael N. Schmitt and Brian T. O'Donnell, 439-455. Newport, RI: Naval War College, 2002.

450   The upcoming CCD COE Frameworks for International Cyber Security: A Compilation of Legal Acts (Draft. CCD COE, 2009) demonstrates the wealth of legal initiatives undertaken by international organisations over the recent years.

# II Observations regarding the threat environment

## Reliance on ICT increases the degree of vulnerability to politically motivated cyber intrusions

Many authors have concluded that the more a society relies on sophisticated information systems, the more vulnerable it is to interference with them.[451] Examples of interference with military information systems date back to mid-90ies.[452] The number of Internet users has grown an average of 380% since 2000, currently comprising about 1,7 billion active users all around the globe. According to Internet World Stats, in 2009, Internet penetration (Internet users per 100 population) in the US is 74,2% and 63,8% in the EU. At the same time, more than 42% of Internet users come from the Asian region.[453]

Estonia 2007 may be the best recent illustration to the correlation between high IT reliance and accompanying vulnerability. The small and highly developed information society was deeply impacted by the wide-scale DDoS attacks in the spring of 2007 – not so much due to the quality of preparedness to handle the incident, but because the services that were attacked were an integral part of the daily life of a large segment of population. This is not to say that cyber conflict only threatens highly sophisticated information societies – the August 2008 DDoS attacks against Georgian governmental web servers and the 2007 Radio Free Europe DDoS attacks also impacted the targets' vital

interest – the ability to disseminate information.

Therefore nations, entities and functions relying on ICT are vulnerable to cyber attacks, but the severity of impact is likely to increase with both higher ICT penetration and criticality of the services rendered. In the Estonian case, both indicators were high. Estonia has largely passed the information society hype curve and accepted ICT as a way of life and organisation of the whole society. Reliance on ICT services is crucial both in terms of quantity – hundreds of services rendered via national information system cover the whole nation – and quality – government working as e-cabinet, parliament and local elections as well as EU parliament elections conducted online, etc. But even in the absence of high ICT penetration, a nation's vulnerability may be increased by a context factor. As demonstrated by the Georgia 2008 example, the damage caused by the attacks was most acutely experienced at the time when the nation was the most dependent on the availability of information channels, even though cyber attacks did not have a major effect on the Georgian Internet infrastructure.

## A territorial approach to law-making and law enforcement has not proved effective in tackling cyber security issues

In 1996, John Perry Barlow drafted his revolutionary Declaration of the Independence of Cyberspace, where he contested that governments' concepts of property, expression, identity, movement, and context do not apply to Cyberspace and proposed that due to their inability to understand and control the culture of the Cyberspace, national governments should abstain from imposing regulations to 'global social space'.[454] He suggested that the "online community" would form their own Social Contract, and hopefully build a more humane and fair civilization than the governments have made before.[455] As many incidents over

---

451  E.g. Johnson, 441; O'Donnell, Brian; Kraska, James C. Humanitarian Law: Developing International Rules for the Digital Battlefield, in: Journal of Conflict & Security Law, April 2003; Kanuck, Sean P. Information Warfare: New Challenges for Public International Law, Harvard International Law Journal Vol. 37 (1996), p. 272.

452  E.g. Aldrich, Richard W. The International Legal Implications of Information Warfare, in Airpower Journal – Fall 1996, p. 100.

453  Internet Usage Statistics: The Internet Big Picture. World Internet Users and Population Stats, 2009. Available at: http://www.internetworldstats.com/stats.htm.

454  Barlow, John Perry. A Declaration of the Independence in Cyberspace. 1996. Available at http://homes.eff.org/~barlow/Declaration-Final.html.

455  Ibid.

past 15 years have shown, this social contract has not been able to prevent the confrontation between the "inhabitants" of cyberspace and "the real world".

At the same time, we can see that neither have the visions of Lessig[456] and Easterbrook[457] materialised – so in 2009, we still need to figure out how to best apply the existing regulation to cyberspace and where the nature of the environment and threat call for introducing new or additional legal instruments.

Johnson contented in his 1999 conclusions on how CNA is different from other means of warfare that geography has ceased to be relevant to the security of information systems that are connected to the Internet or that are accessible by radio.[458] Similar observations were made by Goodman and Brenner in an article dealing with criminal law enforcement issues in cyberspace using the example and case study of the 'Love Bug' virus.[459]

On the other hand, the problem of national borders hindering or preventing effective cyber defence is real. Considering the typology that the four studied incidents present, politically motivated cyber attacks are rarely a matter involving one or two nations only. On the contrary, they routinely involve tens of nations either because the perpetrators are located there or because attacks are directed through networks located in these countries in order to hide the traces. The architecture of the Internet makes it possible to engage in a cyber attack thousands and thousands of PCs irrespective to their physical location, while the arms of any defending government formally only reach to the physical borders of its jurisdiction. Even if extended (extraterritorial) jurisdiction over such crimes is foreseen, its practical usefulness is still dependent on the preparedness of other involved countries to cooperate.

The awareness of end users about the security of their communication, as well as the quality of law enforcement in the particular jurisdiction, are key factors for favourable jurisdiction shopping.

In addition, international cooperation in criminal matters, in its mainly bilateral nature – involving the nation requesting assistance and the nation giving assistance on a two-sided basis – is often ineffective even if both parties are willing and able to cooperate. The Internet facilitates easy splitting up of a given illegal act to several small trails that can be left in a number of countries – such as the formation of a botnet to attack servers in a particular country. Not all countries involved may consider such acts as crimes – or may disagree on the definition of them; there are often differing legal requirements for what is permissible in criminal proceedings in a given country and according to the law dealing with the specific criminal deed; and in some cases the attackers may resort their activities to jurisdictions that the attacked country or the country receiving a request for assistance – does not recognise. The awareness of end users about the security of their communication, as well as the quality of law enforcement in the particular jurisdiction, are key factors for favourable jurisdiction shopping for malicious actors.

The lack of unison of regulation between countries leads to a fragmented solution for a phenomenon that knows no borders. The need to handle such threats calls for a wider platform of multinational cooperation.

## Cyber attacks are easy to launch

According to Johnson the worldwide use of comparable equipment, operating systems, and software greatly facilitates CNA.[460] Although this aspect has not been studied much in regard to recent international cyber attacks, the interoperability and interconnectivity of information

---

456   In his "Code: And Other Laws of Cyberspace", Lessig suggested that the code (i.e. the architecture of IT infrastructure) determines the limits of the permissible in cyberspace and therefore legislative initiatives should be secondary means of shaping behaviour of the online community. See Lessig, Lawrence. Code: And Other Laws of Cyberspace, Version 2.0. Basic Books, 2006.

457   Easterbrook, Frank H. Cyberspace and the Law of the Horse, 1996 U Chi Legal F 207. Easterbrook asserted that cyber law as such is just a sum of legal provisions existing or to be created under other areas of law and it cannot and should not be regarded as a self-standing legal discipline.

458   Johnson, *supra* note 449, p. 441.

459   Goodman, Marc D., Brenner Susan W. The Emerging Consensus on Criminal Conduct in Cyberspace in: International Journal of Law and Information Technology, Summer 2002 Volume 10.

---

460   Johnson, *supra* note 449, p. 441.

systems and services inevitably results in a "collective vulnerability". In the Lithuanian case, we see how a single ISP vulnerability results in defacement of over 300 "random" websites. The key connector between the sites attacked was the fact that they all used the same service provider with the same type of vulnerability within one server that these sites were hosted on. Also, one might think that in Estonia and Georgia, information systems were as different as the climate, culture and language of the two countries. Yet, protocols and standards of the Internet are the same virtually across the globe. Therefore, even though countries may prioritise slightly different types of cyber threats, in their essence, these threats materialise in one global infrastructure – the Internet architecture.

Also, developing at least some capability to interfere with a nation's' information systems is relatively cheap and easy, compared to other modern weapons systems, and the necessary expertise and equipment are widely available.[461] Some held that the DDoS attacks that Estonia went through were experienced with such severity due to the weakness of Estonian ICT infrastructure. However, when falling under a similar attack, no information society has watertight guarantees as to whether its infrastructure will be able to endure. Engaging all the bandwidth could never face the potential of hundreds of thousands or millions of zombie computers that can be used in concert to provide more requests than the information infrastructure is able to persist.

Estonian ICT infrastructure is strong for what it was meant to do – providing information society services to up to 1.3 million inhabitants, and having sufficient backup capability to accommodate foreseeable traffic increases. There are limits, dictated by economic reason, to how much bandwidth capacity an ISP or government infrastructure owner can be required to provide as backup. On the other hand, someone with a malicious purpose can always "buy" botnet bandwidth that is capable of overriding the limits of the system. For small nations and small markets especially, the cost of investment needed to run the race ahead of botnet-renting cyber criminals may be economically unfeasible, considering the foreseeable risk of coming

under cyber attack of a scale that cannot be defined beforehand.

It must be kept in mind that botnet owners derive revenue from organising DDoS attacks and thus have the economic stimulus to spread their structures, and that enlarging a botnet in itself is neither a costly activity nor difficult to arrange. It may be tempting to diagnose a particular case as a "lack of sufficient bandwidth"-incident, but the acceptance of a situation where cyber attacks are viewed as some sort of a natural disaster, the response costs of which must be borne by the ISP or a national government, is ill-advised.[462]

# Information technologies develop rapidly

The speedy development of ICT means, on the one hand, that the methods and devices of cyber attacks develop quickly and make these types of attacks (as well as potential defences) more and more efficient and sophisticated. On the other hand, this tendency also means that governments face difficulties in keeping up with such rapid development, which poses great challenges to regulation and effective proactive defences.

To handle the challenge this rapid advance brings for the regulatory level, the principle of technologically neutral regulation has been proposed. Ideally, such an approach would mean that the "effects of the offline and on-line regulatory environments, including the criminal and civil law, should be as similar as possible", while still allowing for the necessary flexibility if "there [are] occasions when different treatment is necessary to realise an equivalent result."[463]On a more pragmatic level, technologically neutral legislation has been suggested to have the potential of relieving the legislative system of the constant need to keep the legal framework up-to-date with the technological advances, and concentrating on "regulating functions and

---

461  Id.

462  Id., p. 142.
463  E-Policy Principles. UK Office of the e-Envoy, 2003. Available at: http://archive.cabinetoffice.gov.uk/e-envoy/guidelines-eprinciples/$file/principles.htm

effects, not means".[464]

In addition, any proactive defence system builds on technology, human resources, and procedural rules. Regarding the former, governments are normally tied to more or less time-consuming public procurement procedures and accountability rules for use of limited public funds. As for the latter, the exercise of public authority by public officials is limited to the activities that the law prescribes. Both of these constraints are unknown to malicious actors, who therefore have a competitive advantage over governments – which in turn places a very high requirement for awareness and resources to the government, compared to what the criminal industry needs to reckon with.

## Most advances in IT are developed for commercial purposes

Most advances in information technology are developed by individuals or companies for commercial purposes.[465]This explains why defences designed for ICT assets often fail in case of a large-scale, politically motivated (or terrorist) cyber attack. From a business perspective, investments into security of information systems take into account the projected quantity of customers and volume of use, as well as the technical specifications of services rendered to the users. Business entities cannot be expected to have sufficient incentives to invest into network and service security beyond the level of their own sustainable business interest and anticipated return. The collective risks of other market players are normally not calculated into the investment formula of a single enterprise. The role of coordination of "collective defences", as well as that of minimisation of collective risks, is that of the governments.

# III Perceptions in need for revision

As we can see above, many authors have put substantial effort into identifying the factors that are vital to making the cyberspace more secure and reliable. Yet the situation has not considerably improved since the 90ies and different schools exist as regards to the need and means of international cyber security.

To understand why so many scientific and practical approaches to cyber security have not created a coherent standard of protection, one needs to study the contributions to cyber security solutions by different authors over the past 10 years. We have done this, and by categorising these articles and materials by the areas of law providing the legal background perspective of each author, four distinct groups were delineated – those written by experts in the law of armed conflicts and international humanitarian law, contributions from criminal law experts, views of lawyers dealing with IT security and information society law in general, and finally, materials written by non-lawyers on legal issues related to cyber security.

From this, we learned that depending on their particular legal background, legal experts deal with different fragments of cyber security and therefore have different presumptions installed in their argumentation. To a non-lawyer or even a legal expert from another area of law, these prerequisites are often invisible and in case of incorrect assessment of the nature or scale of the incident, or mix or inconsistency in the legal background perspective, legal argument about the situation becomes blurry.

To illustrate this observation, the Estonian case again offers a good example. When commenting on the situation in Estonia, the Estonian politicians, most of them having no legal background and none being intimate with the subject of cyber law, interchangeably used terms such as "cyber war", "cyber attack", "cyber blockade", etc. All these terms have a strong connection with the law of armed conflict, where "attack" and "warfare" are terms to define the conditions under which a nation is entitled to remedies as self-defence and potentially, the use of force against another nation. However, in

---

464   Koops, Bert-Jaap. "Should ICT Regulation be Technology-Neutral?", in: Starting Points for ICT Regulation. Deconstructing Prevalent Policy One-Liners, IT & Law Series, Bert-Jaap Koops, Miriam Lips, Corien Prins & Maurice Schellekens, eds., Vol. 9, pp. 77-108, The Hague: T.M.C. Asser Press, 2006. P.6.
465   Johnson, supra note 449, p. 441.

the jargon of IT specialists, a "cyber attack" can be a mere unauthorised intrusion or jamming of a network and have nothing to do with national interests and mandate. The EU has regulated on this phenomenon from an information society perspective, referring to attacks against information systems as "illegal access" or "interference with an information system or data" and again, presuming no link with state authorities.[466] The problem with such chaotic use of terms lies in the confusion it creates for identifying the suitable level, authority, and means of response: the usage of same or similar terms by experts with different backgrounds leads to confusion as to the details of what is meant, and thereby blurs the focus of the arguments in general.

The terminology confusion reflects the stove-piped view on cyber incidents prevalent among the legal thought in different fields. Few have an interdisciplinary understanding of the different areas of law and an understanding of the role of law as a means for enforcing the necessary measures for cyber security management, based on input from other essential areas of cyber incident management such as diplomacy, military, economics, etc. Even fewer are those national examples where the different legal requirements are considered and de-conflicted as part of a national cyber security legal framework.

This stove-piped view could be part of the reason why real-life cyber incidents differ slightly from what the nations have been preparing for. Unlike what often has been the perception, the incidents we have studied demonstrate that in the majority of cases, state involvement is either lacking completely, cannot be identified, or its threshold is too low to be relevant for the application of LOAC. At the same time, the cases under review do not fit into what nations have perceived to be the effective response under cyber crime regulation. A stove-piped approach where legal discussion is contained in separate legal areas cannot contribute to a coherent or comprehensive cyber security preparedness. Irrelevant of which area of law will be the point of departure for developing an approach to cyber security, a coherent and systematic approach will only be achieved through the combination of different legal areas. The same ap-

plies to other substantial areas of cyber incident handling – law cannot offer a solution without input from technology, military, business and other expert areas. Likewise, a stove-piped approach by entities and nations will not result in a viable protection.

The defences of the cyber domain can best be achieved when combining national approaches on the international level. Also, it is important that these processes are as transparent as possible to allow nations to explore and adopt best practices and openly discuss alternatives.

In a way, the approach to cyber security looks like a pyramid international law only of which forms the very tip. The most important enforcement layer comprises national approaches to cyber security and the fundamental solutions are developed on private entities and end user levels.

Although some decisions need to be taken on the national level – e.g. what activities need to be criminalised from the national point of view, and what would be sufficient sanctions, other issues are international in scope and thus require a wider consensus. The latter especially concerns the impact of national remedies on other countries. Goodman and Brenner have illustrated this with the Love Bug example, where the virus launched in the Philippines inflicted damage in twenty countries but resulted in no legal consequences as launching a virus was not a crime in the Philippines at the time.[467]

# Real-life cyber incidents differ slightly from what the nations have been preparing for

Cyber attacks in general are nothing new as a national security threat – authors like Arquilla[468], Schmitt[469], Wingfield[470] etc. saw them coming more than a decade ago and have proposed a number of approaches to implementation of

---

466  Council Framework Decision 2005/222/JHA of 24 February 2005 on attacks against information systems. OJ L 69/67, 16.03.2005.

467  Goodman, Brenner, supra note 459, p. 142.
468  Arquilla, John. 'Can information warfare ever be just?' In Ethnics and Information Technology 1: 203-212, 1999.
469  Schmitt, supra notes 403 and 410.
470  Wingfield, Thomas C. The Law of Information Conflict: National Security Law in Cyberspace. Aegis Research Corp, 2000.

the law of armed conflicts to this type of threats. The only problem with using their proposals is that the real-life incidents do not reach the threshold of applicability of the law of armed conflicts, thereby rendering all the good advice mostly hypothetical.

As long as there is no state attribution of cyber attacks, LOAC will offer no remedies and the particular incident must be managed under a different area of law. This will most likely be criminal law, but information society law and IT law have useful solutions to offer as well – network security and service quality requirements defined by IT law are essential to building and maintaining a resilient infrastructure and service capacity. In order to build up comprehensive defences, tools from several relevant fields of law are required – e.g. in order to deal with terrorist content of websites, rather than giving the authority to army commanders to deal with this, it is important to have provisions on ISP co-operation and illegal content available and the procedural measures clear for law enforcement to deal with these cases.

The case closest to the application of LOAC was the Georgian case, where cyber attacks against Georgian governmental websites fell into the timeframe of a nationally declared state of war. We have concluded in the Georgian analysis that it would be highly problematic to apply Law of Armed Conflict to the Georgian cyber attacks – the objective evidence of the case is too vague to meet the necessary criteria of both state involvement and gravity of effect. Yet, when looking at the context of when these attacks occurred and how well the desired effect was achieved, if state attribution would be possible, the applicability of LOAC would be much more likely.

# Effective cyber security cannot be achieved by merely cyber crime regulation

When suggesting that most contemporary cyber incidents must be managed under criminal law, we are not saying that we see any particular field of law as the most efficient response framework to the cyber threats the world is currently facing.

The reasons for this position are well reflected in the cases studied in the book. In all of the four incidents, for various reasons, criminal law failed to provided an efficient answer to the incident. In the Estonian case, this was partly due to limitations in substantive and procedural law, and partly because of an issue that national criminal law, but also international law is powerless against: unwillingness to cooperate on the side of the state where the attacks originated in. In the case of Radio Free Europe/Radio Liberty, the problem was that the relevant state refused to view such incidents as a criminal law problem at all. In the Lithuanian case, much of the problem was the weak measurability of attack effects in a situation where the law tied the availability of effective sanctions to the presence of "serious harm". And in Georgia, it was both a problem of insufficient substantive law and lack of international cooperation agreements.

The situation is likely to be similar in most nations. The view of criminal law, as the standard currently stands in many nations, considers cyber crime foremost as an economically motivated activity. Among the international harmonisation initiatives in recent years, the Council of Europe Convention on Cybercrime[471] has rightfully received wide attention; it has the largest number of parties that either have ratified and implemented the instrument in national law or have used it as a *de facto* standard for developing their national cyber crime law.[472]

The Convention sets to "pursue, as a matter of priority, *a common criminal policy* aimed at

---

471  Section 1 of Chapter II of the Convention – that specifies the measures that the acceding nations agree to take at the national level – divides cyber crimes into the following five categories: offences against the confidentiality, integrity and availability of computer data and systems (Title 1), computer-related offences (Title 2), content-related offences (referring to criminalising child pornography) (Title 3), offences related to infringements of copyright and related rights (Title 4), as well as ancillary liability and sanctions for aiding or abetting the commission of any of the offences listed previously (Title 5).

472  The convention is open for ratification also for nations that are not COE members, and four non-COE-countries (Canada, Japan, South Africa, and the United States) have acceded to the treaty, even though only in the latter has it also entered into force (on 1 January 2007). In addition, many countries around the world (including countries in Africa, Asia and Central and South America) have used the convention as a guideline for their national legislative drafting in the field of cyber crime.

the protection of society against cybercrime, inter alia, by adopting appropriate legislation and fostering international co-operation" (our emphasis).

Most of the provisions of the Convention deal with more "traditional" forms of cyber crime, such as computer-related forgery or fraud, acquiring illegal access, unlawful interference into data or systems, or misuse of devices, but also crimes related to copyright infringements or distributing child pornography. While the relevant treaty provisions are not limited to a specific motivation behind the unlawful activities, thereby not restricting the criminalisation and prosecution of politically motivated cyber attacks in principle, the protected legal interest, as expressed in the Explanatory Report of the treaty, is normally the integrity, availability, confidentiality or the proper functioning and use of computer data, programs, or networks, not the wider societal or moral harm caused by such actions. (Harmful activities directly motivated by financial gain are, on the other hand, covered under a separate section.)

As the Estonian incident adequately demonstrates, this traditional prism of cyber crime may not be sufficient to satisfactorily respond to politically motivated cyber attacks. Even if a nation is party to the convention and has implemented its provisions in national law, the functioning of the information society and the threats directed against it from the cyberspace may remain outside the direct scope of its criminal law.

## Information society regulation has little regard to national security interests

The European Union, which has more than two decades of experience of developing a strong legislative base for information society, IT and electronic communications law, has, until recent years, largely refrained from the cyber security and cyber defence debate. The exclusion clauses contained in EU law, which preclude its applicability in the areas of public security and criminal law, have also caused the public and political pressure to be far more aligned towards individual freedoms than public security. In ad-

dition, privacy law and other legal areas related to individual freedoms are much more homogeneous and transparent thanks to the systematic harmonisation efforts. Yet even though security is still an area where EU institutions do not exercise legislative authority even after the entry into force of the Lisbon Treaty, this does not preclude intergovernmental cooperation among EU member states in harmonisation of national cyber security approaches – and the latter should be encouraged. [473]

## Concluding remarks on "perception revision"

To sum up, the elements of legal argument differ by areas of law, and all of them must be carefully considered when addressing international cyber security from a legal point of view. From what we have learned, our suggestion is broadly the following: while the law of armed conflicts approach to cyber security may need a restatement from a "real" cyber perspective – looking more critically into what constitutes state action, what are the criteria of cyber attacks to potentially qualify as "armed attack", and what are the proportionate responses, other areas of law – specifically, criminal law and information society/IT law – are in a similar need for a restatement from an (inter)national security perspective.

Until the "gray area" around these legal fields is filled, it is easy to conduct malicious cyber activities that fall into legal loopholes and therefore devaluate the authority of law. Patriotic hacking is a great example of a disturbing phenomenon that exploits the current situation: residing in the suburbs of criminal law, it takes advantage of the ineffective enforcement mechanism and at the same time uses the shield of state-led

---

473  However, an interesting approach in this question was taken in the so-called Data Retention Directive 2006/24/EC, which justifies the harmonisation of certain aspects of criminal procedure with the fact that "*the legal and technical differences between national provisions [···] present obstacles to the internal market for electronic communications, since service providers are faced with different requirements [···]*." See Directive 2006/24/EC of the European Parliament and of the Council of 15 March 2006 on the retention of data generated or processed in connection with the provision of publicly available electronic communications services or of public communications networks and amending Directive 2002/58/EC. OJ L 13.4.2006, 105/54.

policy to deliver a political message by highly damaging means. All the while it benefits of the cover of its own government that protects the perpetrators from getting prosecuted by the victim nation.

It is likely, in our opinion, that "gray area attacks" will continue until these deficiencies are properly addressed on the international level. At the same time, we do not see the international level currently being the primary level of response to immediate cyber security issues – as long as the criminal policy towards patriotic hacking and other kinds of politically motivated cyber attacks are not reconsidered on national level, there is no likelihood of reaching the international consensus on this matter, not to speak of efficient criminal procedure.

# IV Some recommendations for the way forward

## Know the challenges

The observations above are best to be regarded as continuing challenges to building effective cyber defence. Estonia ran into almost all of the obstacles that were described above in the course of investigating the cyber attacks of spring 2007. Despite international alarm and bold national statements, the only person convicted for a role in the cyber attacks was a local student who was thoughtless enough to boast about his actions on a local Internet forum. Even though mutual assistance requests were issued on the basis of both the applicable international and bilateral agreements between Estonia and Russia, unwillingness to cooperate can be disguised into numerous formal excuses and none of those requests have met any success.[474] Likewise in the Lithuanian incident, tackling a politically motivated cyber attack turned out to depend on the preparedness of national criminal law to efficiently take into account lawful interests that were not purely financial, but the success of cyber deterrence as much also

depended on day-to-day IT security measures that were there (or in the case of the private sector, were not there), but that could be ensured were the proper legal requirements in place. And as the Georgian incident demonstrated, different legal frameworks (LOAC, criminal law, and IT law) all play a role in supporting national cyber security, and where one area of law fails, another might still be able to provide solutions – provided that it has been developed.

## Need to get the terminology right!

A terminology review is, in many ways, a starting point for the successful outcome of the following recommendations, which is why we have listed it first in this section.

Much confusion is currently created by the fact that virtually all cyber attacks are referred to as cyber war and cyber terrorism, which in legal terms may be misleading unless the facts are filtered through the relevant legal frameworks. Not every deviation from, or a violation of everyday IT-security can be regarded as a manifestation of "cyber warfare", terrorists or ordinary criminal act. In some cases, we deal only with breaches of IT security regulations. The point is that it is important to develop a full lexicon that speaks to all legal frameworks, not just terrorism or warfare, and to not assume that every incident is an attack or onset of war.

As Goodman and Brenner observe in the context of criminal law, terms like 'cybercrime', 'computer crime', 'Information Technology crime' and 'high-tech crime' are often used interchangeably to refer to computer offenses.[475] When defining cyber terrorism, Goodman and Brenner refer to it as a premeditated, politically motivated attack against information, computer systems, computer programs, and data which result in violence against non-combatant targets by sub-national groups or clandestine agents.[476] Confusion in terminology also exists in the field of policy – while the term "cyber security" is commonly being used in the United States (US) legislation (e.g. Cyber Security Enhancement

---

474  A more detailed discussion on this topic can be found in Tikk, Eneken; Kaska, Kadri. 'Russia's refusal to cooperate in a criminal proceedings: analysis and proposals'. CCD COE, 2008

475  Goodman, Brenner, supra note 459, p. 144.
476  Ibid.

Act of 2002[477]), and NATO introduced the term "cyber defence" in the Cyber Defence Policy adopted in 2008[478], the EU in its numerous instruments refers to terms such as network and information security (NIS)[479], information and communication technology (ICT) security[480], information technology (IT) security[481], information security[482], network security[483], cyber security[484], etc.

There are rather practical constraints related to the inconsistency of terminology – the one Goodman and Brenner refer to is the inability of the law enforcement and statistical organs

to keep accurate track of the cyber incidents.[485] Also, different terminology makes it difficult to legally qualify the incident and optimize the response in terms of authorities, means and procedures involved. Moreover, terminological inconsistency makes it difficult to legally qualify the incident and optimise the response in terms of authorities, means and procedures involved, and may create legal uncertainty which weakens the ability of law enforcement agencies to take determined action against malicious activities in the cyberspace.

## Legal area-specific responses are not the ultimate answer

Because cyber incidents of most international concern tend to have a political context, accession to and/or ratification of the Council of Europe Convention on Cybercrime even by all EU or NATO nations cannot solve the practical problems related to cyber attacks. Countries that have witnessed and experienced cyber attacks have also recognised that there are significant restrictions as regards the applicability and usefulness of cyber crime provisions to such attacks – the provisions are often incomplete, the punishments are weak, or the investigatory powers are insufficient. Also, given the relatively small number of nations that have ratified the Convention on Cybercrime, there is often no prior certainty for the investigating authorities regarding any useful outcome of the international cooperation. Since among the majority of the 47 nations that are parties to the European Convention on Mutual Assistance in Criminal Matters[486], efficient international cooperation in criminal matters is only available between countries that mutually recognise such actions

---

477  Cyber Security Enhancement Act of 2002, available at: http://thomas.loc.gov/cgi-bin/bdquery/z?d107:h.r.03482:

478  Read more at NATO Defending Against Cyber Attacks, available at: http://www.nato.int/issues/cyber_defence/index.html

479  E.g. Communication COM(2001) 298 final from the Commission to the Council, the European Parliament, the Economic and Social Committee and the Committee of the Regions of 6 June 2001, "Network and Information Security: proposal for a European Policy approach", available at: http://eur-lex.europa.eu/LexUriServ/LexUriServ.do?uri=CELEX:52001DC0298:EN:HTML, hereafter *Communication 2001*

480  E.g. Communication from the Commission to the European Parliament and the Council on Public-Private Dialogue in Security Research and Innovation {SEC(2007) 1138} {SEC(2007) 1139} /* COM/2007/0511 final */, available at: http://eur-lex.europa.eu/LexUriServ/LexUriServ.do?uri=CELEX:52007DC0511:EN:HTML

481  E.g. Commission staff working document - Annex to the Communication from the Commission to the Council, the European Parliament, the European Economic and Social committee and the Committee of the Regions A strategy for a Secure Information Society - "Dialogue, partnership and empowerment" {COM(2006) 251 final} - Impact assessment /* SEC/2006/0656 */ , available at:

482  E.g. the opinion of the European Economic and Social Committee, quoted in Opinion of the European Economic and Social Committee on the Proposal for a Decision of the European Parliament and of the Council on interoperability solutions for European public administrations (ISA), available at: http://eur-lex.europa.eu/LexUriServ/LexUriServ.do?uri=OJ:C:2009:218:0036:01:EN:HTML

483  E.g. Communication from the Commission to the European Parliament and the Council - An area of freedom, security and justice serving the citizen /* COM/2009/0262 final */, available at: http://eur-lex.europa.eu/LexUriServ/LexUriServ.do?uri=CELEX:52009DC0262:EN:HTML

484  The Report on the Implementation of the European Security Strategy (Brussels, 11 December 2008 S407/08) addresses cyber security as one of the key threats to global security: "Modern economies are heavily reliant on critical infrastructure including transport, communication and power supplies, but also the internet. The EU Strategy for a Secure Information Society adopted in 2006 addresses internet-based crime. However, attacks against private or government IT systems in EU Member States have given this a new dimension, as a potential new economic, political and military weapon.

485  Goodman, Brenner, supra note 459, p. 159.

486  European Convention on Mutual Assistance in Criminal Matters, supra note 281.

as crimes[487], the fact that the potential cooperating country has not ratified the Convention on Cybercrime often leaves the investigating country to initial ignorance as to the content of the potential cooperating country's national criminal law, which is a waste in terms of efficiency and resources such as time, manpower and finances.

Thus, while the Convention on Cybercrime is highly relevant and a useful agreement, this instrument in its current scope and implementation practice, as well as status, cannot be the ultimate answer to the problems related to cyber incidents.

As cyber attacks against nation states become more frequent, new approaches to traditional LOAC principles may need to be developed in order to provide effective legal remedies under this area of law. Although the Geneva Conventions (1949) and Additional Protocols (1977) were adopted at a time when nobody could have explicitly defined armed conflicts to include cyber attacks, the latest developments in information warfare welcome such interpretation. The new (and presumably bloodless) types of warfare make estimating the level of suffering difficult; the definition of an "attack" should not be strictly connected with established meanings of death, injury, damage and destruction. Instead the definition of an attack should be consequence-based and bear in mind the final effect on the population.

In addition to these advancements in the

understanding of LOAC and international cooperation, one of the best ways for the international community to protect the global information infrastructure is through the development and enhancement of national ICT legal frameworks. It is this body of law under which the peace-time security standards and business continuity measures are developed and which touches upon many practical aspects of both cyber offense and defence such as ISP liability, data protection, provision of information society services and building trust towards cyberspace in general.

## "Gray area attacks" are (the most) likely

From a legal point of view, given the current and projected future threat environment – increasing threat of asymmetric attacks by non-state entities, less threat of state-sponsored warfare –, there is an increasing likelihood of attacks that fall in poorly defined areas of law. In fact, it is the general murkiness, the lack of clear policies and procedures, the lack of direct evidence of the attacking entity's identity that may make such attacks even more attractive. In such a volatile environment, by deliberately remaining below the threshold of use of force and at the same time using national policy cover as shield against investigations and prosecution, an attacking entity may believe there is less likelihood of reprisal even if the attacker's identity is suspected.

## Defences need to be coordinated through different areas of law

In order to reduce the likelihood of perpetrators "falling in the gaps" of different legal regimes and thus avoiding all legal consequences, defences need to be developed in a coherent and comprehensive approach that involves different relevant areas of law and institutional framework. It may not be the best tactic to focus on defining whose area of responsibility a particular type cyber attack might be – whether it is "an IT security problem" or "a law enforcement problem" or "a military problem". A national-scale cyber attack is a problem affecting the

---

487  Article 5 of the European Convention on Mutual Assistance in Criminal Matters. A list of declarations and reservations can be viewed at: http://conventions.coe.int/ Treaty/Commun/ListeDeclarations.asp?NT=030&CM=1&D F=1/15/2009&CL=ENG&VL=1.
The text of Article 5:
Any Contracting Party may, by a declaration addressed to the Secretary General of the Council of Europe, when signing this Convention or depositing its instrument of ratification or accession, reserve the right to make the execution of letters rogatory for search or seizure of property dependent on one or more of the following conditions:
that the offence motivating the letters rogatory is punishable under both the law of the requesting Party and the law of the requested Party;
that the offence motivating the letters rogatory is an extraditable offence in the requested country;
that execution of the letters rogatory is consistent with the law of the requested Party.
2. Where a Contracting Party makes a declaration in accordance with paragraph 1 of this article, any other Party may apply reciprocity. [Our emphasis]

society, its security and public order as a whole. It is an obligation of the state deriving from natural law to ensure a social order in which universal rights and fundamental freedoms can be fully realised.[488] Therefore, what is needed is a legal framework specifying at what degrees of cyber attacks the different institutions – the ISPs, the national CERT, the law enforcement authorities and the military – are entitled to and obliged to interfere, and what is the procedure and their terms of reference in those cases. Also, in-incident-cooperation between those entities is vital in ensuring a seamless response.

As a first step, the development of an information society needs to be backed up with legal protection of privacy, freedom of speech, consumer rights and other "practical" aspects of a well-functioning peace-time information community. Realising however that the desired harmony needs to be enforced against cyber criminals, nations need to modernise their criminal law – both procedural law and substantive criminal law to make sure that the gaps in procedure do not affect implementation of criminal law (as we partly saw it in the Estonian case). Also, having in mind the vulnerability of vital information systems and command and control functions, one also needs to prepare for cyber war from the legal perspective.

Equally important is that international agreements and uniform standards of best practice are developed between the relevant international umbrella organisations (such as ICANN and IANA), as well as between national incident handlers, specifying the procedural rules and their terms of reference in the event of a cyber attack. On national level, understanding that cyber incidents are often difficult to clearly categorise in legal terms, leads to the need to better coordinate the responsibilities of governmental and military authorities.

## Development of consensus takes time

While an understanding for the necessity for international cooperation and consensus on the legal nature and definition of national-scale cyber incidents is becoming more widespread

among stakeholders, the emergence of such consensus itself is not likely to become manifest in the course of the nearest future. This is partly because of different experiences that different nations have – or do not have – with wide-scale cyber incidents, partly because of the different setup of societies regarding the information systems and services crucial to them, partly because of differences in the legal systems and legal practices already deployed by different nations (that may be hard to reconcile with practices followed by other nations), and partly also because the legislative "windmills" have their own slow pace of running. While nations are tackling these problems, those using cyber attacks to further their aims are bound only by the cost of technology (which is increasingly less a barrier), the advance of technology (which is advancing at geometrical speed), and their own wits. Orientation within a constantly changing playing field is no easy task for national and especially international legal regimes, and therefore, it can be expected that the exact legal pinpointing of what is what in terms of cyber incidents may remain an unachievable aspiration.

Thus far, only 26 countries have ratified the Convention on Cybercrime[489] and only few have been in the position to truly test their national defences in terms of law. Furthermore, the concerns and preparedness of countries in the field of cyber security are different. The lack of experience and the perception of threat are the key reasons that make the developing of an international consensus on these matters a time-consuming undertaking.

## Define and share available remedies and resources

As an important step towards a coherent cyber defence, it is useful to rely on what currently already exists in national and international law that nations can use in order to achieve the goals of international and national cyber defence strategies and policies, while at the same time analysing the usefulness of analogies and having national responses in mind. To this end, it is also important to identify best practices in

---

488  See the United Nations Universal Declaration of Human Rights, preamble and article 28.

489  With the addition of Moldova on 1 September 2009, the Convention is currently binding for 26 nations; 46 nations altogether have signed it.

individual nations, entities and organisations for the prevention, detection or investigation of cyber attacks. Based on national best practices, a checklist for legally supported measures of cyber defence can be created. Such a checklist would enable nations to conduct analyses of their respective national laws and decide which additional legal measures are welcome or needed.

Countries that prioritise the development of IT-based services for future progress should pay closer attention to legal protection mechanisms concerning information security and possible cyber attacks. This can be done by developing national strategic approaches that take into account jurisdiction-specific threat assessments, preparedness, national cyber security organisation and available resources to defend against those threats.

Legal mechanisms need to be established for national and international authorities' involvement in a cyber incident. To avoid long reaction time and unclear lines of authority, countries and organisations must analyse the relevance of a cyber incident for their particular jurisdictions and mandates.

# INCIDENT TIMELINES

# Estonia 2007

*Friday, 27 April*

- Simultaneous attacks against multiple websites of the Estonian government and government agencies.

- Access to websites temporarily limited for users located outside of Estonia.

*Saturday, 28 April*

- Multiple-sourced DDoS attacks.

*Sunday, 29 April*

- Malicious attacks originating from outside of Estonia.

- Access for users situated outside of Estonia limited due to technical countermeasures taken to handle the attacks.

*Monday, 30 April*

- Cyber attacks continue.

- Attempts to halt the functioning of the entire public sector data communications network.

*Tuesday, 1 May*

- Increased attacks against the Estonian cyber space in the early hours of the morning. The volume of attacks has gradually increased, but the situation remains under control.

- Attacks mainly targeted against the web and name servers of government entities.

- Short breaks in the availability of websites within Estonia, but these were caused by implementing new technical countermeasures.

- Three serious attacks against web traffic at 8 PM, midnight, and 1 AM, after which the situation normalised.

*Wednesday, 2 May*

- Communications networks operate normally, and websites of the Estonian government agencies (or at least their minimised versions) were viewable both in- and outside of Estonia.

*Thursday, 3 May*

- Volume of Internet traffic still above the normal range.

- Data communications networks were kept up by implementing security measures and adding extra server capacity.

- In addition to government entities, attacks against online media outlets and private enterprises.

- A large DDoS attack against government Internet traffic and web servers, which was put off in cooperation between Internet Service Providers.

*Friday, 4 May*

- Reports of increased volumes of spam-email.

- In early morning, the availability of Estonian websites unstable for users located abroad.

*Saturday, 5 May*

- The situation is relatively calm.

*Sunday, 6 May*

- The situation is relatively calm.

*Monday, 7 May*

- International cooperation in fending off the attacks is starting to clearly pay off.

- In order to minimise possible risks, all government and private sector IT specialists, as well as home users, were requested to pay special attention to security settings of their computers and networks in order to avoid being taken under hacker control.

*Tuesday, 8 May*

- At 11 PM, a large cyber attack commenced that carried on for a long time.

- The primary targets were still government websites and data communications networks.

*Wednesday, 9 May*

- Cyber attacks appear to be attempting a "cyber blockade" of Estonia.

- Dissemination of information hindered from Estonia to the outside world.

*Thursday, 10 May*

- Continued cyber attacks attempting a cyber blockade.

- Many parallel large-volume attacks that lasted

a long time.

- Both the public and the private sector targeted.

- The work of Hansabank (the country's largest bank) Internet channels disturbed.

*Saturday, 12 May to Sunday, 13 May*

- No major attacks reported.

*Monday, 14 May*

- Minister of Defence raises the issue of cyber attacks against Estonia at a meeting with EU defence ministers.

*Tuesday, 15 May*

- Attacks against the second largest commercial bank, SEB Eesti Ühispank.

*Wednesday, 16 May*

- By midnight, single large attacks had subsided to weekend level.

*Friday, 18 May*

- Continued filtering of network traffic in cooperation among IT security staff of public and private sector entities in coordination with CERT-EE.

*Source of data: State Informatics Centre*

# Radio Free Europe/ Radio Liberty 2008

*Saturday, 26 April*

- The website of RFE/RL Belarus service hit by a DDoS attack at 8 AM.

- In a few hours, DDoS attacks expand against seven other RFE/RL websites: RFE/RL in Kosovo, Azerbaijan, Tatar-Bashkir, South Slavic, Tajik, and Radio Farda.

*Saturday, 27 April*

- Attacks continue.

*Monday, April 28*

- Most of the RFE/RL Internet sites restored.

- Radio Svaboda back online in the evening.

# Lithuania 2008

*Saturday, 28 June*

- Cyber attacks commence against Lithuanian websites.

*Sunday, 29 June*

- Attacks peak at 5 to 6 PM.

- 300 internet sites defaced at the peak of the attacks.

*Monday, 30 June*

- Attacks still ongoing.

*Tuesday, 1 July*

- Most sites restored to original content.

# Georgia 2008

*Saturday, 19 July to Sunday, July 20*

- The website of Georgian President Mikheil Saakashvili becomes unavailable for more than 24 hours due to a multi-pronged DDoS attack. The website temporarily moves to US server.

*Friday, 8 August (7 August according to some sources)*

- DDoS attacks begin against Georgian government sites.

- Coordinated cyber attacks against Georgia's Internet infrastructure. Several Georgian state computer servers come under external control.

- The Georgian government switches to hosting locations to the USA; the Ministry of Foreign Affairs opens a Blogspot account to disseminate information.

- Multiple C&C servers attacking websites that are Georgian or sympathetic to the country.

- Prolonged attacks against the websites of the Georgian President, the central government, the Ministry of Foreign Affairs and Ministry of Defence. The latter three remain unavailable at least until 11 August.

- Some commercial websites taken over.

*Saturday, August 9*

- Tulip Systems Inc. (USA) offers help to the Georgian government and transfers the web sites of the President and of a prominent Georgian TV station to company servers in the USA.

- In early morning, the largest commercial bank of Georgia comes under cyber attack.

*Saturday, 9 August to Sunday, 10 August*

- Signs of a concerted effort found by international IT security researchers: evidence presented about distribution of lists of targets over Russian web forums, about instructions and downloadable DoS tools provided for attacking Georgian websites, etc.

*Sunday, 10 August*

- New DDoS attacks against websites from several C&C servers. The attacks were no longer limited to government websites but included Georgian news sites. Among those hit were the website of a Russian opposition politician and news websites from the neighbouring country, Azerbaijan.

*Monday, 11 August*

- Georgian Ministry of Foreign Affairs reports that "[a] cyber warfare campaign by Russia is seriously disrupting many Georgian websites, including that of the Ministry of Foreign Affairs."

- The defaced website of President Saakashvili remains under a sustained DDoS attack.

- A Georgian news portal (civil.ge) comes under DDoS attack and is switched to a Blogger account.

*Wednesday, 13 August*

- Large-scale ICMP-attacks directed against Georgian governmental websites from numerous Russian computers from several different ISPs throughout the country, covering both dialup and broadband users. Russian blogs, forums, and websites spreading a Microsoft Windows batch script designed to attack Georgian websites; the effect of the latter is recorded by observers of the Georgian events.

- Arbor Networks records a set of coordinated cyber attacks, mostly TCP SYN floods. The attacks were all globally sourced, suggesting a botnet (or multiple botnets) behind them.

*Wednesday, 27 August*

- The last large cyber attack (HTTP requests) against Georgian websites, with the Georgian Ministry of Foreign Affairs as a main target.

- Services for other Georgian websites disrupted as a side effect of the HTTP.

*Thursday, 28 August*

- Attacks winding down due to the successful blocking of most attackers.

- Occurrences of minor cyber attacks that are indistinguishable from regular traffic and are probably conducted by regular civilians.

*Sources of data: Dancho Danchev; Steven Adair (Shadowserver);*
*Georgian Ministry of Foreign Affairs*

# ABBREVATIONS AND GLOSSARY

*While efforts were taken to ensure the technical neutrality of the definitions provided here, the definitions in the glossary do not lay claim to universal validity and rather reflect the context in which the terms are used in the text.*

### bandwidth

a measure of available or consumed data communication resources (expressed in bit/s (bits per second, also bps) or multiples of it (kbit/s, Mbit/s etc). Bandwidth may refer to *bandwidth capacity/available bandwidth* (reflecting the maximum throughput of a logical or physical communication path in a digital communication system) or *bandwidth consumption*, corresponding to the average rate of *successful* data transfer through a communication path.

### bot

a piece of software that automates routine, repetitive tasks and performs them much more quickly than a human operator could. A given bot may or may not be malicious, depending on how it is used. In the context of cyberwarfare, the term refers specifically to a parasitic program that hijacks a networked computer and uses it to carry out automated cyberattacks on behalf of a hacker. Individual bots can be building blocks for powerful conglomerations of bots known as botnets or bot armies. A computer wholly or partially controlled by a bot is known as a "zombie."

### bot herder (bot wrangler)

a program designed to produce bots autonomously, a tedious and time-consuming process for a human hacker. Individual bots can be building blocks for powerful conglomerations of bots known as botnets or bot armies.

A bot herder can replicate itself and create additional bot herders as well as bots. By using these wranglers, hackers can construct massive networks of bots and use these herders essentially as *command and control* nodes.

### botnet (bot army)

a collective computing network consisting of many bots and bot herders under the control of a single hacker, giving the hacker access to the computing power of many thousands of machines simultaneously, and allowing the hacker to accomplish tasks that would otherwise be impossible with a single computer. Once these botnets are established, it can be extremely difficult to disband them and counter their decentralised attacks.

### CERT - Computer Emergency Response Team

an organisation whose role is to work with the Internet community to facilitate its response to computer security events involving Internet hosts, to take proactive steps to raise the community's awareness of computer security issues and to conduct research targeted at improving the security of existing systems.

### CDMA - Code Division Multiple Access

a mobile digital radio communication technology standard

### computer network

a group of computers that are physically and logically linked to enable mutual communication and sharing of resources and information

### cracker

an individual who attempts to gain unauthorised access to a computer system. These individuals are often malicious and have many means at their disposal for breaking into a system.

### cross-site scripting (XSS)

a type of computer security vulnerability typically found in web applications which allow code injection by malicious web users into the web pages viewed by other users. Examples of such code include client-side scripts. An exploited cross-site scripting vulnerability can be used by attackers to bypass access controls such as the same origin policy. Vulnerabilities of this kind have been exploited to craft powerful phishing attacks and browser exploits. Cross-site scripting carried out on websites were roughly 80% of all documented security vulnerabilities as of 2007. Often during an attack "everything looks fine" to the end-user who may be subject to unauthorized access, theft of sensitive data, and financial loss.

### data exchange layer of information systems

the common tier used by the Estonian state information system to integrate state databases through user interfaces to a common network and enabling the user to search data from national databases that have joined the system

### DDoS (DDOS) attack - Distributed Denial of Service attack

DoS attacks accomplished by using multiple systems — often large numbers of systems like botnets — to direct overwhelming numbers of signals or requests to a target or group of targets. A single hacker can orchestrate such an attack by hijacking other computers and servers with malicious bots and organizing them into large botnets.

DDoS attacks are capable of shutting down Web sites, servers and backbone nodes; generating massive emailing and spamming campaigns; and disseminating viruses.

### DNS - Domain Name System

a hierarchical naming system for computers, services, or any resource participating in the Internet. It associates information with domain names assigned to such participants and translates domain names meaningful to humans into the numerical (binary) identifiers associated with networking equipment for the purpose of locating and addressing these devices worldwide.

### DNS Server - Domain Name System Server

a server that acts as an Internet directory or phone book, translating domain names or hostnames into numerical IP addresses that computer networks use to relay information

### Domain Name

a name that identifies computers or devices on a network (including the Internet)

### DoS (DOS) Attack - Denial of Service attack

a concerted malevolent effort to deny access to any electronic device, computer, server, network or Internet resource by its intended users. This can be accomplished in numerous ways, e.g. by ping-flood, UDP flood, malformed queries, and other means.

One common method of attack involves saturating the target (victim) machine with external communications requests, such that it cannot respond to legitimate traffic, or responds so slowly as to be rendered effectively unavailable. In general terms, DoS attacks are implemented by either forcing the targeted computer(s) to reset, or consuming its resources so that it can no longer provide its intended service or obstructing the communication media between the intended users and the victim so that they can no longer communicate adequately.

DoS attacks are considered violations of the Internet Architecture Board's Internet Proper Use Policy. They also commonly constitute violations of the laws of individual nations.

### exploit (exploitation)

a flaw or bug in a program, piece of software, command sequence or code that allows a user to use programs, computers or systems in unexpected or unauthorized ways;

a security hole or an instance of taking advantage of a security hole.

### firewall

integrated collection of security measures designed to prevent unauthorised electronic access to a networked computer system; a device or set of devices configured to permit, deny, encrypt, decrypt, or proxy all computer traffic between different security domains based upon a set of rules and other criteria.

Firewalls can be implemented in both hardware and software, or a combination of both.

### forum

a type of virtual messaging board or discussion room where users submit postings for all to read and discussion ensues.

### generic traffic flood

type of DDoS attack

### hacker

an individual who possesses an intimate working knowledge of computers, electronic systems and computer network. The term can have either a complimentary or a derogatory connotation, depending on its use; it has developed an increasingly derogatory meaning due to increased public use as a term for individuals who use computer skills to bypass the security of a given system and explore its functions and limitations.

### hacktivism; hacktivist

the use of hacker skills and techniques to accomplish political goals or advance political ideologies;

a person engaging in hacktivism, i.e hacker techniques in order to promote a political ideology

### host; Internet host

a computer connected to a network, including the Internet. Each host has a unique IP address, and can host information as well as client and/ or server software.

### IANA = Internet Assigned Numbers Authority

the entity that oversees global IP address allocation, root zone management for the Domain Name System (DNS), media types, and other Internet protocol assignments. It is operated by ICANN.

### ICANN=Internet Corporation for Assigned Names and Numbers

a non-profit corporation responsible for managing the assignment of domain names (generic and country code Top Level Domain name system management) and IP addresses, preservation of the operational stability of the Internet; promoting competition, a; to achieve broad representation of global Internet community; and to develop policies appropriate to its mission through bottom-up, consensus-based processes.

### ICMP, ICMP Echo Request (ping), ICMP Echo Reply (See ping), ICMP flood

a type of DDoS attack, accomplished by sending excessive number of pings or UDP packets to the target system, thereby causing the system to slow down or lock up.

### IP address - Internet Protocol Address

the unique 32 bit number assigned to each computer connected to the Internet and used by the TCP/IP protocol to route packets of data to their destinations, thus enabling devices to communicate with one another

### IRC - Internet Relay Chat

a form of real-time Internet text messaging (chat) or synchronous conferencing. It is mainly designed for group communication in discussion forums, called *channels*, but also allows one-to-one communication via private message, as well as chat and data transfers via Direct Client-to-Client.

### ISP - Internet Service Provider

an organisation that offers access to the Internet to its customers

### LAN
### Local Area Network

a data communications network which is geographically limited (typically to a 1 km radius) allowing easy interconnection of terminals, microprocessors and computers within adjacent buildings

### malformed query

a type of DoS attack

### malware

short for "malicious software", a category of software encompassing viruses, worms, Trojans and any other program designed to hijack, compromise or damage computers

### network

a collection of terminals, computers and servers that are interconnected to allow data transmission among them

### operating system

software that manages the operations of a computer or a computer system. It allocates memory, manages system requests, controls input and output devices, manages files, and acts as an interface to allow a user to control various other functions of a system.

### packet

a formatted unit of data, carried by a packet mode computer network (as opposed to the traditional *circuit switched* point-to-point telecommunications links where data is transmitted as a series of data). When data is formatted into packets, the bitrate of the communication medium can better be shared among users than if the network were *circuit switched.*

### ping

a computer network tool used to test the reachability of computer or network destinations across an IP network. This is done by sending "ICMP Echo Request" packets to the target host and listening for "ICMP echo response" replies. Ping measures the round-trip time and records any packet loss.

### ping flood

a simple DoS attack where the attacker overwhelms the victim with ICMP Echo Request (ping) packets. The attack is successful if the attacker has more bandwidth than the victim or can combine bandwidth with other attackers simultaneously. See also ping.

### ping of death

a type of attack on a computer that involves sending a malformed or otherwise malicious ping to a computer, e.g. sending an IP packet larger than the maximum IP packet size (65,535 bytes) that crashes the target computer or sending a fragmented packet exceeding the maximum IP packet size that the target system cannot reassemble, causing a system crash.

### port

an application-specific or process-specific software construct serving as a communications endpoint

### protocol

a convention or standard that controls or enables the connection, communication, and data transfer between computing endpoints. Protocols may be implemented by hardware, software, or a combination of the two.

### query

a user's (or agent's) request for information, generally as a formal request to a database or search engine.

### Rally Around the Flag

an ideological motivation, similar to nationalism, that can emerge when a compelling cause other than national interest (one that is controversial, substantial and out of the ordinary) arises to unify substantial numbers of hackers suddenly and temporarily

### request

a signal from one computer to another or to a server asking for a specific piece of information or data

### script

a set of instructions that directs how a piece of software, an application or a program is to perform and be processed by the computer that is running it

### script kiddies

a derogatory term used to describe those who use scripts or programs developed by others to attack computer systems and networks.

### server farm (also server cluster, computer farm)

a group of networked servers that are housed in one location and are used to streamline internal processes by distributing the workload between the individual components of the farm, and to expedite computing processes by harnessing the power of multiple servers. When one server in the farm fails, another can step in as a backup.

### spoofing

a situation in which one person or program successfully masquerades as another by falsifying data and thereby gaining an illegitimate advantage.

### SQL injection

An SQL injection is a code injection technique that exploits a security vulnerability occurring in the database layer of an application. The vulnerability is present when user input is either incorrectly filtered for string literal escape characters embedded in SQL statements or user input is not strongly typed and thereby unexpectedly executed.

SQL (Structured Query Language) is a database computer language designed for the retrieval and management of data in relational database management systems (RDBMS), database schema creation and modification, and database object access control management.

### TCP SYN flood

a type of DDoS attack, conducted by taking advantage of the flaw of TCP three-way handshaking behaviour. The attacker makes connection requests aimed at the victim server with packets with unreachable source addresses. The server is not able to complete the connection requests and, as a result, the victim wastes all of its network resources. A relatively small flood of false packets will tie up memory, CPU, and applications, resulting in shutting down a server.

### Transmission Control Protocol (TCP)

one of the core protocols of the Internet Protocol Suite, handling end systems (e.g. a Web browser and a Web server) and providing reliable, ordered delivery of a stream of bytes from one program on one computer to another program on another computer.

### Trojan

a class of computer threats (malware) that appears to perform a desirable function but in fact performs undisclosed malicious functions that allow unauthorised access to the host machine, thereby enabling unauthorised control over the computer

### UDP flood

UDP flood attack is a type of DoS attack using the User Datagram Protocol (UDP), a sessionless/connectionless computer networking protocol by sending UDP packets to a random port on the victim system. When the victim system receives a UDP packet, it will determine what application is waiting on the destination port. When it realizes that there is no application that is waiting on the port, it will generate an ICMP packet of destination unreachable to the forged source address. If enough UDP packets are delivered to ports on victim, the system will go down.

### URL - Uniform Resource Locator

a resource identifier that describes the location of a particular piece of information, including the protocol used to retrieve that information

### virus

a type of malware that propagates from computer to computer by attaching itself to other software. It is generally inadvertently triggered by the user (e.g., by downloading an infected file or opening an infected email attachment).

### WiFi

wireless networking technology that uses radio waves to provide wireless high-speed Internet and network connections

### WiMax - Worldwide Inter-operability for Microwave Access

a telecommunications technology that provides wireless transmission of data using a variety of transmission modes, from point-to-multipoint links to portable and fully mobile internet access.

### worm

a type of malware that propagates itself inside a network, often autonomously, without necessarily attaching itself to another program (as a virus does). Worms are often much more harmful than viruses because they can spread on their own and, while they might not damage their targets, they can also cause complications for the broader network or Internet by consuming bandwidth and processing power

### WWW - World Wide Web

the collection of interlinked, interactive documents published as Web pages and accessible via the Internet

### zombie

a computer wholly or partially controlled by a malicious bot

*Sources of definitions: Techdictionary.com;*
*Stratfor Today;*
*Webopedia; Free Online Dictionary of*
*Computing (FOLDOC);*
*Wikipedia; State Informatics Centre (Estonia);*
*Advanced Networking Management Lab (IN,*
*USA)*

# BIBLIOGRAPHY

[1] 'A Brief History of RFE/RL'. RFE/RL. Available at: http://www.rferl.org/info/history/133.html..

[2] 'Acquisition of state share of JSC 'United Telecommunications Company of Georgia'. Press release by BTA Bank, 16 May 2006. Available at bta.kz/en/press/news/2006/05/16/1043/.

[3] Adair, Steven. 'Georgian Attacks: Remember Estonia?' Shadowserver Foundation, 13 Aug 2008. Available at: http://www.shadowserver.org/wiki/pmwiki.php/Calendar/20080813.

[4] Adair, Steven. 'Georgian Websites Under Attack - DDoS and Defacement'. Shadowserver Foundation, Aug 11, 2008. Available at: http://www.shadowserver.org/wiki/pmwiki.php/Calendar.20080811.

[5] Akavita.com: Рейтинг белорусских сайтов. Новости и СМИ. Рейтинг за: среднесуточный. (In Belarus). Available at: http://top.akavita.com/Mass_Media_and_News/daily/visitors/by/.

[6] Aldrich, Richard W. The International Legal Implications of Information Warfare, in Airpower Journal – Fall 1996, p. 100.

[7] 'All commercial banks in Georgia are operating business as usual'. National Bank of Georgia, Aug 18, 2008. Available at: http://www.nbg.gov.ge/index.php?m=340&newsid=832.

[8] Almann, Lauri. Presentation at the Conference Board of Canada conference 'Cyber Security: Proactive Defence of Critical Systems and Information'. 5 Nov 2008.

[9] 'Alustati kriminaalasi küberrünnakute uurimiseks.' Press release by the State Prosecutor's Office 2 May 2007. Available at: http://www.prokuratuur.ee/28707.

[10] An Expert Look at Chinese Information Operations Theory. IntelliBriefs, 10 November 2008. Available at: http://intellibriefs.blogspot.com/2008/11/expert-look-at-chinese-information.html.

[11] An Overview of Events, compiled by the CCD COE activation team on 8 May 2007.

[12] Armin, J. 'Atrivo – Cyber Crime USA: White Paper - Atrivo and their Associates'. Vers: 1.1, September 2008. Available at: hostexploit.com/downloads/Atrivo%20white%20paper%20090308ad.pdf ..

[13] Arnold, Chloe. 'Russian Group's Claims Reopen Debate On Estonian Cyberattacks.' RFE/RL, 30 March 2009. Available at: http://www.estemb.org/news/aid-2526.

[14] Arnoldy, B. Cyberspace: New Frontier in Conflicts. ABC News, 17 Aug 2008. Available at: abc-news.go.com/Technology/AheadoftheCurve/Story?id=5590834&page=2.

[15] Arquilla, John. 'Can information warfare ever be just?' In Ethnics and Information Technology 1: 203-212, 1999.

[16] 'Arthur D. Little Global M-Payment Update 2005'. Available at: http://www.3mfuture.com/articles_epayment/Global_M-Payment-Report_Update_Arthur_D_Little_2005.pdf.

[17] Barlow, John Perry. A Declaration of the Independence in Cyberspace. 1996. Available at http://homes.eff.org/~barlow/Declaration-Final.html.

[18] Behind The Estonia Cyberattacks. Radio Free Europe/Radio Liberty, 6 March 2009. Available at http://www.rferl.org/Content/Behind_The_Estonia_Cyberattacks/1505613.html .

[19] Belarus. CIA World Factbook, 2009. Available at: https://www.cia.gov/library/publications/the-world-factbook/geos/bo.html.

[20] Berendson, Risto. 'Küberrünnakute taga seisavad profid.' (IN Estonian.) Postimees, 3 May 2007 Available at http://www.tarbija24.ee/120507/esileht/siseuudised/258409.php .

[21] Bidgoli, Hossein. 'Handbook of information security', Volume 3. John Wiley and Sons, Inc, 2003.

[22] Brownlie, Ian. 'The rule of law in international affairs: international law at the Fiftieth Anniversary of the United Nations'. The Hague Academy of International Law, 1998. Pp. 202-203.

[23] Cenne polskie wsparcie dla Gruzji (in Polish), RMF FM, 9 Aug, 2008. Available at: http://www.rmf.fm/fakty/?id=141305.

[24] CERT-EE Report on status in Georgia, 14 August 2008. Available at the website of the Estonian Informatics Centre at http://www.ria.ee/index.php?lang=en. .

[25] Clover, Charles. Kremlin-backed group behind Estonia cyber blitz. Financial Times, 11 March 2009. Available at http://www.ft.com/cms/s/0/57536d5a-0ddc-11de-8ea3-0000779fd2ac.html?nclick_check=1 .

[26] Coalson, Robert. 'Behind The Estonia Cyberattacks'. RFE/RL, 6 March 2009. Available at: http://www.rferl.org/Content/Behind_The_Estonia_Cyberattacks/1505613.html.

[ 27 ]   Commission Communication COM(2002)276 of 5 June 2002 on Impact Assessment (available at http://eur-lex.europa.eu/LexUriServ/LexUriServ.do?uri=CELEX:52002DC0276:EN:NOT). .

[ 28 ]   Commission on Human Rights resolution 2000/38, 'The right to freedom of opinion and expression'. The United Nations High Commissioner for Human Rights, 2000. Available at: http://www.unhchr.ch/Huridocda/Huridoca.nsf/0/a10988ef7018d21d802568d4004d04a7?Opendocument.

[ 29 ]   Commission staff working document - Annex to the Communication from the Commission to the Council, the European Parliament, the European Economic and Social committee and the Committee of the Regions A strategy for a Secure Information Society - "Dialogue, partnership and empowerment" {COM(2006) 251 final} - Impact assessment /* SEC/2006/0656 */

[ 30 ]   Communication COM(2001) 298 final from the Commission to the Council, the European Parliament, the Economic and Social Committee and the Committee of the Regions of 6 June 2001, "Network and Information Security: proposal for a European Policy approach", available at: http://eur- lex.europa.eu/LexUriServ/LexUriServ.do?uri=CELEX:52001DC0298:EN:HTML, hereafter *Communication 2001*

[ 31 ]   Communication from the Commission to the European Parliament and the Council on Public-Private Dialogue in Security Research and Innovation {SEC(2007) 1138} {SEC(2007) 1139} /* COM/2007/0511 final */, available at: http://eur-lex.europa.eu/LexUriServ/LexUriServ.do?uri=CELEX:52007DC0511:EN:HTML

[ 32 ]   Communication from the Commission to the European Parliament and the Council - An area of freedom, security and justice serving the citizen /* COM/2009/0262 final */, available at: http://eur-lex.europa.eu/LexUriServ/LexUriServ.do?uri=CELEX:52009DC0262:EN:HTML

[ 33 ]   Council of Europe Parliamentary Assembly Resolution 1633 (2008) on 'The consequences of the war between Georgia and the Russian Federation'. Available at assembly.coe.int/Mainf.asp?link=/Documents/AdoptedText/ta08/ERES1633.htm.

[ 34 ]   Council of Europe. Convention on Cybercrime: Status as of 25 Aug 2009. Available at: http://conventions.coe.int/Treaty/Commun/ChercheSig.asp?NT=185&CM=&DF=&CL=ENG.

[ 35 ]   Craciun, G. 'President of Georgia Web Page Down after Hacker Attack - The Russians are believed to be behind it', *Security News Editor*. Available at: news.softpedia.com/news/President-of-Georgia-Web-Page-Down-after-Hacker-Attack-90420.shtml.

[ 36 ]   Cyber Attack Against Lithuania. Official Statement by Lithuanian Embassy (by e-mail), 1 July 2008.

[ 37 ]   Cyber attacks against the Republic of Estonia. 10 May 2007. An overview by the Cooperative Cyber Defence Centre of Excellence project team.

[ 38 ]   'Cyber Attacks Disable Georgian Websites'. Georgian Ministry of Foreign Affairs, 11 Aug 2008. Available at: georgiamfa.blogspot.com/2008/08/cyber-attacks-disable-georgian-websites.html.

[ 39 ]   Cyber Security Enhancement Act of 2002, available at: http://thomas.loc.gov/cgi-bin/bdquery/z?d107:h.r.03482:

[ 40 ]   Cyber Security Strategy. Cyber Security Strategy Committee, Ministry of Defence. Tallinn 2008. The English version of the Estonian Cyber Security Strategy is available at: http://www.mod.gov.ee/static/sisu/files/Estonian_Cyber_Security_Strategy.pdf.

[ 41 ]   'Cyberjamming'. The Wall Street Journal, 29 April 2008. Available at: http://online.wsj.com/article/SB120942466671951083.html.

[ 42 ]   'Cyberwarfare: a glossary of useful terms'. Stratfor today, 1 March 2008. Available at http://www.stratfor.com/analysis/cyberwarfare_glossary_useful_terms .

[ 43 ]   Danchev, Dancho. '300 Lithuanian Sites Hacked By Russian Hackers'. Zero Day, 2 July 2008. Available at: blogs.zdnet.com/security/?p=1408.

[ 44 ]   Danchev, Dancho. 'Coordinated Russia vs Georgia cyber attack in progress'. 11 Aug 2008. Available at: blogs.zdnet.com/security/?p=1670.

[ 45 ]   Danchev, Dancho. 'DDoS Attack Graphs from Russia vs Georgia's Cyberattacks'. 15 Oct 2008. Available at: ddanchev.blogspot.com/2008/10/ddos-attack-graphs-from-russia-vs.html .

[ 46 ]   Danchev, Dancho. 'Lithuania Attacked by Russian Hacktivists, 300 Sites Defaced'. Circle ID, 8 July 2008 . Available at: http://www.circleid.com/posts/87870_lithuania_internet_attack_russian_hacktivists/.

[ 47 ]   Daniszewski, John. 'Election Fraud Belarus'. 11 Sept 2001, Los Angeles Times. http://articles .latimes.com/2001/sep/11/news/mn-44558.

[48] Declaration of Principles by the World Summit on the Information Society, 'Building the Information Society: a global challenge in the new Millennium'. Geneva 2003. Available at: http://www.itu.int/wsis/outcome/booklet/declaration_A.html.

[49] 'Demonstrating respect for rights? A human rights approach to policing protest.' UK Human Rights Joint Committee Seventh Report, 2009. Sections 15, 17, and 29 Available at: http://www.publications.parliament.uk/pa/jt200809/jtselect/jtrights/47/4705.htm.

[50] Department of Economic and Social Affairs of the United Nations Secretariat. 'UN e-Government Survey 2008: From e-Government to Connected Governance.' United Nations, 2008.

[51] DG Information Society and Media. e-Inclusion Policy. Country Profile: Lithuania. European Commission, 2008. Available at: ec.europa.eu/information_society/activities/einclusion/policy/a_documents/lithuania_einclusion.doc.

[52] Draft Articles on the Responsibility of States for Internationally Wrongful Acts. (Text as it appears in the annex to General Assembly resolution 56/83 of 12 December 2001)

[53] Dyomkin, Denis. 'Russia condemns rewriting of World War Two history,' Reuters, 23 June 2008. Available at: uk.reuters.com/article/worldNews/idUKL221014120080623?pageNumber=1&virtualBrandChannel=0&sp=true.

[54] Easterbrook, Frank H. Cyberspace and the Law of the Horse, 1996 U Chi Legal F 207.

[55] 'E-Communications Household Survey'. Special Eurobarometer 293. TNS opinion & social/European Commission, June 2008.

[56] Eesti aitab Gruusiat küberrünnete tõrjumisel (in Estonian), Estonian Informatics Centre, Aug 12, 2008. Available at: http://www.ria.ee/index.php.

[57] Ehlers, Dirk (Ed.) 'European fundamental rights and freedoms.' De Gryter Recht, 2007.

[58] E-Policy Principles. UK Office of the e-Envoy, 2003. Available at: http://archive.cabinetoffice.gov.uk/e-envoy/guidelines-eprinciples/$file/principles.htm

[59] Estland im Visier: Ist ein Internetangriff der Ernstfall?. Frankfurter Allgemeine Zeitung, 18.06.2007, Nr. 138 / Seite 6. (in German). Available at: http://www.faz.net/s/RubDDB-DABB9457A437BAA85A49C26FB23A0/Doc~E7CCF88CEFB6F467BB8D75A400C07B959~ATpl~Ecommon~Scontent.html; Ottis, Rain. Overview of Events, 7 May 2007. CCD COE Activation Team, TDCCIS.

[60] Estonia hit by Moscow cyber war. BBC News, 1 7 May 2007. Available at http://news.bbc.co.uk/2/hi/europe/6665145.stm.

[61] Estonia. CIA World Factbook, November 2008. Available at: https://www.cia.gov/library/publications/the-world-factbook/geos/en.html .

[62] 'Estonian DDoS - a final analysis'. Heine Online, 31 May 2007. Available at http://www.h-online.com/security/news/item/Estonian-DDoS-a-final-analysis-732971.html.

[63] EurActiv. 'Estonia first country in the world to introduce internet voting'. 12 October 2005. Available at http://www.euractiv.com/en/egovernment/estonia-country-world-introduce-internet-voting/article-145735 .

[64] European Parliament recommendation of 26 March 2009 to the Council on strengthening security and fundamental freedoms on the Internet (2008/2160(INI)). Available at: http://www.europarl.europa.eu/sides/getDoc.do?type=TA&language=EN&reference=P6-TA-2009-0194.

[65] European Parliament resolution on freedom of expression on the Internet, P6_TA(2006)0324. Available at: http://www.europarl.europa.eu/sides/getDoc.do?pubRef=-//EP//NONSGML+TA+P6-TA-2006-0324+0+DOC+PDF+V0//EN.

[66] 'European Union External Relations: Georgia'. European Commission. Available at: ec.europa.eu/external_relations/georgia/index_en.htm.

[67] Evron, Gadi. 'Battling Botnets and Online Mobs. Estonia's Defence Efforts during the Internet War'. Georgetown Journal of International Affairs, Winter/Spring 2008, p 121-126.

[68] Evron, Gadi. 'Georgia Cyber Attacks From Russian Government? Not So Fast'. CSO, 13 Aug 2009. Available at http://www.csoonline.com/article/443579/Georgia_Cyber_Attacks_From_Russian_Government_Not_So_Fast.

[69] 'Expert: Cyber-attacks on Georgia websites tied to mob, Russian government'. Los Angeles Times, 13 Aug 2008. Available at latimesblogs.latimes.com/technology/2008/08/experts-debate.html .

[70] Explanatory Memorandum to the Draft Act on the Amendment of the Penal Code (116 SE). (In Estonian.) December 2007. Available at: http://www.riigikogu.ee/?page=pub_file&op=emsplain&content_type=application/msword&u=20090902161440&file_id=198499&file_name=KarS%20seletuskiri%20(167).doc&file_size=66048&mnsensk=166+SE&etapp=03.12.2007&fd=29.10.2008.

[71] Explanatory Report to the European Convention on Mutual Assistance in Criminal Matters, available at: http://conventions.coe.int/Treaty/en/Reports/Html/030.htm

[72] Finley, Julie. 'Statement on Cyber-attacks Against Radio Free Europe in Belarus', Statement to the OSCE Permanent Council, 8 May 2008. Available at: http://www.america.gov/st/texttrans-english/2008/May/20080508115033e aifas0.3709833.html.

[73] Finn, Peter. ' Cyber Assaults on Estonia Typify a New Battle Tactic,' Washington Post, 19 May 2007. Available at http://www.washingtonpost.com/wp-dyn/content/article/2007/05/18/AR2007051802122.html .

[74] Freedom Of The Press - Belarus (2008). Freedom House, 2009. Available at: http://www.freedomhouse.org/inc/content/pubs/pfs/inc_country_detail.cfm?country=7351&year=2008&page=16&view=mopf&pf.

[75] Freedom of the Press 2009 Table of Global Press Freedom Rankings (pp. 1-5); Freedom of the Press 2009: Press Freedom Rankings by Region: Central And Eastern Europe / Former Soviet Union (p. 10). Available at: http://www.freedomhouse.org/uploads/fop/2009/FreedomofthePress2009_tables.pdf.

[76] General Assembly Resolution 58/63, 28.01.2002, Annex (Draft Articles).

[77] 'Georgia targeted in cyber attack.' AFP, 12 Aug 2008. Available at http://afp.google.com/article/ALeqM5iRuGsssizXAKVgmPqAXOxqB5uH-sQ.

[78] 'Georgia, Russia: The Cyberwarfare Angle'. Stratfor Today, Aug 12, 2008. Available at: http://www.stratfor.com/analysis/georgia_russia_cyberwarfare_angle. .

[79] Georgia. CIA World Factbook (Updated as of 6 November 2008). Available at: https://www.cia.gov/library/publications/the-world-factbook/geos/gg.html.

[80] Georgia: Electronic Communications Market Turn Over Exceeds GEL 1 bln. Caucas Euronews, 8 Jun 2007. Available at: http://www.caucaz.com/home_eng/depeches.php?idp=1723&PHPSESSID=d7e84d535388fb8344927152099c6967.

[81] Georgia's Caucasus Online Invests $40 Mln in Fibre Optic Link to W. Europe via Bulgaria. SeeNews - The Corporate Wire 20 Nov 2008. Available at http://www.seenews.com/news/latestnews/georgiancaucasusonlinelaunchesfibreopticprojectinbulgariaonfriday-153906/.

[82] Germain, Jack M. 'The Winds of Cyber War'. TechNewsWorld, 16 Sept 2008, available at: http://www.technewsworld.com/rss-tory/64494.html?wlc=1263369698.

[83] 'Global Cyber Attack Against Radio Free Europe/Radio Liberty'. Radio Free Europe/Radio Liberty, 28 April 2008. Available at: http://www.rferl.org/content/PressRelease/1110126.html.

[84] Global Online Freedom Act of 2006 (H.R. 4780). 109th Congress, 2005-2006. Available at: http://www.govtrack.us/congress/bill.xpd?tab=main&bill=h109-4780.

[85] Global Online Freedom Act of 2007 (H.R. 275) . 110th Congress, 2007-2008. Available at: http://www.govtrack.us/congress/bill.xpd?bill=h110-275.

[86] Global Online Freedom Act of 2009 (H.R. 2271). 111th Congress, 2009-2010. Available at: http://www.govtrack.us/congress/bill.xpd?bill=h111-2271.

[87] 'Good Law — Bad Implementation'. Interview with Andrei Richter. Published from 'Media Expert', Russian-Byelorussian quarterly. The Centre for Journalism in Extreme Situations at the Russian Union of Journalists, #4, 2004. Available at: http://www.medialaw.ru/e_pages/publications/goodlaw.htm.

[88] Goodin, Dan. 'Radio Free Europe hit by DDoS attack', SecurityFocus, 1 May 2008. Available at: http://www.securityfocus.com/news/11515?ref=rss.

[89] Goodman, Marc D., Brenner Susan W. The Emerging Consensus on Criminal Conduct in Cyberspace in: International Journal of Law and Information Technology, Summer 2002 Volume 10.

[90] Gorman, Siobhan. 'Hackers Stole IDs for Attacks'. Wall Street Journal, 24 Aug 2009, available at: http://online.wsj.com/article/SB125046431841935299.html.

[91] Hansapanka tabas küberrünne. Postimees 10 May 2007 (In Estonian). Available at http://www.tarbija24.ee/180507/esileht/majandus/259920.php.

[92] Hardabkhadze, V., Kvernadze, L. Georgia. (Part of a report produced for the European Commission on the electronic communications markets in Central and Eastern Europe) Available at: ec.europa.eu/information_society/activities/internationalrel/docs/pi_study_rus_ukr_arm_azerb_bel_geor_kaz_mold/7_georgia.pdf .

[93] Heil, Andy. E-mail to Kadri Kaska/CCD COE, 23 Oct 2009.

[94] Hustad, Richard. 'International Human Rights Law: Substantive Rights'. Lecture 2: Freedom of Expression (HUMR 5120/4120/1120). Norwegian Centre for Human Rights, 2008.

[95] Hoffman, Stefanie. 'Russian Cyber Attacks Shut Down Georgian Websites'. ChannelWeb, 12 Aug 2008. Available at http://www.crn.com/security/210003057 .

[96] Hyppönen, Mikko. 'Unrest in Estonia'. April 28, 2007. http://www.f-secure.com/weblog/archives/00001181.html .

[97] Hyppönen, Mikko. 'Update on the Estonian DDoS attacks.' F-Secure Weblog, 30 April 2007. Available at http://www.f-secure.com/weblog/archives/00001183.html .

[98] Implementation Plan 2007-2008 of the Estonian Information Society Strategy. Available at http://www.riso.ee/en/information-policy/policy-document/implementation_plan.

[99] Information about the latest developments in Georgia, *President of the Republic of Poland*. Available at: http://www.president.pl/x.node?id=479.

[100] Information for Press. Georgian Ministry of Foreign Affairs, 8 Aug 2008. Available at: http://www.mfa.gov.ge/index.php?lang_id=ENG&sec_id=461&info_id=7193&date=2008-08-08&new_month=08&new_year=2008.

[101] International Covenant on Civil and Political Rights. New York, 16 December 1966. Available at: http://treaties.un.org/Pages/ViewDetails.aspx?src=TREATY&mtdsg_no=IV-4&chapter=4&lang=en.

[102] Internet access a fundamental right, says French court'. Rediff Business, 12 June 2009. Available at: http://business.rediff.com/report/2009/jun/12/net-access-a-fundamental-right-says-french-court.htm.

[103] Internet Usage Statistics: The Internet Big Picture. World Internet Users and Population Stats, 2009. Available at: http://www.internetworldstats.com/stats.htm.

[104] Internet users per 100 population, 2006. Available at: data.un.org/Data.aspx?d=MDG&f=seriesRowID:605.

[105] Inventory of CERT Activities in Europe, ENISA. Available at: www.enisa.europa.eu/cert_inventory/pages/03_li.htm.

[106] ITU ICT Statistics Database (ICT Eye). Internet indicators: subscribers, users and broadband subscribers: 2008. Available at: http://www.itu.int/ITU-D/icteye/Reporting/ShowReportFrame.aspx?ReportName=/WTI/InformationTechnologyPublic&RP_intYear=2008&RP_intLanguageID=1.

[107] Jinks, Derek. 'State Responsibility for the Acts of Private Armed Groups', Chicago Journal of International Law, 4 (2003), 83-95.

[108] Johnson, M. 'Georgian Websites Under Attack - Don't Believe the Hype', Shadowserver Foundation, Aug 12, 2008. Available at: http://www.shadowserver.org/wiki/pmwiki.php/Calendar.20080812.

[109] Johnson, Phillip A. Is It Time for a Treaty on Information Warfare?' In International Law Studies, Vol. 76, edited by Michael N. Schmitt and Brian T. O'Donnell, 439-455. Newport, RI: Naval War College, 2002.

[110] Judgment of 31 May 2007 by the Administrative Chamber of the National Court 3-3-1-20-07 (Kalda) (In Estonian) RT III 2007, 23, 193.

[111] Judgment of Harju County Court of 13 December 2007 in criminal matter No 1-07-15185 (Galushkevich).

[112] Kaasik, Peeter. 'Common grave for and a memorial to Red Army soldiers on Tõnismägi, Tallinn. Historical statement' (*In Estonian*). Estonian Foundation for the Investigation of Crimes Against Humanity, 2006. Available at http://www.valitsus.ee/brf/failid/ajalooline_oiend_2006_en.pdf .

[113] Kanuck, Sean P. Information Warfare: New Challenges for Public International Law, Harvard International Law Journal Vol. 37 (1996).

[114] Karnej, Ihar; Whitmore, Brian. 'Belarus: RFE/RL Cites Online 'Solidarity' In Face Of Cyberattack' RFE/RL, 29 April 2008. http://www.rferl.org/content/article/1109649.html.

[115] Kash, Wyatt. 'Lauri Almann: Lessons from the cyberattacks on Estonia'. GCN Interview with Lauri Almann, Estonia's permanent undersecretary of Defence. Government Computer News, 13 Jun 2008. .

[116] Kelsey, Jeffrey T. G. 'Hacking into International Humanitarian Law: The Principles of Distinction and Neutrality in the Age of Cyber Warfare', 106 Michigan Law Review, 1427-1452 (2008). P. 1442-1443.

[ 117 ] Kirk, Jeremy 'Lithuania: Attacks Focused on Hosting Company'. PC World, 4 July 2008. Available at: http://www.pcworld.com/article/147960/lithuania_attacks_focused_on_hosting_company.html.

[ 118 ] Kirk, Jeremy. 'Update: Estonia, Poland Help Georgia Fight Cyberattacks,' IDG News Service, August 12, 2008, http://www.computerworld.com/action/article.do?command=viewArticleBasic&articleId=9112399&source=rss_news50 .

[ 119 ] Kosachev, Konstantin. 'An insult to our war dead'. The Guardian, 6 Mar 2007. Available at http://www.guardian.co.uk/commentisfree/2007/mar/06/comment.secondworldwar .

[ 120 ] Krebs, Brian 'Lithuania Weathers Cyber Attack, Braces for Round 2,' 3 July 2008. Available at: voices.washingtonpost.com/securityfix/2008/07/lithuania_weathers_cyber_attac_1.html.

[ 121 ] Krebs, Brian. 'Internet Shuns U.S. Based ISP Amid Fraud, Abuse Allegations' Washington Post, 22 Sept 2008; available at voices.washingtonpost.com/securityfix/2008/09/internet_shuns_us_based_isp_am.html.

[ 122 ] Krebs, Brian. 'Report: Russian Hacker Forums Fueled Georgia Cyber Attacks' on Computer Security, 16 Oct 2008, The Washington Post. Available at voices.washingtonpost.com/securityfix/2008/10/report_russian_hacker_forums_f.html.

[ 123 ] Krebs, Brian. 'Shadowy Russian Firm Seen as Conduit for Cybercrime', Washington Post, Oct 13, 2007. Available at: http://www.washingtonpost.com/wp-dyn/content/article/2007/10/12/AR2007101202461_pf.html (last accessed: 27 Aug 2008).

[ 124 ] Koops, Bert-Jaap. 'Should ICT Regulation be Technology-Neutral?', in: Starting Points for ICT Regulation. Deconstructing Prevalent Policy One-Liners, IT & Law Series, Bert-Jaap Koops, Miriam Lips, Corien Prins & Maurice Schellekens, eds., Vol. 9, pp. 77-108, The Hague: T.M.C. Asser Press, 2006.

[ 125 ] Käo, Merike. 'Cyber Attacks on Estonia: Short Synopsis'. 2007

[ 126 ] 'Küberründed ei ole vaibunud'. Postimees, 10 May 2007 (in Estonian). Available at: http://www.tarbija24.ee/110507/esileht/krimi/259961.php.

[ 127 ] 'Küberrünnete korraldajaid ähvardab ELi vahistamismäärus'. BNS, 12 March 2009. Available at: http://www.postimees.ee/?id=93564 .

[ 128 ] [Labott, E., Gotsadze, E.] Russian warplanes target Georgia. CNN, August 9, 2008. Available at: edition.cnn.com/2008/WORLD/europe/08/09/georgia.ossetia/index.html?eref=rss_topstories.

[ 129 ] Landler, Mark; Markoff, John. 'In Estonia, what may be the first war in cyberspace.' International Herald Tribune. 28 May 2007. Available at http://www.iht.com/articles/2007/05/28/business/cyberwar.php .

[ 130 ] Lessig, Lawrence. Code: And Other Laws of Cyberspace, Version 2.0. Basic Books, 2006.

[ 131 ] Liik, Kadri. 'Tee sõtta'. (In Estonian) International Centre for Defence Studies. 11 Aug 2008. Available at http://www.icds.ee/index.php?id=73&type=98&L=0&tx_ttnews[tt_news]=262&tx_ttnews[backPid]=214&cHash=4de7396400. .

[ 132 ] Linnamäe, L. 'Küberrünnakute kahjusid hakatakse arvutama hiljem' (in Estonian). Postimees, 5 May 2007. Available at: suusk24.postimees.ee/110507/esileht/majandus/259796.php.

[ 133 ] List of declarations made with respect to treaty No. 185. Available at: http://conventions.coe.int/Treaty/Commun/ListeDeclarations.asp?NT=185&CV=1&NA=4&PO=999&CN=999&VL=1&CM=9&CL=ENG.

[ 134 ] Lithuania. CIA World Factbook, November 2008. Available at: https://www.cia.gov/library/publications/the-world-factbook/geos/lh.html.

[ 135 ] 'Lithuanian tax office website hit by cyber attack'. Reuters, 21 July 2008. Available at: http://www.reuters.com/article/rbssTechMediaTelecomNews/idUSMAR14153920080721.

[ 136 ] Long-Term Development Strategy of the State. Adopted by resolution No. IX-1187 of the Seimas of the Republic of Lithuania on 12 November 2002. Official translation available at: www3.lrs.lt/pls/inter3/dokpaieska.showdoc_l?p_id=219184.

[ 137 ] Maksymiuk, Jan. 'Belarus: The Slow-Boiling Dictatorship'. RFE/RL, 14 June 2005. Available at: http://www.rferl.org/content/article/1059266.html.

[ 138 ] Marcinkevicius, Markas from Lithuanian Cyber Crime Bureau in an e-mail (8 Dec 2008) to the CCD COE Legal Team.

[ 139 ] Markoff, John. 'Before the gunfire, cyberattacks,' International Herald Tribune, Aug 13, 2008. Available at: http://www.iht.com/articles/2008/08/13/technology/13cyber.php.

[140] Marson, James. 'Belarus: Can Europe Change Its 'Last Dictatorship'?'. The Time, 25 March 2009. Available at: http://www.time.com/time/world/article/0,8599,1887513,00.html; .

[141] Maskeliūnas, Saulius; Otas, Alfredas. 'Development and Application of Information Society Strategies in Lithuania.' Institute of Mathematics and Informatics, Kaunas University of Technology, 2008. Available at: http://www.scholze-simmel.at/starbus/ws3/lithuania.pdf.

[142] Mchedlishvili, Niko. 'Georgia cuts access to Russian websites, TV news'. Reuters, 19 Aug 2008. Available at http://www.reuters.com/article/internetNews/idUSLJ36223120080819?sp=true

[143] McMillan, Robert. 'Hackers Hit Scientology With Online Attack'. IDG News Service, 26 Jan 2008 Available at http://www.pcworld.com/article/141839/hackers_hit_scientology_with_online_attack.html.

[144] Meikar, Silver. 'Perestroika imelaps Valgevene' (in Estonian). Diplomaatia, nr 63, November 2008. International Centre for Defence Studies.

[145] Member States of the United Nations. Available at: http://www.un.org/en/members/index.shtml .

[146] 'Military and Paramilitary Activities in and against Nicaragua' – ICJ Reports, 1986.

[147] Millman, Rene. 'DDoS attacks on Estonia 'not from Kremlin''. ITPro. 1 June 2007. Available at http://www.itpro.co.uk/114570/ddos-attacks-on-estonia-not-from-kremlin .

[148] Mills, Elinor. 'Radio Free Europe DDOS Attack Latest by Hactivists', CNET News, 1 May 2008. Available at: http://news.cnet.com/8301-10784_3-9933746-7.html.

[149] Morsink, Johannes. 'The Universal Declaration of Human Rights'. University of Pennsylvania Press, 1999.

[150] Mueller, Milton. 'Net Neutrality as Global Principle in Internet Governance'. School of Information Studies, Syracuse University, 2007. Available at: http://www.internetgovernance.org/pdf/NetNeutralityGlobalPrinciple.pdf. Pp. 2-3.

[151] Myers, Steven Lee. 'Youth Groups Created by Kremlin Serve Putin's Cause'. New York Times, 8 July 2007. Available at: http://www.nytimes.com/2007/07/08/world/europe/08moscow.html?_r=1.

[152] 'NATO Defending Against Cyber Attacks', available at: http://www.nato.int/issues/cyber_defence/index.html

[153] 'NATO Sees Recent Cyber Attacks on Estonia as Security Issue. DW staff / AFP / dpa (nda) 26 May 2007. Available at http://www.dw-world.de/dw/article/0,2144,2558579,00.html .

[154] Nazario, Jose (Arbor Networks); DiMino, Andre M. (Shadowserver Foundation). 'An In-Depth Look at the Georgia-Russia Cyber Conflict of 2008'. October 2008. Available at: http://www.shadowserver.org/wiki/uploads/Shadowserver/BTF8_RU_GE_DDOS.pdf.

[155] Nazario, José. 'Georgia DDoS Attacks - A Quick Summary of Observations', Arbor Networks, 12 Aug 2008. Available at: asert.arbornetworks.com/2008/08/georgia-ddos-attacks-a-quick-summary-of-observations.

[156] Nazario, José. 'Radio Free Europe DDoS', Arbor Networks, 29 April 2008. Available at: http://asert.arbornetworks.com/2008/04/radio-free-europe-ddos/.

[157] Nazario, Jose. 'Estonian DDoS Attacks - A summary to date'. Arbor Networks, 17 May 2007. Available at asert.arbornetworks.com/2007/05/estonian-ddos-attacks-a-summary-to-date/ .

[158] 'Nicaragua recognizes South Ossetia, Abkhazia'. Reuters. 3 Sep 2008. Available at: http://www.reuters.com/article/gc07/id-USN0330438620080903.

[159] 'No agreement on reform of telecom legislation'. European Parliament press release, 06 May 2009. Available at: http://www.europarl.europa.eu/news/expert/infopress_page/058-55086-124-05-19-909-20090505IPR55085-04-05-2009-2009-true/default_en.htm.

[160] O'Donnell, Brian; Kraska, James C. Humanitarian Law: Developing International Rules for the Digital Battlefield, in: Journal of Conflict & Security Law, April 2003.

[161] Ojala, Agnes. Pronksiöö hinda mõõdetakse sadades miljonites. Äripäev 10.07.2007. (in Estonian).

[162] Opinion of the European Economic and Social Committee, quoted in Opinion of the European Economic and Social Committee on the Proposal for a Decision of the European Parliament and of the Council on interoperability solutions for European public administrations (ISA), available at: http://eur-lex.europa.eu/LexUriServ/LexUriServ.do?uri=OJ:C:2009:218:0036:01:EN:HTML

[163] Ottis, Rain. Overview of Events, 30 April 2007. CCD COE Activation Team, TDCCIS.

[164] Ottis, Rain. Overview of Events, 2 May 2007. CCD COE Activation Team, TDCCIS.

[ 165 ] Ottis, Rain. Overview of Events, 3 May 2007. CCD COE Activation Team, TDCCIS.

[ 166 ] Ottis, Rain. Overview of Events, 7 May 2007. CCD COE Activation Team, TDCCIS.

[ 167 ] Ottis, Rain. Overview of Events, 9 May 2007. CCD COE Activation Team, TDCCIS.

[ 168 ] Ottis, Rain. Overview of Events, 10 May 2007. CCD COE Activation Team, TDCCIS.

[ 169 ] Ottis, Rain. Overview of Events, 14 May 2007. CCD COE Activation Team, TDCCIS.

[ 170 ] Ottis, Rain. Overview of Events, 15 May 2007. CCD COE Activation Team, TDCCIS.

[ 171 ] Ottis, Rain. Overview of Events, 16 May 2007. CCD COE Activation Team, TDCCIS.

[ 172 ] Overview of Events, 4 May 2007. CCD COE Activation Team, TDCCIS.

[ 173 ] Pääbo, Heiko 'War of Memories: Explaining 'Memorials War' in Estonia,' Baltic Security & Defence Review, Vol. 10, (2008), 5-28.

[ 174 ] 'Pankadel on üle 1,6 miljoni internetipanga kliendi'. Delfi Online, 8 Jan 2009 (in Estonian). Available at http://www.delfi.ee/news/eesti/eesti_uudised/article.php?id=20829300.

[ 175 ] Pastukhou, Mikhail; Taparashau, Yury. 'Authorities to eliminate independent media'. Charter97.org, 13 June 2008. Available at: http://charter97.org/en/news/2008/6/13/7407/.

[ 176 ] Pau, Aivar. 'Venemaa keeldus koostööst küberrünnakute uurimisel'. EPLOnline, 6 July 2007. Available at: http://www.epl.ee/artikkel/392271.

[ 177 ] Pauluchenka, Fyodar. 'Internet censorship in Belarus: Politically motivated DDoS-attacks on http://www.charter97.org'. A presentation given at the CCD COE Cyber Warfare Conference on 18 June 2009.

[ 178 ] Pavilenene, Danuta 'Cyber attacks against Lithuania do not stop,' The Baltic Course, 30 June 2008. Available at: http://www.baltic-course.com/eng/Technology/?doc=2807.

[ 179 ] Petriashvili, Diana. 'Georgia Pins Investment Hopes on Kazakhstan.' Eurasianet.org 17 April 2007. Available at http://www.eurasianet.org/departments/insight/articles/eav041707a.shtml.

[ 180 ] Pictet, J. (ed.). Commentary on the Geneva Convention for the Amelioration of the Condition of the Wounded and Sick in Armed Forces in the Field. ICRC, Geneva, 1952. .

[ 181 ] 'Politsei viis Eesti lipu lehvitaja minema'. Delfi.ee, 9 May 2006 (In Estonian). Available at: http://www.delfi.ee/news/paevauudised/eesti/article.php?id=12845410.

[ 182 ] Preliminary conclusions on 'Cyberattack against Georgia'. Swedish National Defence University, August 2008. E-mail to CCD COE.

[ 183 ] Presidency Conclusions of European Council, 23 and 24 March 2000, Lisbon. Available at: http://www.europarl.europa.eu/summits/lis1_en.htm.

[ 184 ] President Dmitri Medvedev. Statement on the Situation in South Ossetia. 8 August 2008. The Kremlin, Moscow. Available at kremlin.ru/eng/speeches/2008/08/08/1553_type82912type82913_205032.shtml.

[ 185 ] Press release of the President of Georgia. Declaration of Universal Mobilization by Georgian President Mikheil Saakashvili. 8 Aug 2008. Available at: http://www.president.gov.ge/?l=E&m=0&sm=1&st=0&id=2689.

[ 186 ] Prince, Brian. 'Security Researcher Asserts Russian Role in Georgia Cyber-attacks'. eWeek, 13 Aug 2008. Available at http://www.eweek.com/c/a/Security/Security-Researcher-Asserts-Russian-Role-in-Georgia-Cyber-Attacks/.

[ 187 ] 'Profile: Alexander Lukashenko'. BBC News, 9 January 2007. Available at: http://news.bbc.co.uk/2/hi/europe/3882843.stm.

[ 188 ] Project Grey Goose. Phase I Report Russia/Georgia Cyber War – Findings and Analysis. 17 October 2008. http://www.scribd.com/doc/6967393/Project-Grey-Goose-Phase-I-Report.

[ 189 ] 'Pronkssõdur avati taas rahvale vaatamiseks'. Postimees Online, 30 April 2007. (in Estonian) Available at http://www.postimees.ee/300407/esileht/siseuudised/258058.php .

[ 190 ] Prosecutor v. Tadic - ICTY Case No. IT-94-1, 1999.

[ 191 ] 'Putin defies Convention on Cybercrime'. Computer Crime Research Center, March 28, 2008. http://www.crime-research.org/news/28.03.2008/3277/.

[ 192 ] 'Q & A: Violence in South Ossetia'. Human Rights Watch, 15 Aug 2008. Available at: http://www.hrw.org/en/news/2008/08/15/q-violence-south-ossetia; .

[ 193 ] Rahutuste ajal Reformierakonna kodulehte rünnanud noormees sai trahvi. (In Estonian) Postimees, 23 Jan 2008. Available at http://www.postimees.ee/250108/esileht/krimi/307821.php .

[ 194 ] Rainys, Rytis, RRT. E-mail (10 Dec 2008) to the CCD COE Legal Team.

[ 195 ] Rand, Erik. 'Ansip: pronkssõdur viiakse Tõnismäelt minema'. Postimees, 29 March 2007 (In Estonian). Available at: http://www.epl.ee/artikkel/380087.

[ 196 ] Rand, Erik. 'Gruusia välisministeeriumi kodulehekülg paigutati Eesti serverisse' (in Estonian). EPLOnline. August 12, 2008. Available at: http://www.arileht.ee/artikkel/438306; .

[ 197 ] Randel, Tarmo. CERT Eesti tegevuse aastakokkuvõte (CERT-EE Annual Report; in Estonian). Estonian Informatics Centre, 2007.

[ 198 ] Rantanen, Miska. 'Virtual harassment, but for real.' Helsingin Sanomat International Edition, 6 May 2007. Available at http://www.hs.fi/english/article/Virtual+harassment+but+for+real+/1135227099868 .

[ 199 ] Report on the Implementation of the European Security Strategy (Brussels, 11 December 2008 S407/08).

[ 200 ] 'RFE/RL Belarus Service Director Discusses Cyberattack'. RFE/RL 28, April 2008. Available at: http://www.rferl.org/content/article/1109643.html.

[ 201 ] 'RFE/RL In Brief. RFE/RL'. Available at: http://www.rferl.org/info/facts/200.html.

[ 202 ] 'RFE/RL Websites Hit By Mass Cyberattack'. Radio Free Europe/Radio Liberty, 28 April 2008. Available at: http://www.rferl.org/content/article/1109642.html.

[ 203 ] 'RFE/RL's Belarus service'. RFE/RL. Available at: http://www.rferl.org/info/facts/184.html.

[ 204 ] Rhodin, Sara 'Hackers Tag Lithuanian Web Sites With Soviet Symbols,' The New York Times, 1 July 2008. Available at: http://www.nytimes.com/2008/07/01/world/europe/01baltic.html .

[ 205 ] Richter, Andrei. 'Belarus: New Media Law Adopted'. IRIS 2008-8:7/9. Media Law and Policy Centre, 2008. Available at: http://merlin.obs.coe.int/iris/2008/8/article9.en.html.

[ 206 ] 'Riigiprokuratuur: Vene saatkond esitas valeväiteid'. Postimees, 11 July 2007 (In Estonian). Available at: http://www.euro.postimees.ee/120707/esileht/siseuudised/271694.php.

[ 207 ] Roudik, Peter 'Lithuania: 'Constitutional Law - Ban on Nazi and Soviet Symbols,' Law Library of Congress, 2 July 2008. Available at: http://www.loc.gov/lawweb/servlet/lloc_news?disp3_487_text.

[ 208 ] Ruiz, Maricelle (ed). 1nternet Law - Should We Go To War Over A Massive Cyber-Attack?' Internet Business Law Services, 23 May 2007. Available at http://www.ibls.com/internet_law_news_portal_view.aspx?id=1762&s=latestnews; .

[ 209 ] 'Russia 'ends Georgia operation''. BBC, 12 Aug 2008. Available at news.bbc.co.uk/go/pr/fr/-/2/hi/europe/7555858.stm.

[ 210 ] 'Russia Warns Lithuania on US Missile Defense'. The Moscow News, 3 July 2008. Available at: mnweekly.rian.ru/news/20080703/55335914.html.

[ 211 ] 'Russian Cyber Attack on Georgia, Government Websites Down or Replaced With Fakes'. Telegraph.co.uk, 11 Aug 2008 .

[ 212 ] Sarke Infromation Agency. Daily News. November 17, 2008. Available at http://www.sarke.com/cgi/search/issue.asp?Day=17&Month=11&Year=2008&Type=1#5.

[ 213 ] Schmitt, Michael N. 'Computer Network Attack and the Use of Force in International Law: Thoughts on a Normative Framework.' Research Publications 1, Information Series (1999).

[ 214 ] Schmitt, Michael N. 'Wired Warfare: Computer Network Attack and jus in bello', IRRC June 2002, Vol. 84, No. 846.

[ 215 ] Seger, Alexander. 'The Convention on Cybercrime: a Global Framework'. IGF, Geneva, 2009.

[ 216 ] Shachtman, Noah; 'Estonia, Google Help 'Cyberlocked' Georgia (Updated),' Wired Blog Network/Danger Room, August 11, 2008, http://blog.wired.com/defense/2008/08/civilge-the-geo.html#more.

[ 217 ] Sharp, Walter Gary. 'Cyberspace and the Use of Force'. Falls Church, Va.: Aegis Research Corp., (1999).

[ 218 ] Socor, Vladimir. 'Moscow stung by Estonian ban on totalitarianism's symbols'. Eurasia Daily Monitor, The Jamestown Foundation, 26 Jan 2007. Available at http://www.jamestown.org/single/?no_cache=1&tx_ttnews[tt_news]=32427.

[ 219 ] SoftLayer Technologies - Does the Cyber War 'Buck' Stop There?. Intelfusion. Available at: http://intelfusion.net/wordpress/?p=452.

[ 220 ] Some key events in tense Russia-Georgia relations. Associated Press, 17 August 2008. Available at: http://www.aol.com.au/news/story/Some-key-events-in-tense-Russia-Georgia-relations/827601/index.html.

[ 221 ] Sootak, Jaan; Pikamäe, Priit. Karistusseadustik: kommenteeritud väljaanne. 2nd ed. Juura, 2009 .

[ 222 ] Special Investigation Service of the Republic of Lithuania. Annual Performance Report 2003. Available at: http://http://www.stt.lt/en/files/report_2003.pdf. .

[ 223 ] Statement by President of Russia Dmitry Medvedev on August 26, 2008. Available at: kremlin.ru/eng/speeches/2008/08/26/1543_type82912_205752.shtml; .

[ 224 ] Statistics Estonia. Statistical Database. Population by Sex, Ethnic Nationality And County, 1 January 2007. pub.stat.ee/px-web.2001/Dialog/statfile1.asp.

[ 225 ] Stephens, Hampton. 'Belarusian Cyber Attack', World Politics Review Blogs, 28 April 2008. Available at: http://www.worldpoliticsreview.com/blog/blog.aspx?ID=2012.

[ 226 ] Swaine, Jon. 'Georgia: Russia 'conducting cyber war'. The Telegraph. 11 Aug 2008. Available at http://www.telegraph.co.uk/news/worldnews/europe/georgia/2539157/Georgia-Russia-conducting-cyber-war.html.

[ 227 ] Swartz, Kristie E. 'Tulip Systems Tries to Keep Other Georgia's Web Sites Safe,' The Atlanta Journal-Constitution, August 17, 2008, http://www.ajc.com/business/content/business/stories/2008/08/17/tulip_systems_georgia.

[ 228 ] Talihärm, Anna-Maria. 'Estonia 2007: A Possible Model For Cyberterrorism?' Stockholms Universitet, 2008.

[ 229 ] Tere, Juhan. 'Russian Hackers Plan Cyber Attacks on Baltic Countries and Ukraine,' Baltic Course, 25 June 2008. Available at: http://www.baltic-course.com/eng/baltics_cis/?doc=2699.

[ 230 ] 'The most popular websites to be blocked for Belarusians'. Charter97.org, 16 June 2008. Available at: http://charter97.org/en/news/2008/6/16/7428/.

[ 231 ] Tikk, Eneken; Kaska, Kadri. 'Russia's refusal to co-operate in a criminal proceedings: analysis and proposals'. CCD COE, 2008

[ 232 ] Tikk, Eneken; Oorn, Reet. 'Legal and Policy Evaluation: International Coordination of Prosecution and Prevention of Cyber Terrorism.' In 'Responses to Cyber Terrorism'. COE DAT, 2008. Pp. 89-103;.

[ 233 ] Tiks, Oliver. 'Küberrünnakuid tõrjuvad sajad spetsialistid' (In Estonian). Postimees Online, 2 May 2007. Available at http://www.tarbija24.ee/120507/esileht/siseuudised/258274.php .

[ 234 ] Tiks, Oliver. 'Pahatahtlikud küberründed Eesti vastu tulevad välismaalt'. (In Estonian.) Postimees Online, 29 April 2007. Available at http://www.tarbija24.ee/110507/esileht/siseuudised/257862.php .

[ 235 ] Traynor, Ian. 'Russia accused of unleashing cyberwar to disable Estonia.' The Guardian, 17 May 2007. Available at http://www.guardian.co.uk/world/2007/may/17/topstories3.russia .

[ 236 ] 'Tyco to construct undersea fibre-optic system for Caucasus'. Invest In Georgia Investment Agency. Available at: http://www.investingeorgia.org/news/view/274.

[ 237 ] UK Enterprise Development Impact Assessment Information Service. Available at: http://www.enterprise-impact.org.uk/word-files/CoreText-1-WhatisImpactAssessment.doc.

[ 238 ] Urkis, Marius. A comment by head of the Academic and Research Network Computer Emergency Response Team of Lithuania. Available at: http://www.pcworld.com/article/147960/lithuania_attacks_focused_on_hosting_company.html.

[ 239 ] US Department of State – Bureau of European and Eurasian Affairs. Background Notes – Belarus. Available at: http://www.state.gov/r/pa/ei/bgn/5371.htm; .

[ 240 ] 'Valitsus kiitis heaks küberjulgeoleku strateegia rakendusplaani aastateks 2009–2011'. Postimees, 14 May 2009. Available at: http://uudisvoog.postimees.ee/?DATE=20090514&ID=204872.

[ 241 ] Vamosi, Robert. 'Hundreds of Lithuanian Websites defaced'. 1 July 2008. Available at: http://news.cnet.com/8301-10789_3-9983940-57.html.

[ 242 ] Värk, René. 'State Responsibility for Private Armed Groups in the Context of Terrorism'. XI Juridica International, 2006, 184-193.

[ 243 ] 'Vene saatkond: Eesti ei saatnud korrektset teabenõuet'. Postimees, 10 May 2007 (In Estonian). Available at: http://www.euro.postimees.ee/100707/esileht/siseuudised/viimased_sundmused/271542.php.

[ 244 ] 'Venemaa keeldub endiselt koostööst küberrünnakute uurimisel'. ERR, 13 Dec 2008. Available at: http://uudised.err.ee/index.php?06147571 .

[ 245 ] Waterman, Shaun. 'Analysis: Russia-Georgia Cyberwar Doubted'. United Press International, 18 August 2008. Available at: http://www.spacewar.com/reports/Analysis_Russia-Georgia_cyberwar_doubted_999.html.

[ 246 ] Web Hosting Companies in Lithuania. Web-hosting.info. Available at: http://www.webhost-ing.info/webhosts/tophosts/Country/LT .

[ 247 ] Weiss, Michael. 'Here Come the Cyber Wars. Are We Ready?' Reason.com August 17, 2007. http://www.reason.com/news/show/121896.html.

[ 248 ] West, Larry. 'Chernobyl Nuclear Accident'. About.com. Available at: http://environment.about.com/od/chernobyl/p/chernobyl.htm.

[ 249 ] Wingfield, Thomas C. The Law of Information Conflict: National Security Law in Cyberspace. Aegis Research Corp, 2000.

[ 250 ] Yasmann, Victor. 'Monument Dispute With Estonia Gets Dirty'. Russia Report May 8, 2007. Radio Free Europe/Radio Liberty, 8 May 2007. Available at http://www.rferl.org/content/Article/1347550.html .

[ 251 ] Židonis, Evaldas 'The Development of Informa-tion Society in Lithuania – Achievements and Problems,' Information Society Development Committee under Government, 2006. Available at: www3.lrs.lt/home/ivairus/ECPRD_ICT2006/EvaldasZidonis_ICT2006.ppt.

[ 252 ] Zmijewski, E. 'Georgia Clings to the 'Net', Rene-sysblog, Aug 11, 2008. Available at: http://www.renesys.com/blog/2008/08/georgia_clings_to_the_net.shtml.

[ 253 ] Zuckerman, E. 'Cyber Attacks: Misunderstand-ing Cyberwar in Georgia', Postchronicle, Aug 17, 2008. Available at: http://www.postchroni-cle.com/news/technology/article_212165469.shtml.

[ 254 ] Zuckerman, E. 'Misunderstanding Cyberwar', Aug 18, 2008. Available at: http://www.world-changing.com/archives/008381.html.

[ 255 ] 'На сайте МИД Грузии появился коллаж с Гитлером' (in Russian), Lenta.Ru. Available at: http://www.lenta.ru/news/2008/08/09/de-faced/.

# LEGAL ACTS

*International treaties*

[1]  Additional Protocol to the European Convention on Mutual Assistance in Criminal Matters. Strasbourg, 17.III.1978. Available at: http://conventions.coe.int/Treaty/EN/Treaties/Html/099.htm.

[2]  Convention for the Protection of Human Rights and Fundamental Freedoms as amended by Protocol No. 11, Council of Europe. (CETS No.: 005) Rome, 4.XI.1950. Available at: http://conventions.coe.int/Treaty/en/Treaties/Html/005.htm.

[3]  Convention on Cybercrime, Council of Europe (ETS 185). 23.XI.2001. Available at: conventions.coe.int/Treaty/EN/Treaties/Html/185.htm.

[4]  European Convention on Mutual Assistance in Criminal Matters. Council of Europe. (ETS 030). 20.IV.1959. Available at: http://conventions.coe.int/Treaty/EN/Treaties/Html/030.htm.

[5]  International Covenant on Civil and Political Rights; New York, 16 December 1966.

[6]  Rights and Duties of Neutral Powers and Persons in Case of War on Land (Hague V); The Hague, 18 October 1907.

[7]  Rights and Duties of Neutral Powers in Naval War (Hague XIII); The Hague, 18 October 1907.

[8]  Universal Declaration on Human Rights (UDHR); Paris, 10 December 1948.

*European Union law*

[9]  Council Framework Decision 2005/222/JHA of 24 February 2005 on attacks against information systems. OJ L 69/67, 16.03.2005.

[10]  Directive 97/66/EC of the European Parliament and of the Council of 15 December 1997 concerning the processing of personal data and the protection of privacy in the telecommunications sector).

[11]  Directive 1999/5/EC of the European Parliament and of the Council of 9 March 1999 on radio equipment and telecommunications terminal equipment and the mutual recognition of their conformity. OJ L 91, 7.4.1999, pp. 0010–0028.

[12]  Directive 2002/19/EC of the European Parliament and of the Council of 7 March 2002 on access to, and interconnection of, electronic communications networks and associated facilities (Access Directive).

[13]  Directive 2002/20/EC of the European Parliament and of the Council of 7 March 2002 on the authorisation of electronic communications networks and services (Authorisation Directive).

[14]  Directive 2002/21/EC of the European Parliament and of the Council of 7 March 2002 on a common regulatory framework for electronic communications networks and services (Framework Directive). OJ L 108, 24/04/2002 pp. 0033-0050.

[15]  Directive 2002/22/EC of the European Parliament and of the Council of 7 March 2002 on universal service and users' rights relating to electronic communications networks and services (Universal Service Directive).

[16]  Directive 2002/58/EC of the European Parliament and of the Council of 12 July 2002 concerning the processing of personal data and the protection of privacy in the electronic communications sector (Directive on privacy and electronic communications). OJ L 201, 31.7.2002 pp. 0037 – 0047.

[17]  Directive 2006/24/EC of the European Parliament and of the Council of 15 March 2006 on the retention of data generated or processed in connection with the provision of publicly available electronic communications services or of public communications networks and amending Directive 2002/58/EC. OJ L 105 , 13/04/2006 pp. 0054 – 0063. Available at: eur-lex.europa.eu/LexUriServ/LexUriServ.do?uri=OJ:L:2006:105:0054:0063:EN:PDF.

*Estonia*

[18]  Avaliku teabe seadus (*Public Information Act*) (RT I 2000, 92, 597; 2009, 39, 262). An unofficial English tran slation is available at: http://www.legaltext.ee/et/andmebaas/tekst.asp?loc=text&dok=X40095K3&keel=en&pg=1&ptyyp=RT&tyyp=X&query=avaliku+teabe.

[19]  Digitaalallkirja seadus (*Digital Signatures Act*) (RT I 2000, 26, 150; 2009, 1, 3). Passed 8 March 2000, entered into force 15 December 2000. An unofficial English translation is available at http://www.legaltext.ee/et/andmebaas/paraframe.asp?loc=text&lk=et&sk=en&dok=X30081K5.htm&query=digitaalallkirja&tyyp=X&ptyyp=RT&pg=1&fr=no.

[20]  Eesti Vabariigi ja Poola Vabariigi vaheline leping õigusabi osutamise ja õigussuhete kohta tsiviil-, töö- ning kriminaalasjades (RT II 1999, 4, 22). (*Agreement on Legal Assistance and Legal Relations between the Republic of Estonia and Republic of Poland in Civil, Labour and Criminal Cases.*) Signed on 27 November 1998, entry into force 17 May 1996.

[21]  Eesti Vabariigi ja Ukraina leping õigusabi ja õi-
      gussuhete kohta tsiviil- ning kriminaalasjades
      (RT II 1995, 13/14, 63). (*Agreement on Legal
      Assistance and Legal Relations between the
      Republic of Estonia and the Ukraine in Civil and
      Criminal Cases.*) Signed on 15 February 1995,
      entry into force 7 February 2000 .

[22]  Eesti Vabariigi ja Vene Föderatsiooni leping õi-
      gusabi ja õigussuhete kohta tsiviil-, perekonna-
      ja kriminaalasjades (RT II 1993, 16, 27). (*Agree-
      ment on Legal Assistance and Legal Relations
      between the Republic of Estonia and Russian
      Federation in Civil, Family and Criminal Cases.*)
      Signed on 26 January 1993, entry into force 19
      March 1995.

[23]  Haldusmenetluse seadus (*Administrative Proce-
      dure Act*) (RT I 2001, 58, 354; 2009, 1, 3). Passed
      6 June 2001, entered into force 1 January 2002.
      An unofficial English translation is available at:
      http://www.legaltext.ee/et/andmebaas/para-
      frame.asp?loc=text&lk=et&sk=en&dok=X4007
      1K3.htm&query=haldusmenetluse&tyyp=X&pt
      yyp=RT&pg=1&fr=no.

[24]  Jälitustegevuse seadus (*Surveillance Act*) (RT I
      1994, 16, 290; 2008, 35, 213). Passed 22 February
      1994, entered into force 18 March 1994. An un-
      official English translation is available at: http://
      www.legaltext.ee/et/andmebaas/paraframe.as
      p?loc=text&lk=et&sk=en&dok=X30011K7.htm
      &query=j%E4litustegevuse&tyyp=X&ptyyp=RT
      &pg=1&fr=no.

[25]  Karistusseadustik (*Penal Code*) (RT I 2001, 61,
      364; 2009, 51, 348). An unofficial English transla-
      tion is available at: http://www.legaltext.ee/et/
      andmebaas/tekst.asp?loc=text&dok=X30068K
      8&keel=en&pg=1&ptyyp=RT&tyyp=X&query=
      karistusseadustik.

[26]  Kriminaalmenetluse seadustik (*Code of Crimi-
      nal Procedure*) (RT I 2003, 27, 166; 2009, 39, 261).
      Passed 12 February 2003, entered into force 1
      July 2004. An unofficial English translation is
      available at: http://www.legaltext.ee/et/and-
      mebaas/paraframe.asp?loc=text&lk=et&sk=en
      &dok=X60027K5.htm&query=kriminaalmenetl
      use&tyyp=X&ptyyp=RT&pg=1&fr=no.

*Belarus*

[27]  Statute on Mass Media. Available at http://
      pravo.by/webnpa/text.asp?RN=h10800427 (*in
      Belarus*).

*Lithuania*

[28]  Lithuanian Criminal Code (text provided by Cy-
      bercrime Investigation Board, Lithuanian Cyber
      Crime Bureau, December 2008).

*Georgia*

[29]  Georgian Criminal Code (text provided by the
      Ministry of Internal Affairs of Georgia via the
      OSCE Mission in Georgia in August 2008).

*Russia*

[30]  Constitution of the Russian Federation.
      Available at: http://www.constitution.ru/
      en/10003000-01.htm.